AF469061

Perfect DARTMOOR

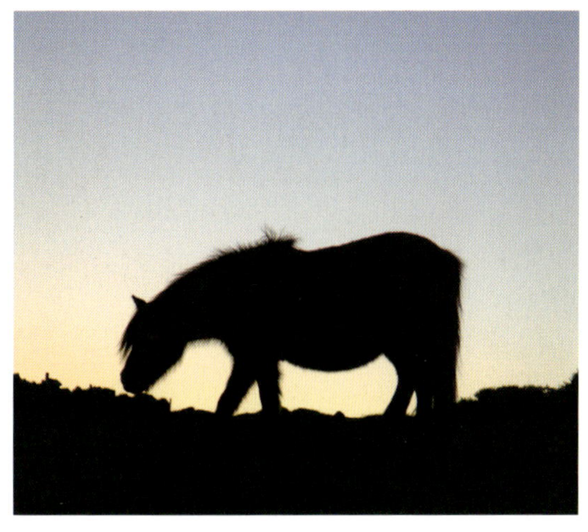

ADRIAN OAKES

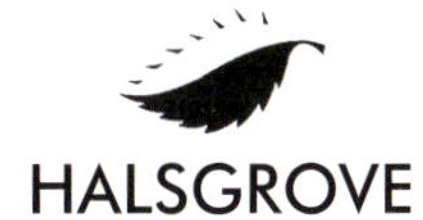

HALSGROVE

First published in Great Britain in 2008

British Library Cataloguing-in-Publication Data
A CIP record for this title is available from the British Library

ISBN 978 1 84114 713 0

HALSGROVE
Halsgrove House
Ryelands Industrial Estate
Bagley Road, Wellington,
Somerset TA21 9PZ
Tel: 01823 653777
Fax: 01823 216796
email: sales@halsgrove.com
website: www.halsgrove.com

Printed and bound by D'Auria Industrie Grafiche, Italy

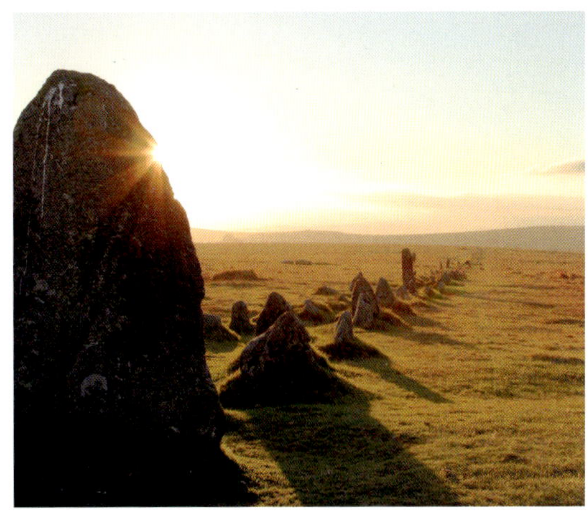

INTRODUCTION

Dartmoor is diverse and totally unique. The moor became a National Park in 1951, eventually encompassing an area of 369 square miles. Dartmoor is the home and workplace for over 30 000 people as well as a location for visitors, climbers and walkers.

The ancient rocks of Dartmoor were formed approximately 280 million years ago, and are composed mostly of granite, as are the outcrops of rock known as tors, created through the action of erosion over millions of years. These towering piles of stone dominate the landscape and are its most prominent and well-known feature.

Much of what we see in the landscape today is the result of human habitation, with evidence of agriculture dating back to prehistoric times. These early inhabitants left curious features, many of them ritualistic, including standing stones, cairns, burial chambers, and stone rows – all visible today. In more recent times quarrying and mining have left their scars.

Dartmoor is not huge but is easily large enough to get lost in. This is especially true if you are not prepared, as changes in the weather can be sudden and violent. The Moor must be treated with respect. Yet the highest and lowest parts of the Moor remain accessible, which further adds to its appeal to walkers. Often my long walks are lengthened by having to circumnavigate bogs, rivers, rocks and gorse, regularly stopping to spread my worn Landranger map on a rock to check my directions. Many a time I have turned back due to the deteriorating weather, and concerns, not so much for my well being, as for the camera equipment. I always set off well prepared with the correct clothing, compass, map, phone, water and food.

My inspiration for this book has come in many forms. I think back to my days climbing tors for views and exploring forests looking for that all important shot. Early rises, especially in winter, are rewarded by wonderful walks and very satisfying photographs. There seems to be a never-ending supply of locations, often with the discovery of remarkably well-preserved prehistoric and medieval artefacts and settlements. The sharp contrast in seasons, combined with varied colour, light and weather conditions, add up to many photographic possibilities.

There is also the human side of Dartmoor: the people that work and live on the moor. I have met many, including thatchers, dry-stone wallers and farmers who often have an fascinating story to tell, while their skills and lifestyle hold great interest. And there is Dartmoor at play: a recreational paradise for walkers, climbers, horse riders and cyclists. Parts of the moor are extensively used by the Military and are often out of bounds.

A particular place that captured my imagination was Wistman's Wood, one of the last remaining areas of ancient woodland that once covered much of the moor. The stunted oaks, covered in lichen and moss, are hundreds of years old. Sunrise in this spooky place is an experience not to be forgotten!

One of my favourite aspects of the moor are the views from the tors. From many you have an uninterrupted 360° view far across Devon. For example, if you venture up to Rippon Tor on a clear morning, you can see right over to Shaldon and the Teign estuary, east towards Exeter, and west to Plymouth, and you actually find yourself looking down over Dartmoor's most visited tor, Hay Tor.

Coming back from the moor, I feel exhilarated from the exercise, having enjoyed the views and its distinctive mood and atmosphere. It can also be a very restful place to sit and contemplate, which I often have to do to get the shot I want, waiting for the sun to be in a particular spot while rising or setting.

The moor will always be to me a special place to spend my time, as I am sure many others will agree.

Adrian Oakes 2008
www.adrianoakes.com

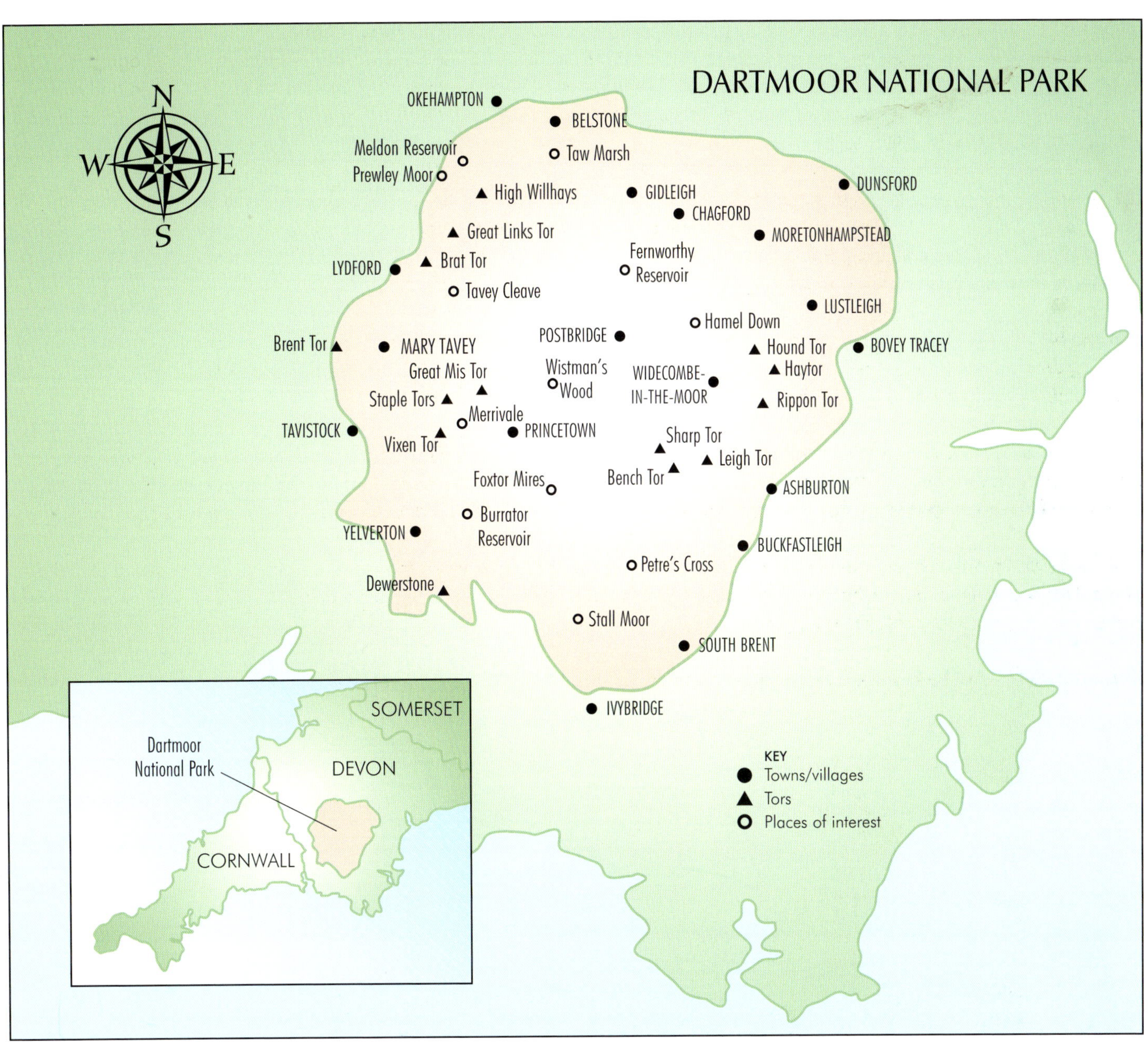
DARTMOOR NATIONAL PARK
N
S
E
W
OKEHAMPTON
BELSTONE
Meldon Reservoir
Taw Marsh
Prewley Moor
High Willhays
GIDLEIGH
DUNSFORD
CHAGFORD
Great Links Tor
MORETONHAMPSTEAD
Fernworthy Reservoir
LYDFORD
Brat Tor
Tavey Cleave
LUSTLEIGH
Hamel Down
POSTBRIDGE
Brent Tor
MARY TAVEY
Hound Tor
BOVEY TRACEY
Haytor
Great Mis Tor
Wistman's Wood
WIDECOMBE-IN-THE-MOOR
Staple Tors
Rippon Tor
Merrivale
TAVISTOCK
PRINCETOWN
Sharp Tor
Vixen Tor
Leigh Tor
Bench Tor
Foxtor Mires
ASHBURTON
Burrator Reservoir
YELVERTON
BUCKFASTLEIGH
Petre's Cross
Dewerstone
Stall Moor
SOUTH BRENT
IVYBRIDGE
SOMERSET
Dartmoor National Park
DEVON
CORNWALL
KEY
Towns/villages
Tors
Places of interest

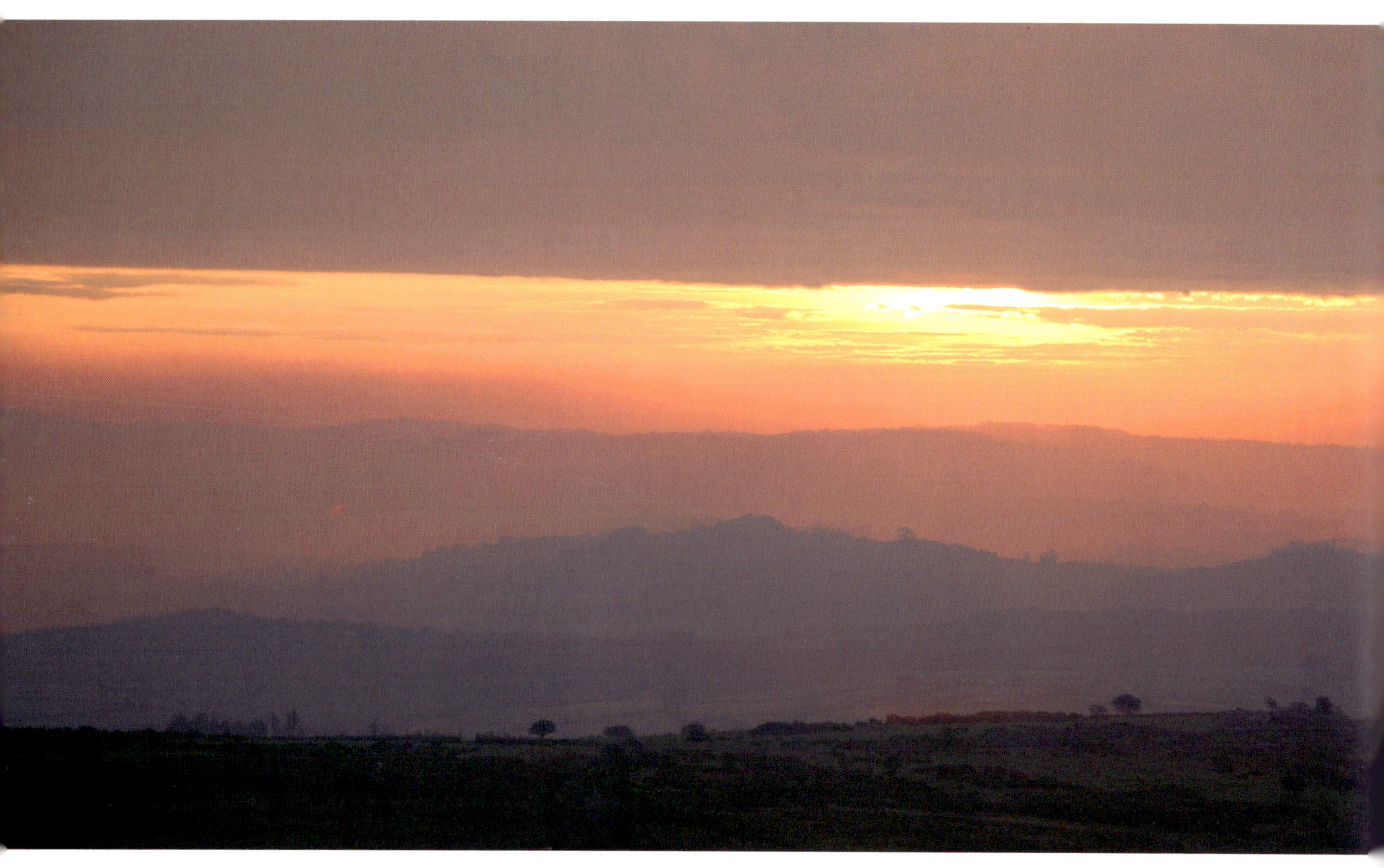

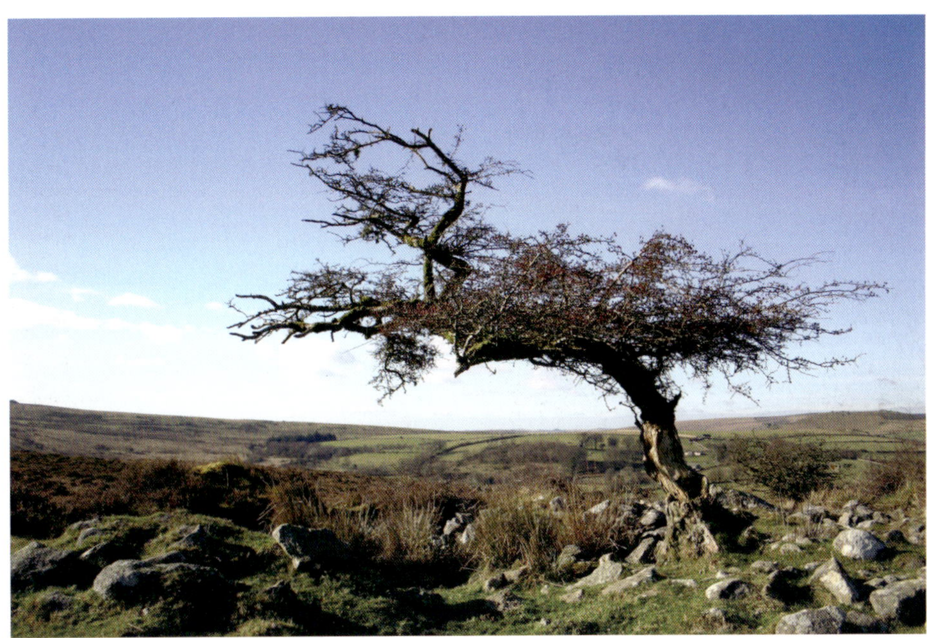

The harsh environment of the open Moor is reflected in the trees that grow twisted and leaning from a life in heavy weather and strong winds.

The depth of the landscape is illuminated by a warm colourful sunrise, looking East from Saddle Tor.

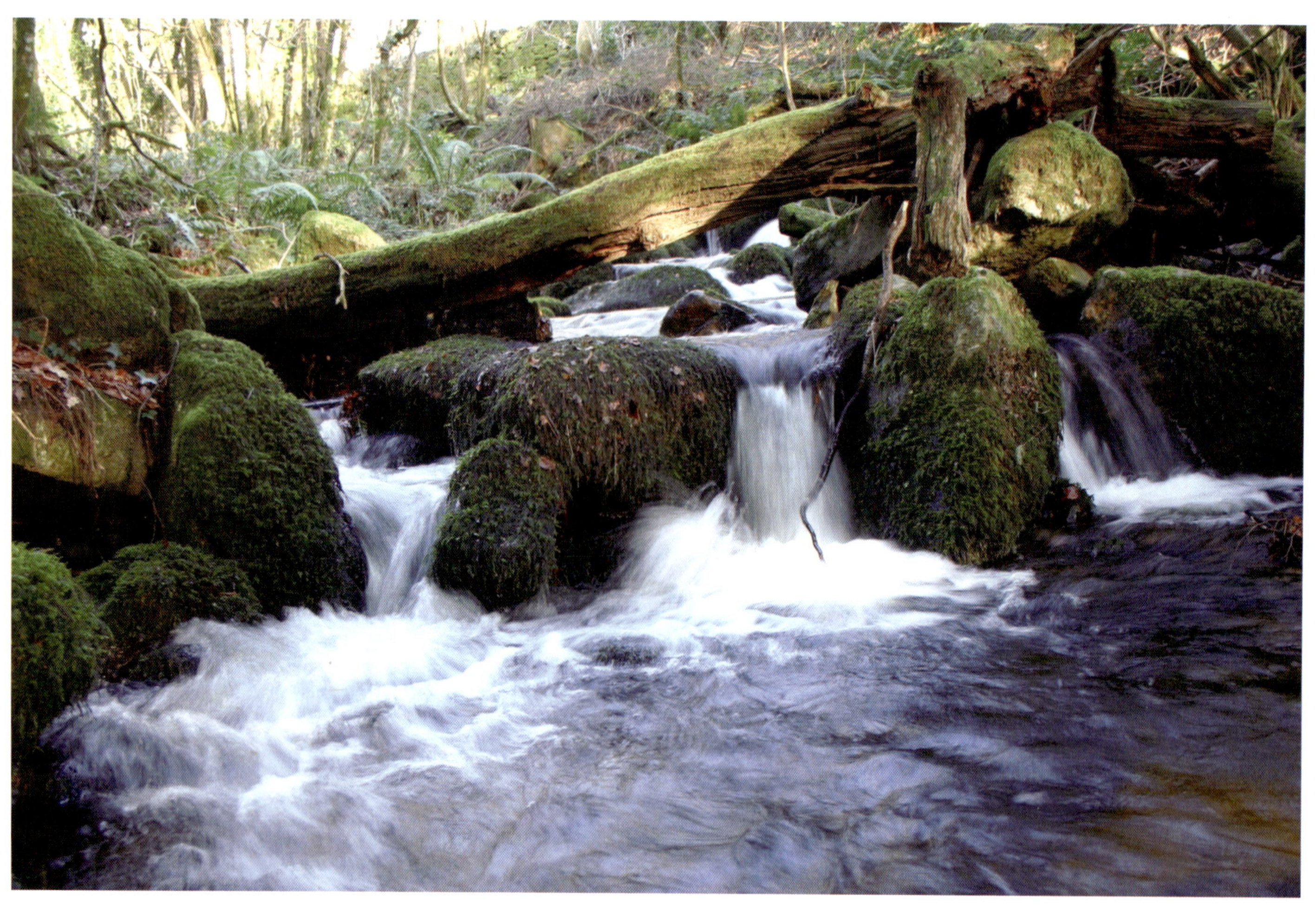

The moor is littered with streams, each with moss-covered rocks and waterfalls. This one is near Buckland.

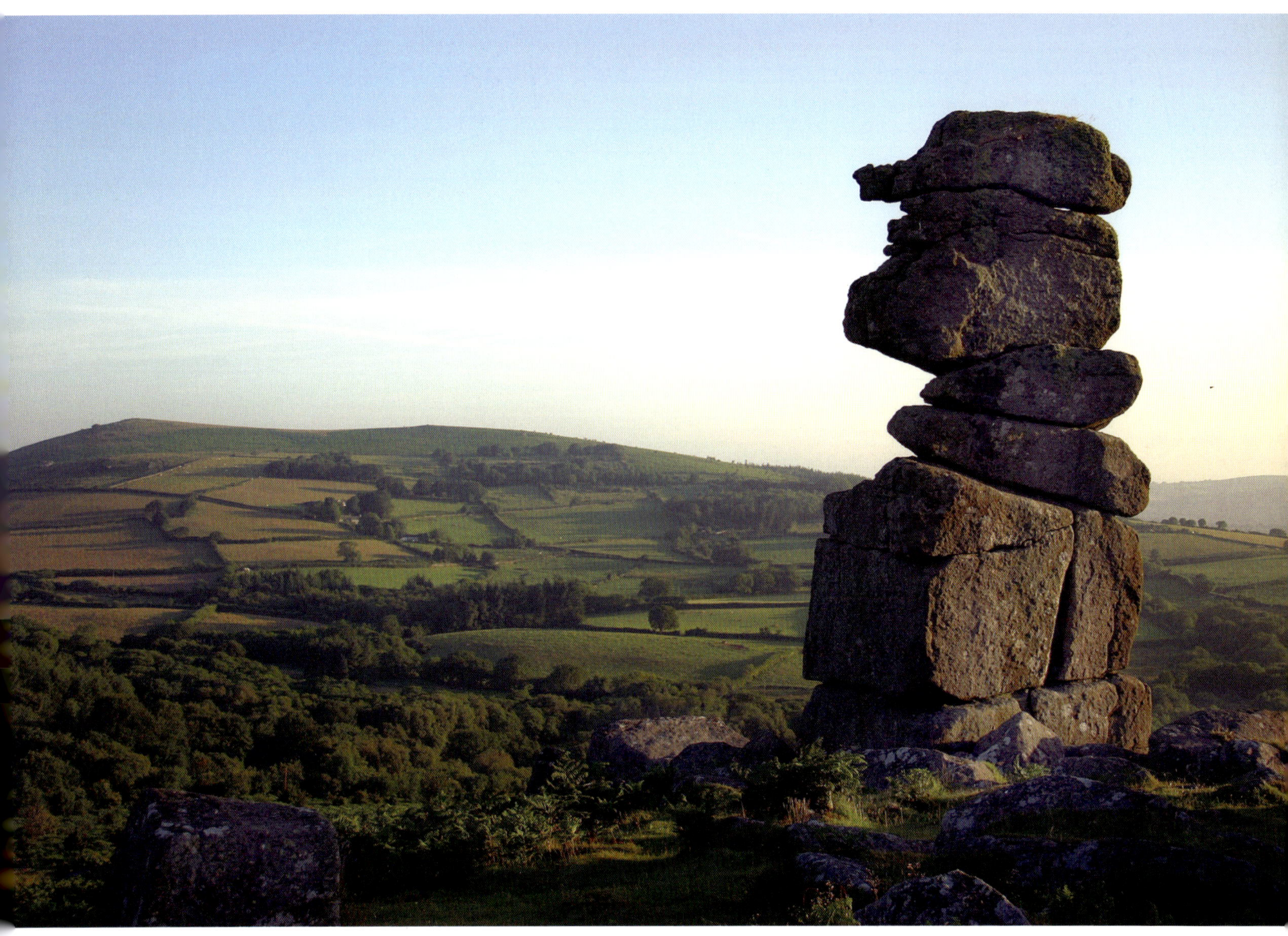

Bowerman's Nose at sunrise. This is one of Dartmoor's most recognisable natural landmarks. Legend has it that the rock is the remains of a hunter, Bowerman, who was turned to stone by witches.

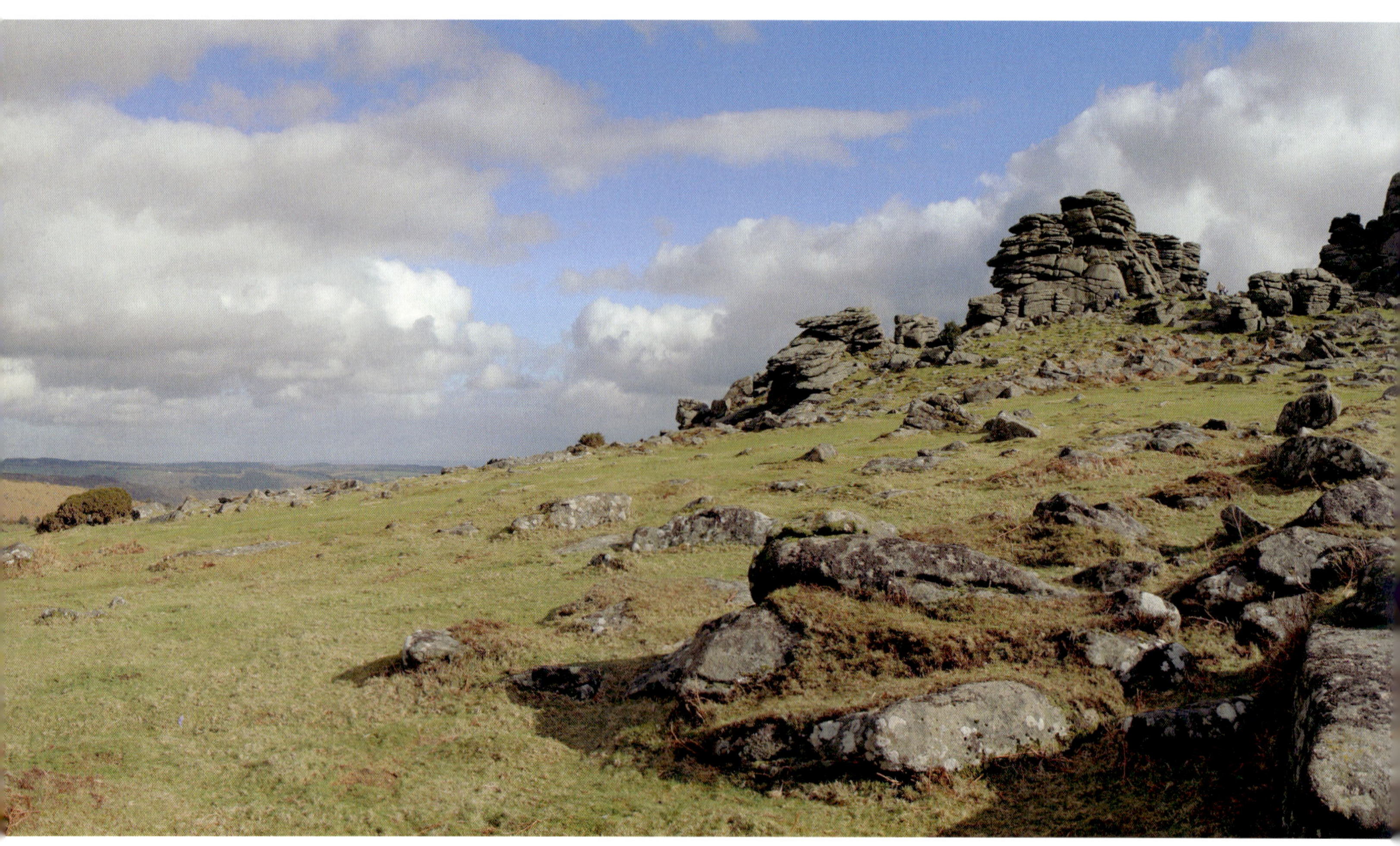

Bowerman's Nose stands nearby Hound Tor. The jumbled rocks are said to be Bowerman's hounds, also turned to stone, hence the tor's name.

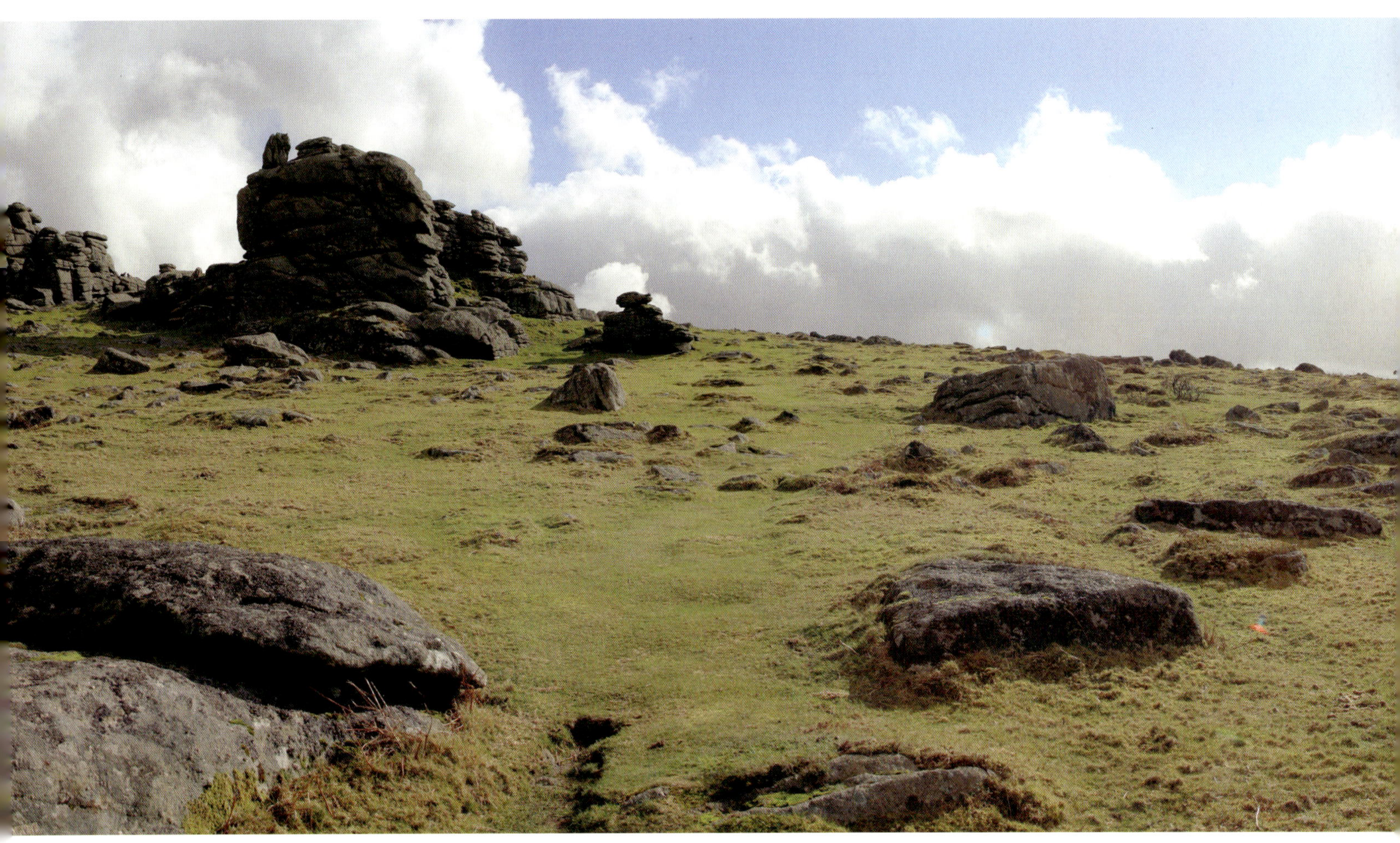

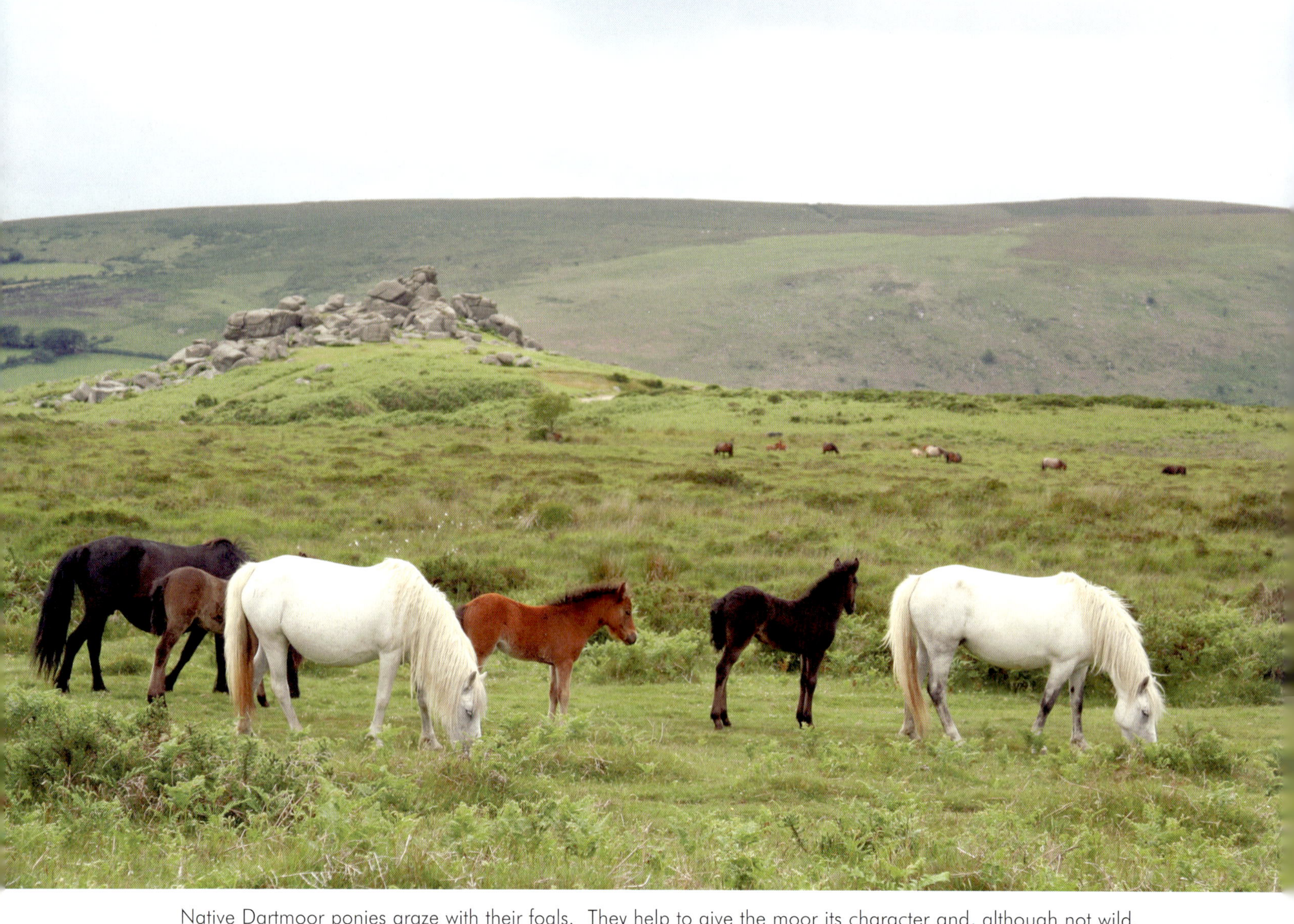

Native Dartmoor ponies graze with their foals. They help to give the moor its character and, although not wild, most of them roam freely all year round. Farmers herd them from certain areas in the autumn. This is called the 'drift'.

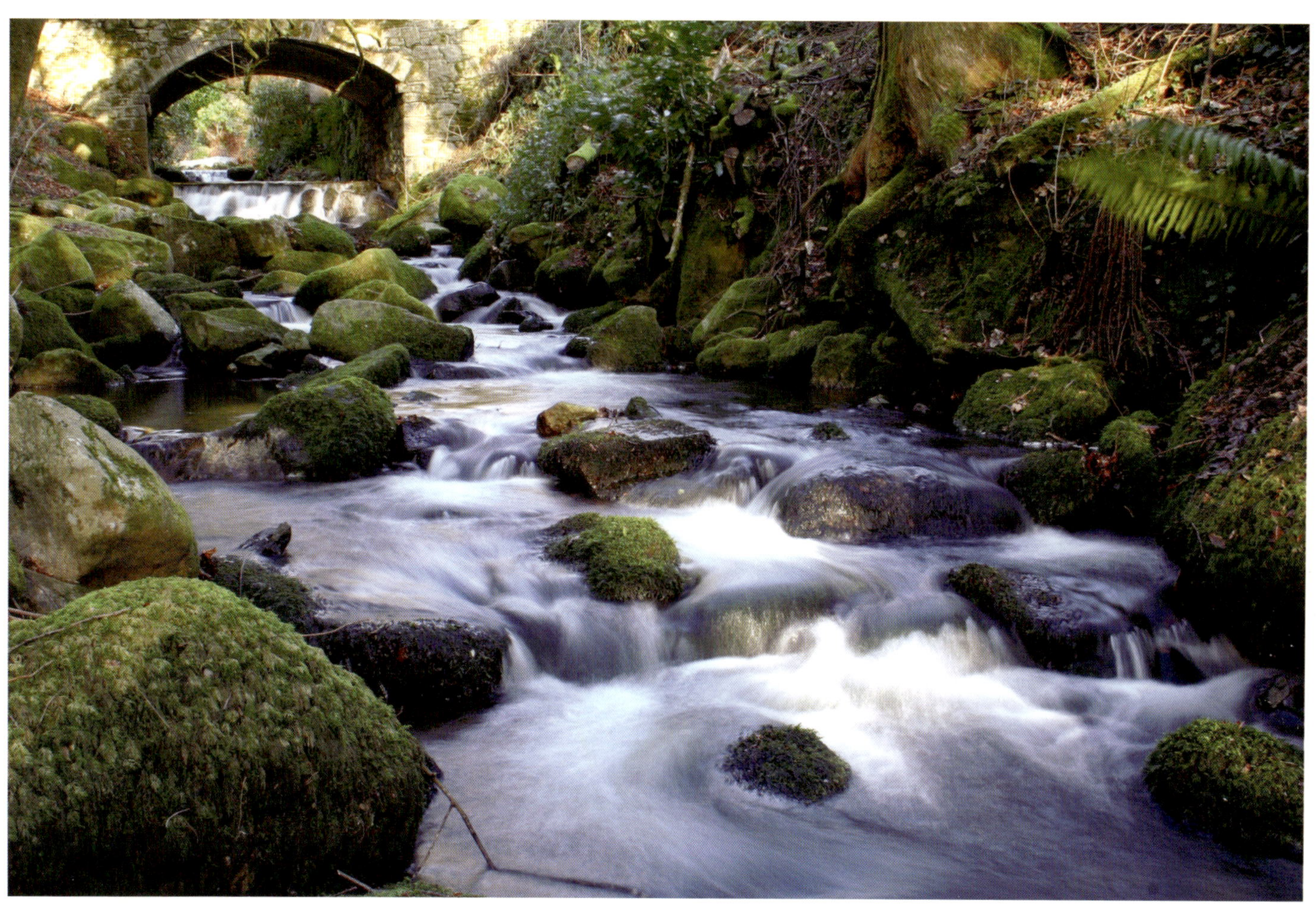

Below the bridge at Buckland in the Moor.

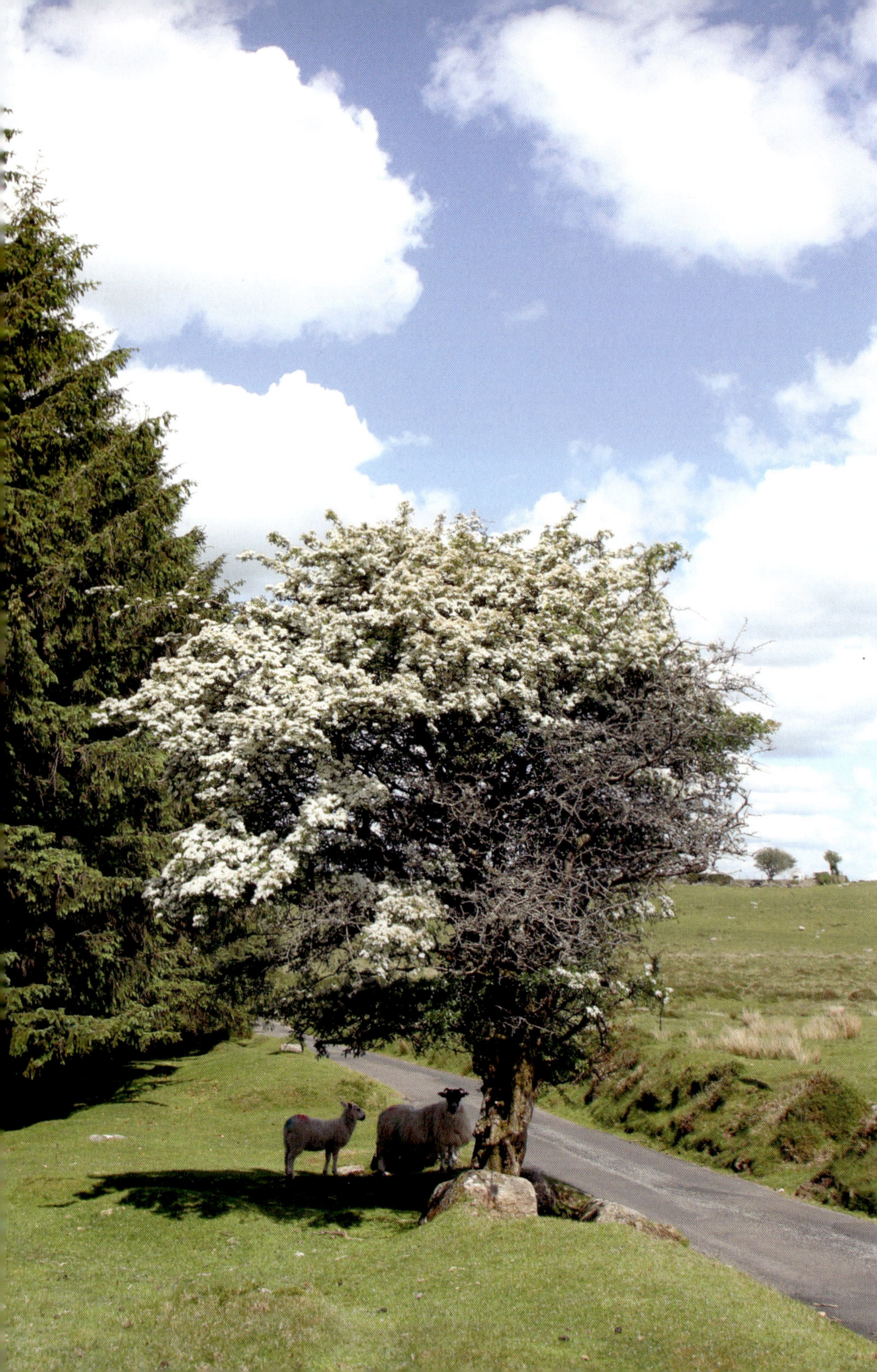

Virtually everywhere you look when walking the moor you see sheep in great numbers. I came across these in the shade created by spring blossom near Bellever.

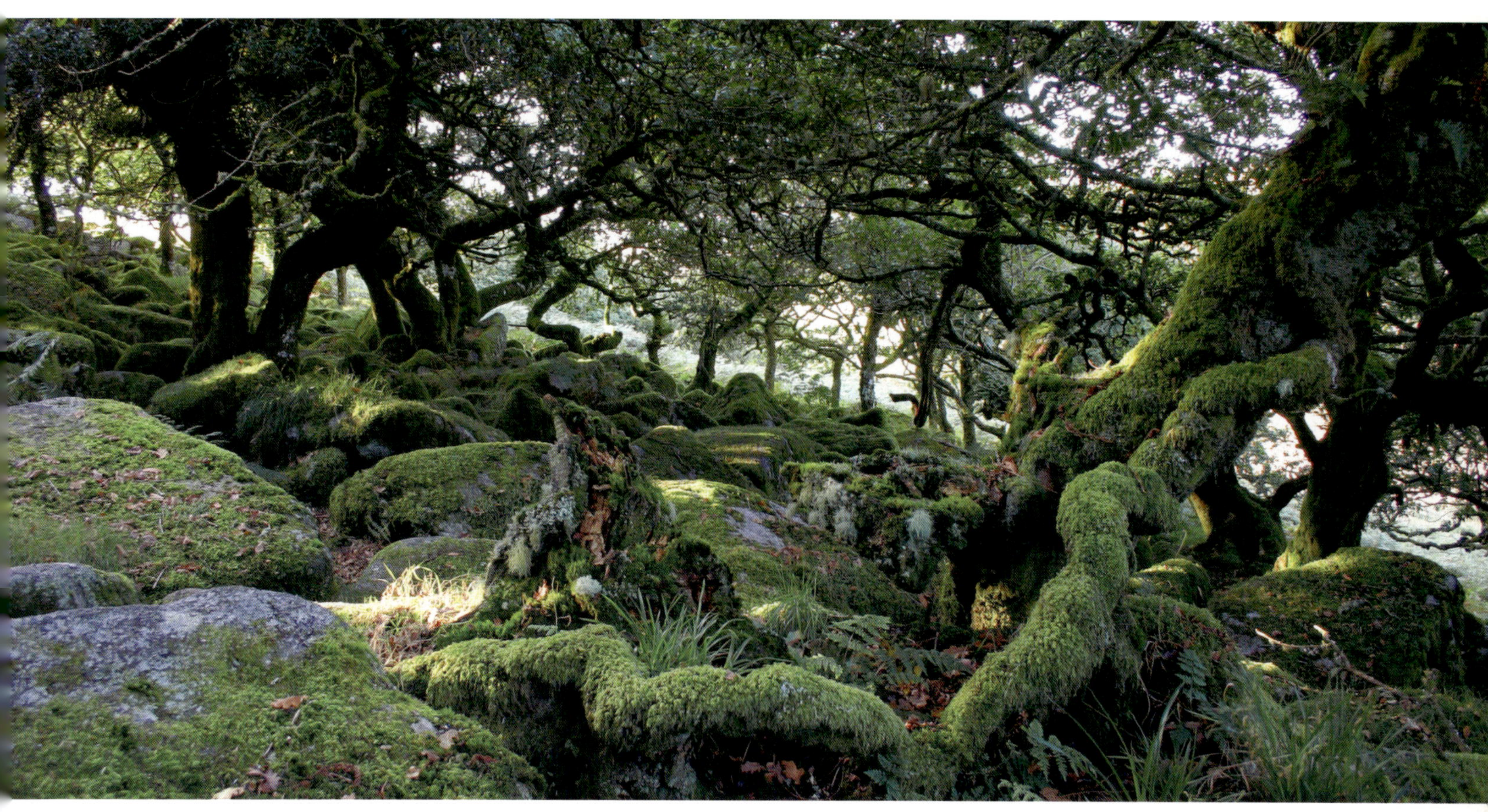

Wistman's Wood is thought to be one of the last remaining areas of ancient woodland which date from prehistoric times, It has a unique atmosphere, especially just after sunrise. This area of stunted oaks, covered in moss and lichen, is said in legend to be haunted by a pack of black hounds that from here start their hunt across the moor.

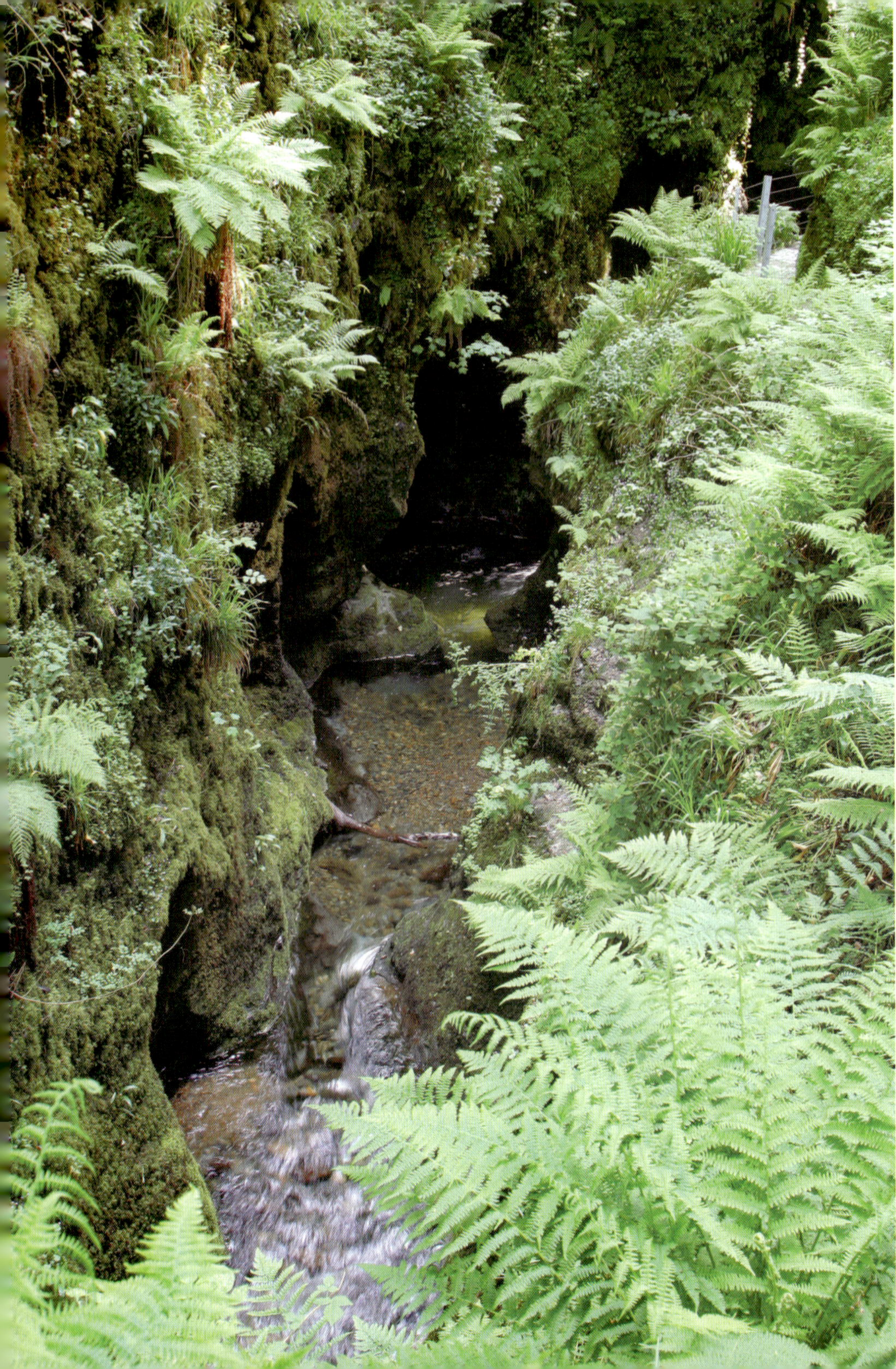

Among the many cuttings,
streams and gorges
ferns and bracken abound.

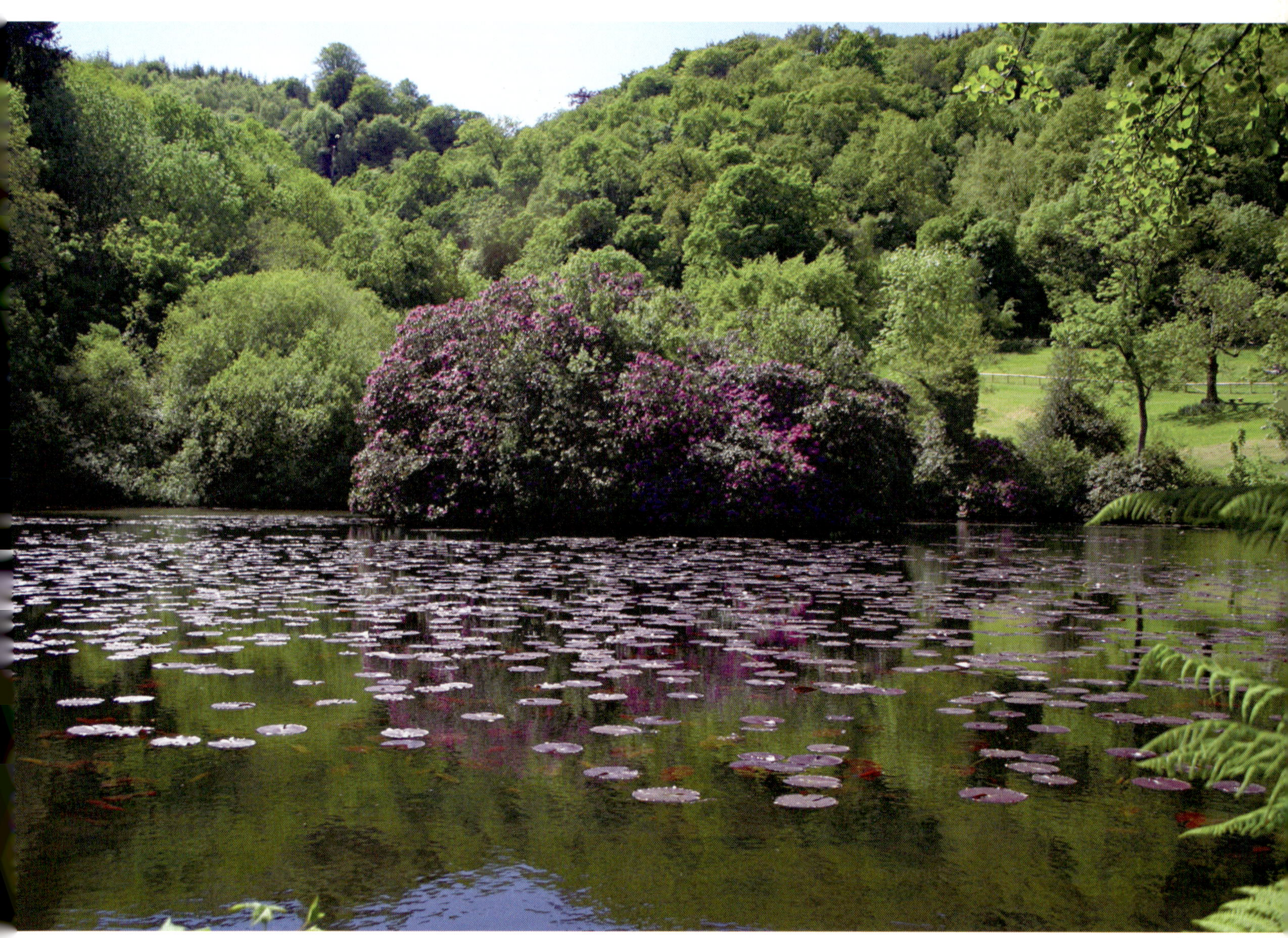

The rhododendron island at Canonteign Falls.

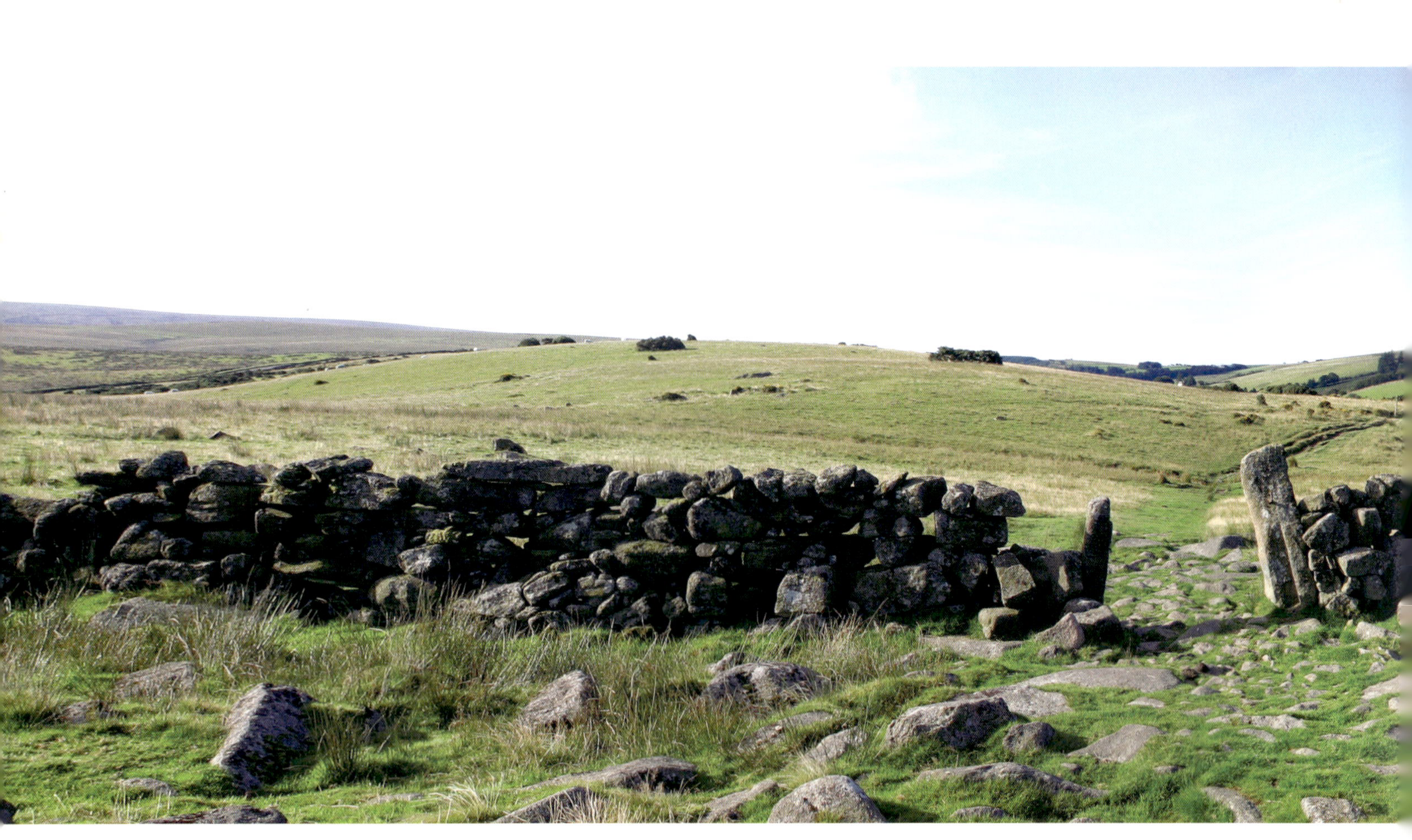

During a walk from Two Bridges I came across this 'gateway on the moor'.

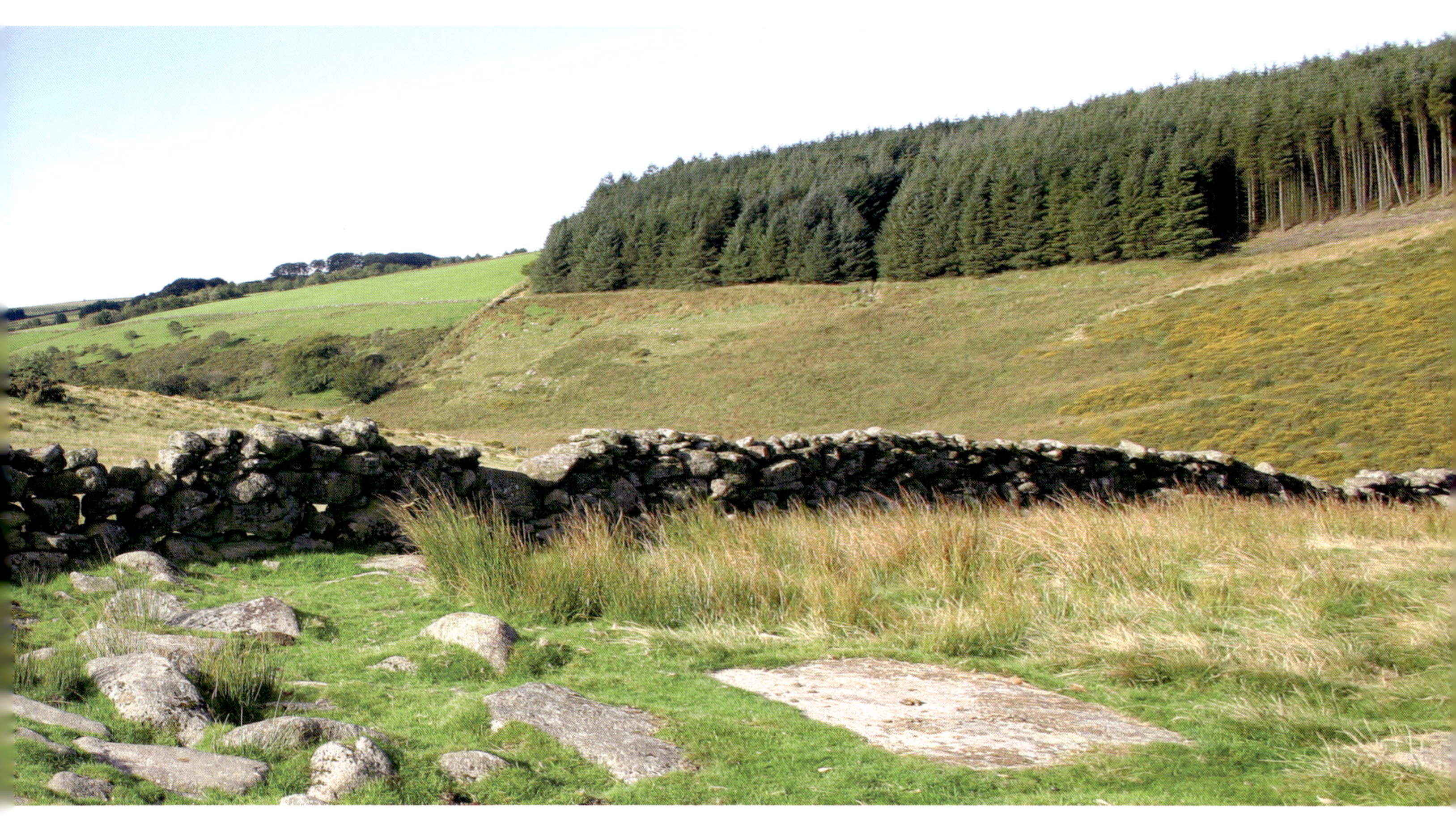

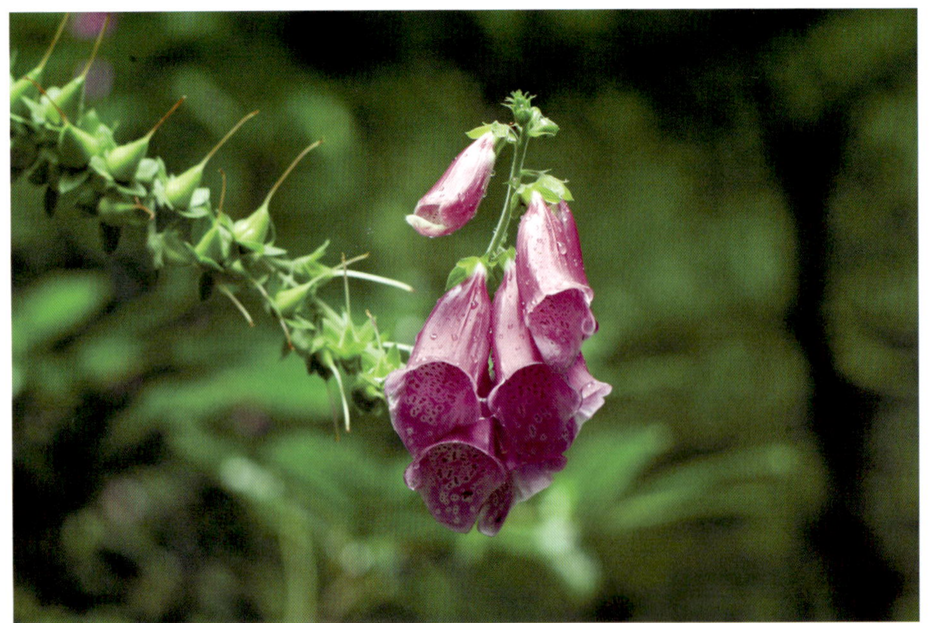

In spring foxgloves appear in large numbers; along the sides of the lanes and in the woodland. This one caught my eye as it was bathed in soft light and was still wet from the early dew.

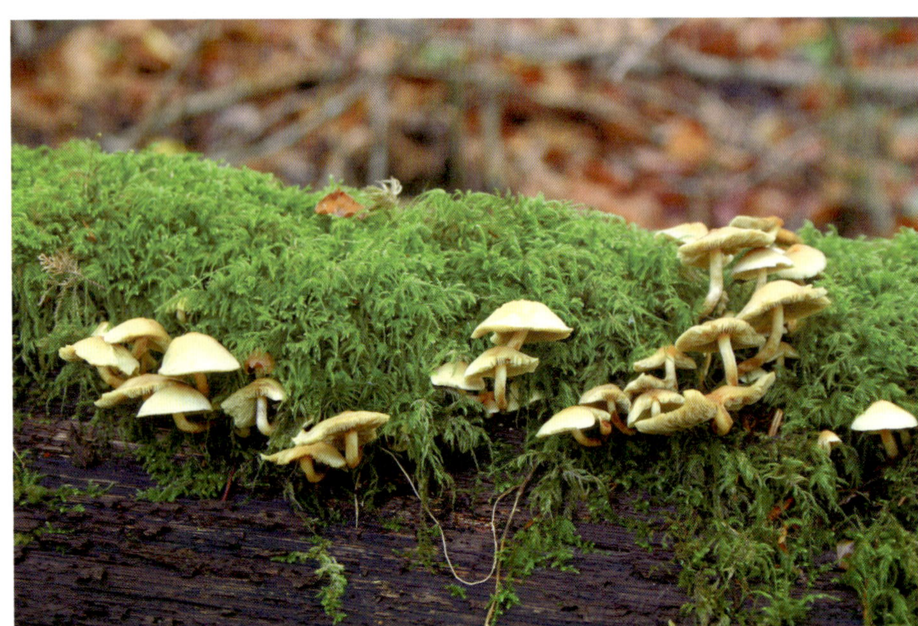

Honey-fungus and nature's rich green velvet thrive together on a rotten tree stump.

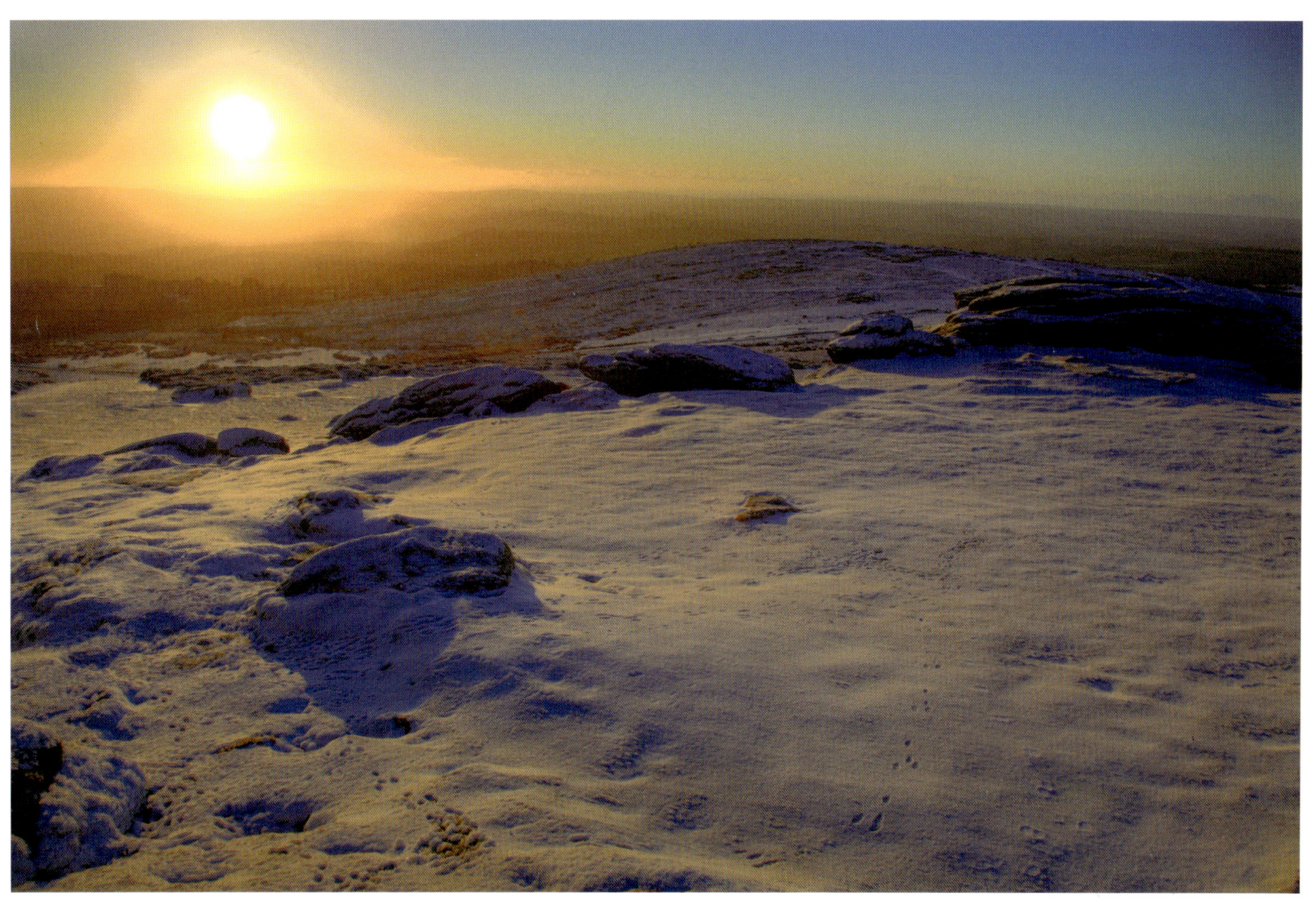

A cold winter sunrise at Haytor.

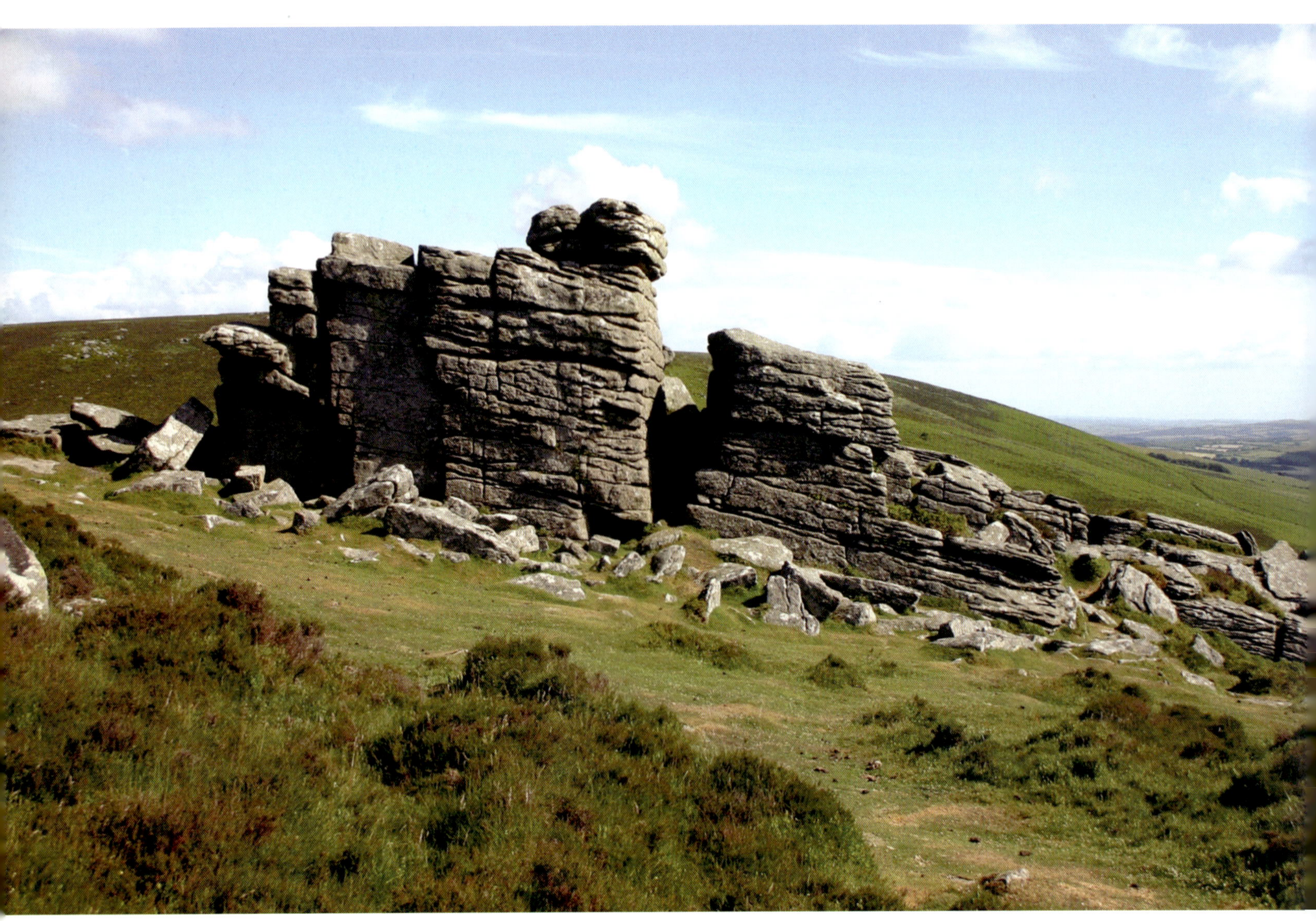

A panoramic view from Hookney Tor towards Widecombe-in-the-Moor.

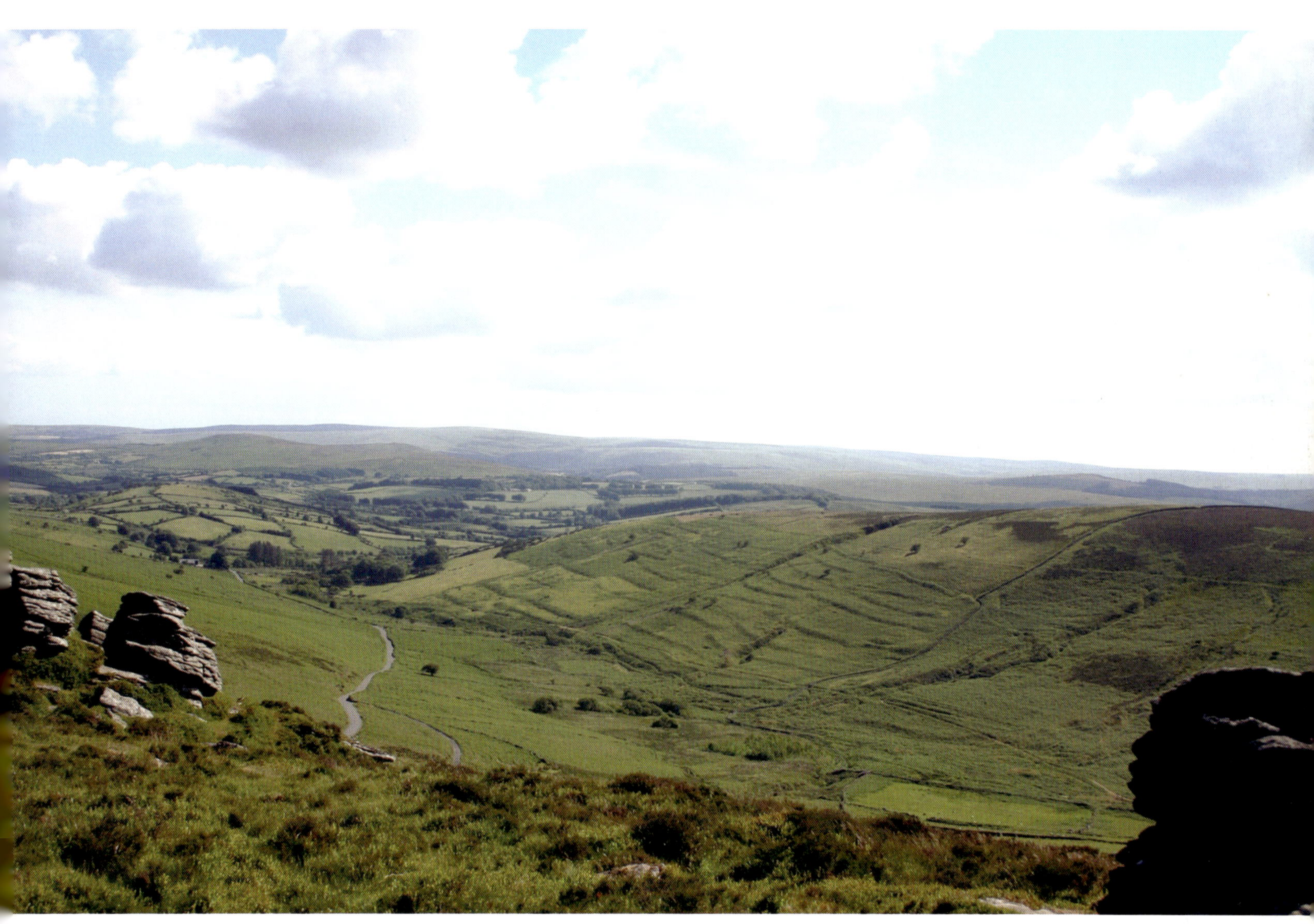

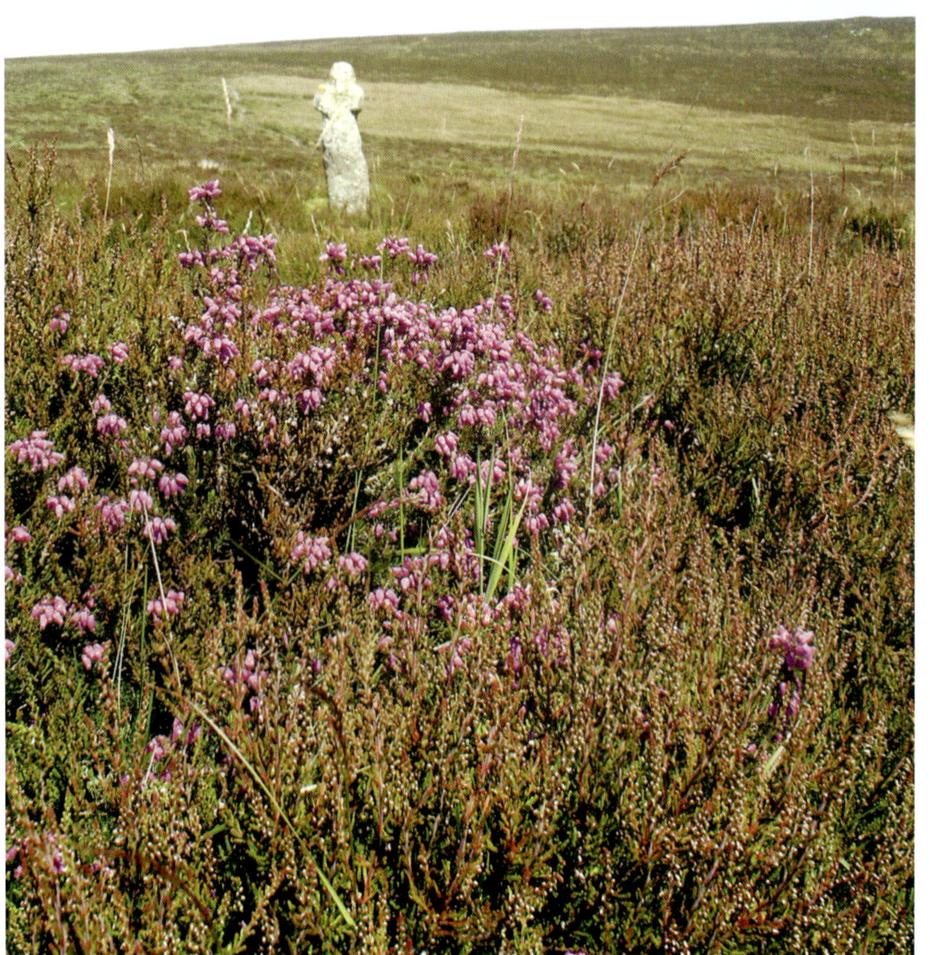

Dartmoor has many stone crosses, some hidden. Bennett's Cross, one of the best known, sits amongst the flowering heather

Opposite:
Rushing water of the River Teign near Fingle Bridge.

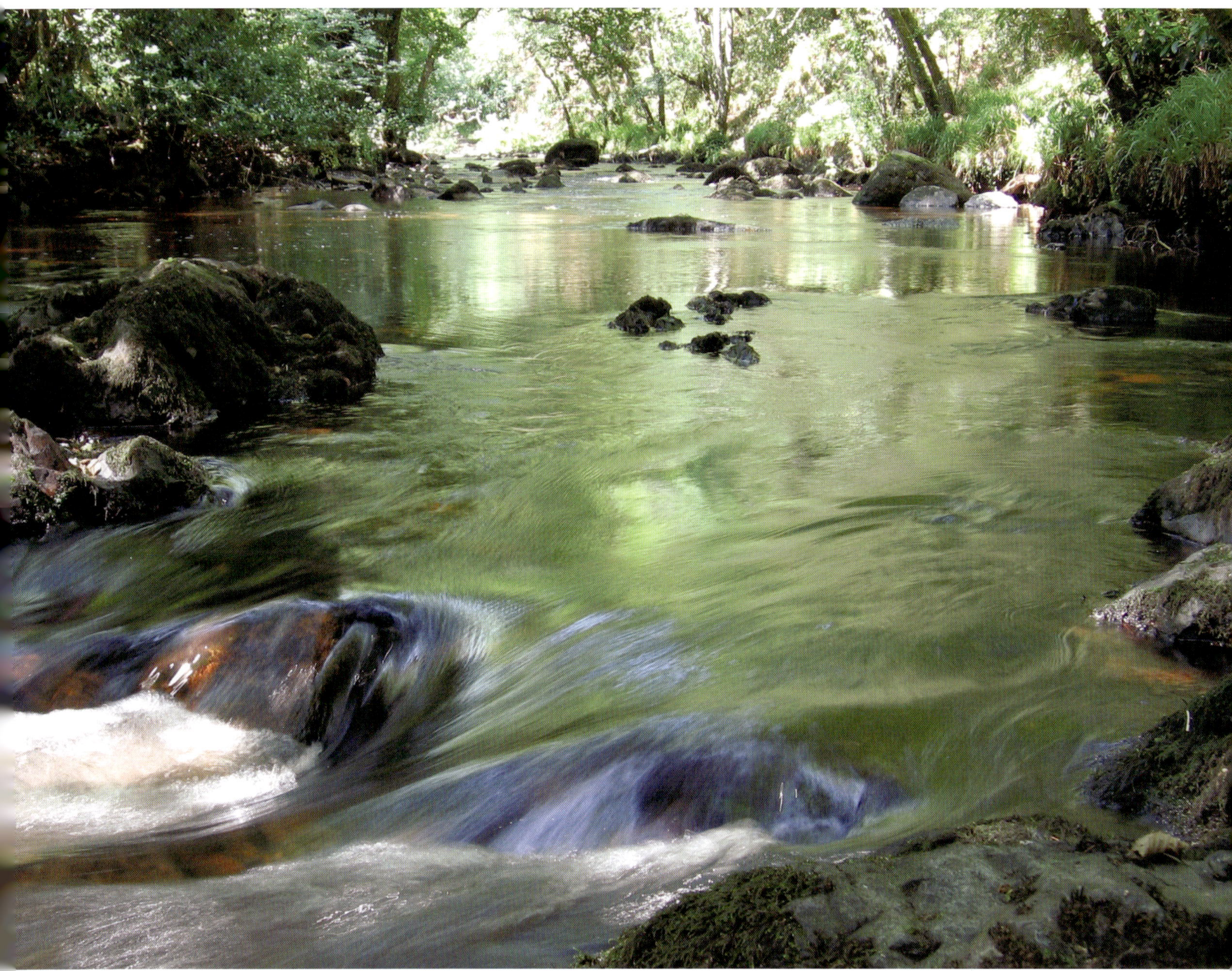

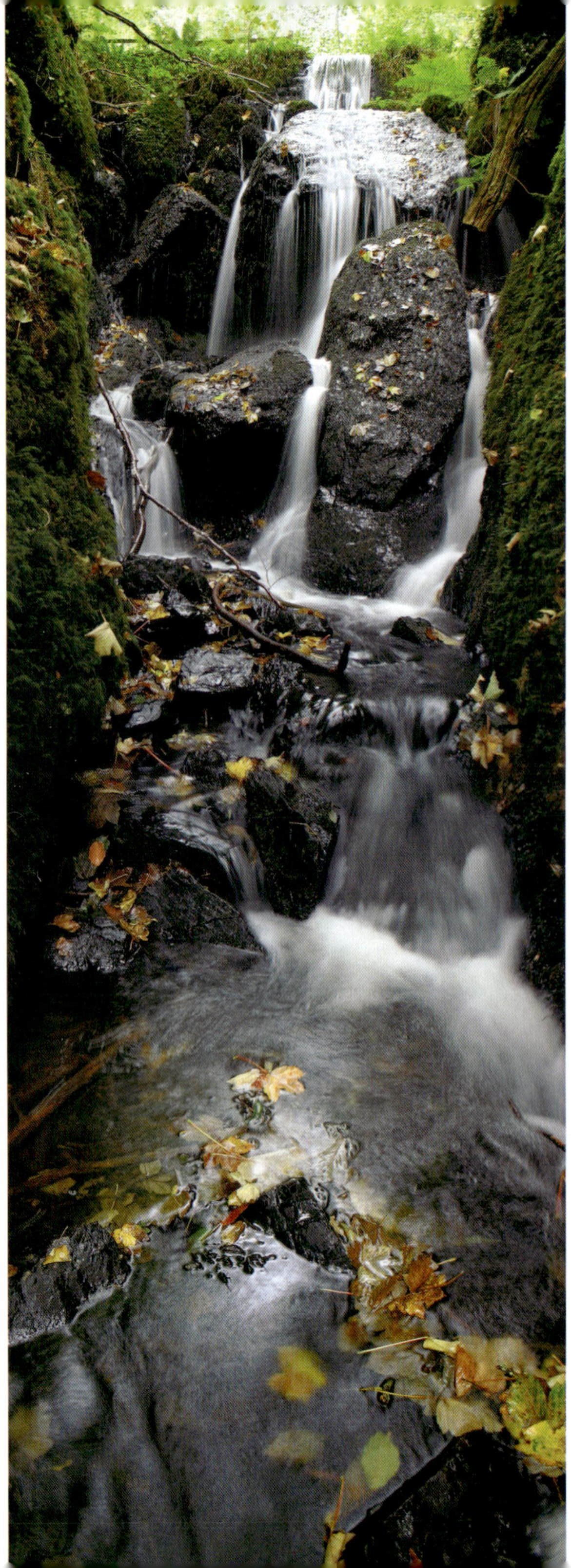

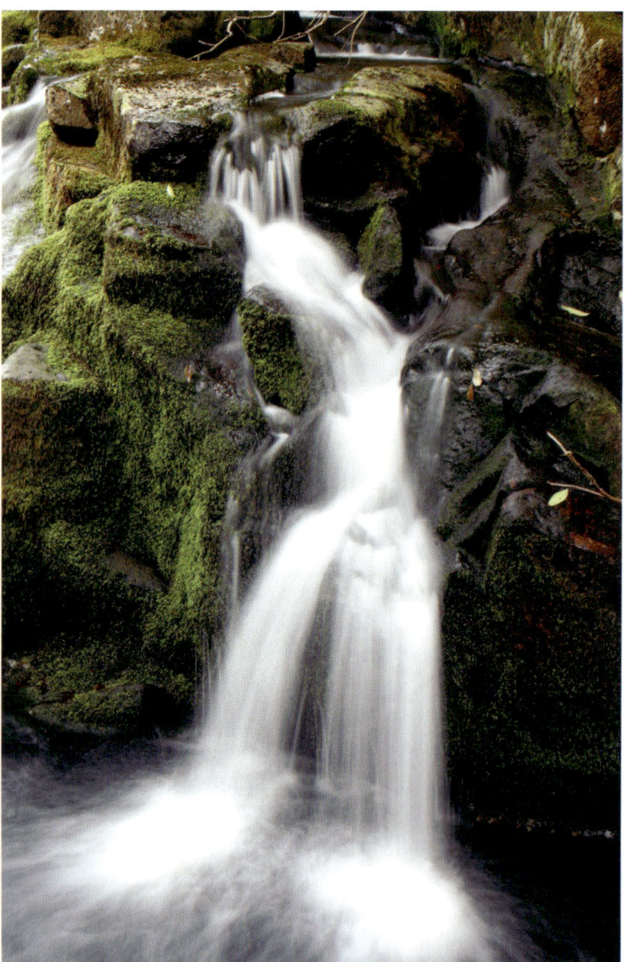

Dartmoor has many falls, some of the more interesting ones are not so easy to find. This one, near Shipley Bridge, captured my imagination.

And one of the most beautiful falls on the moor (left) Clampitt Fall at Canonteign.

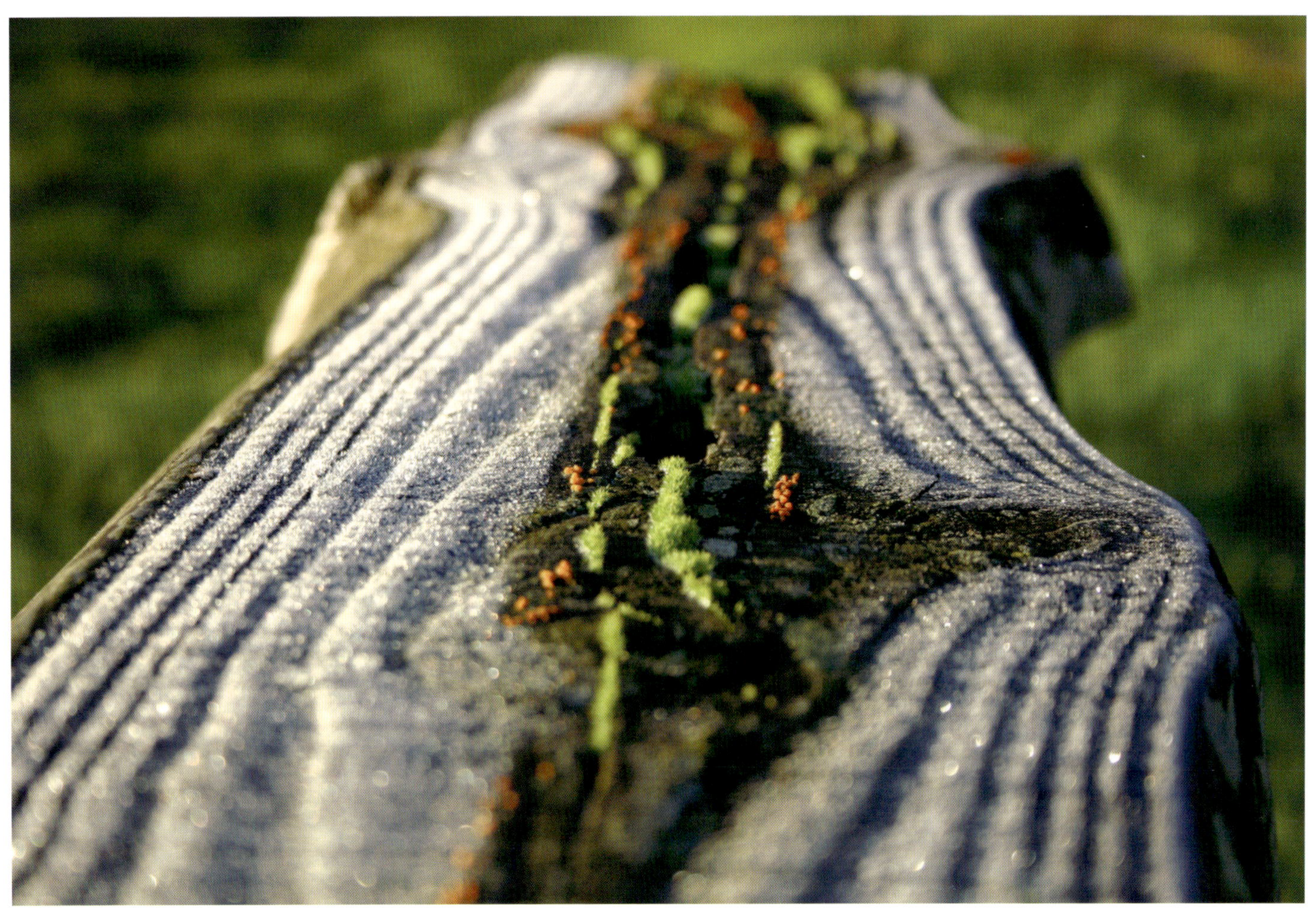

I almost walked past this old wooden bench. On closer inspection it was covered in tiny fungi and patches of moss amongst the early morning frost. Much of Dartmoor's beauty can be found in miniature.

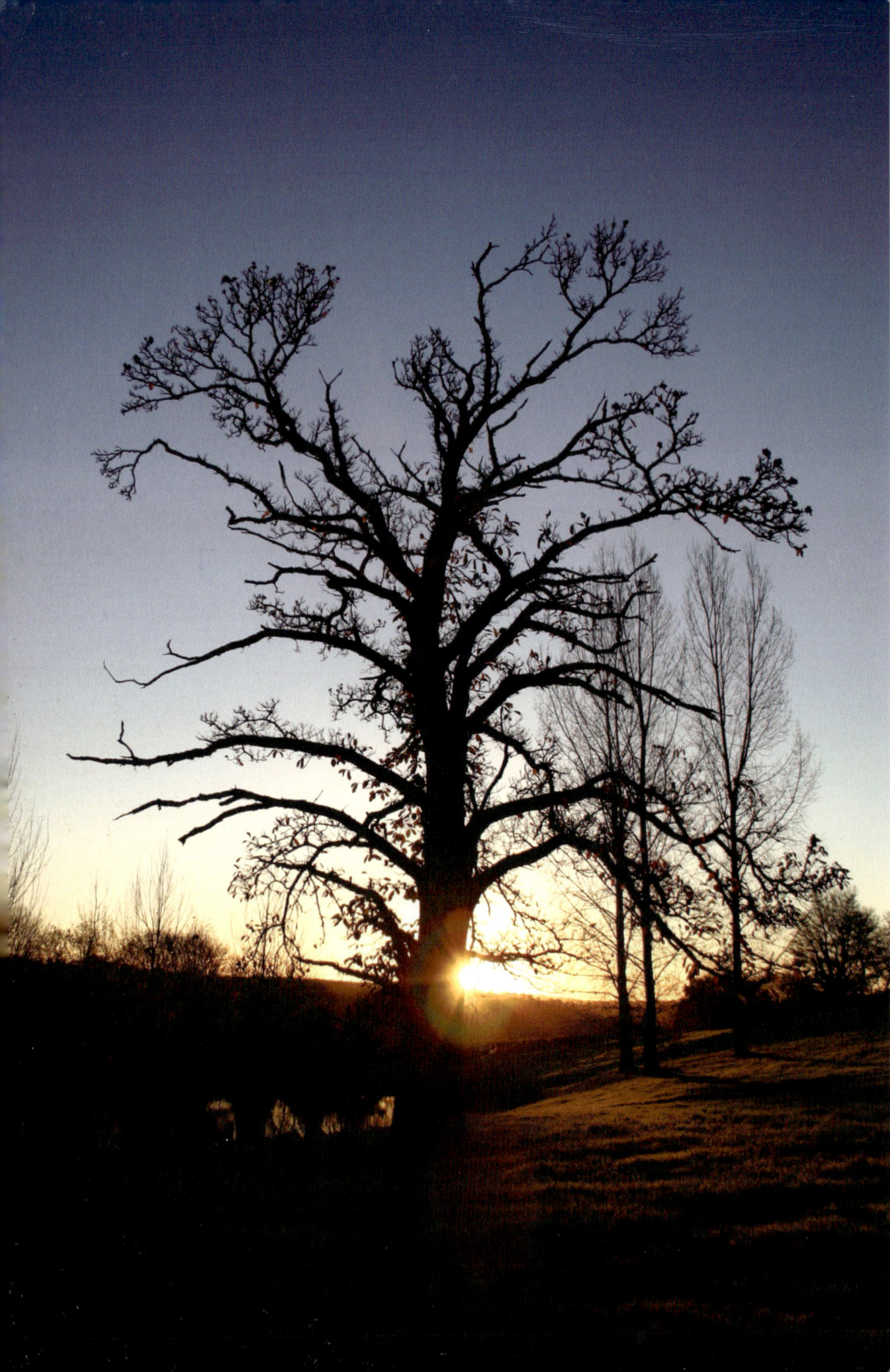

An ancient Dartmoor oak
silhouetted at sunrise.

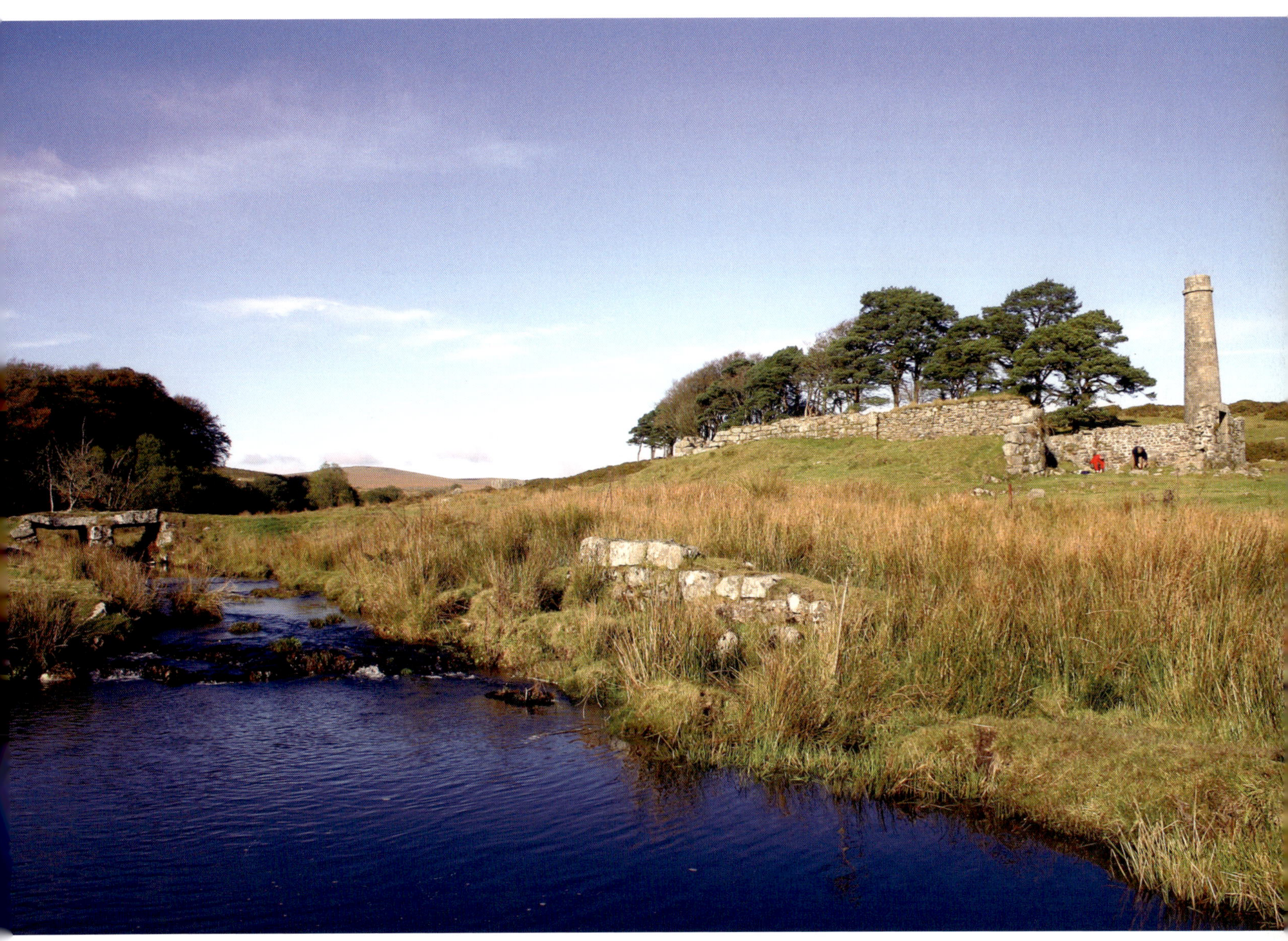

Walkers rest at the remains of the Powder Mills. This was the site of a gunpowder making factory that ceased production on 1897. As shown in the image, a well-preserved clapper bridge can be found here.

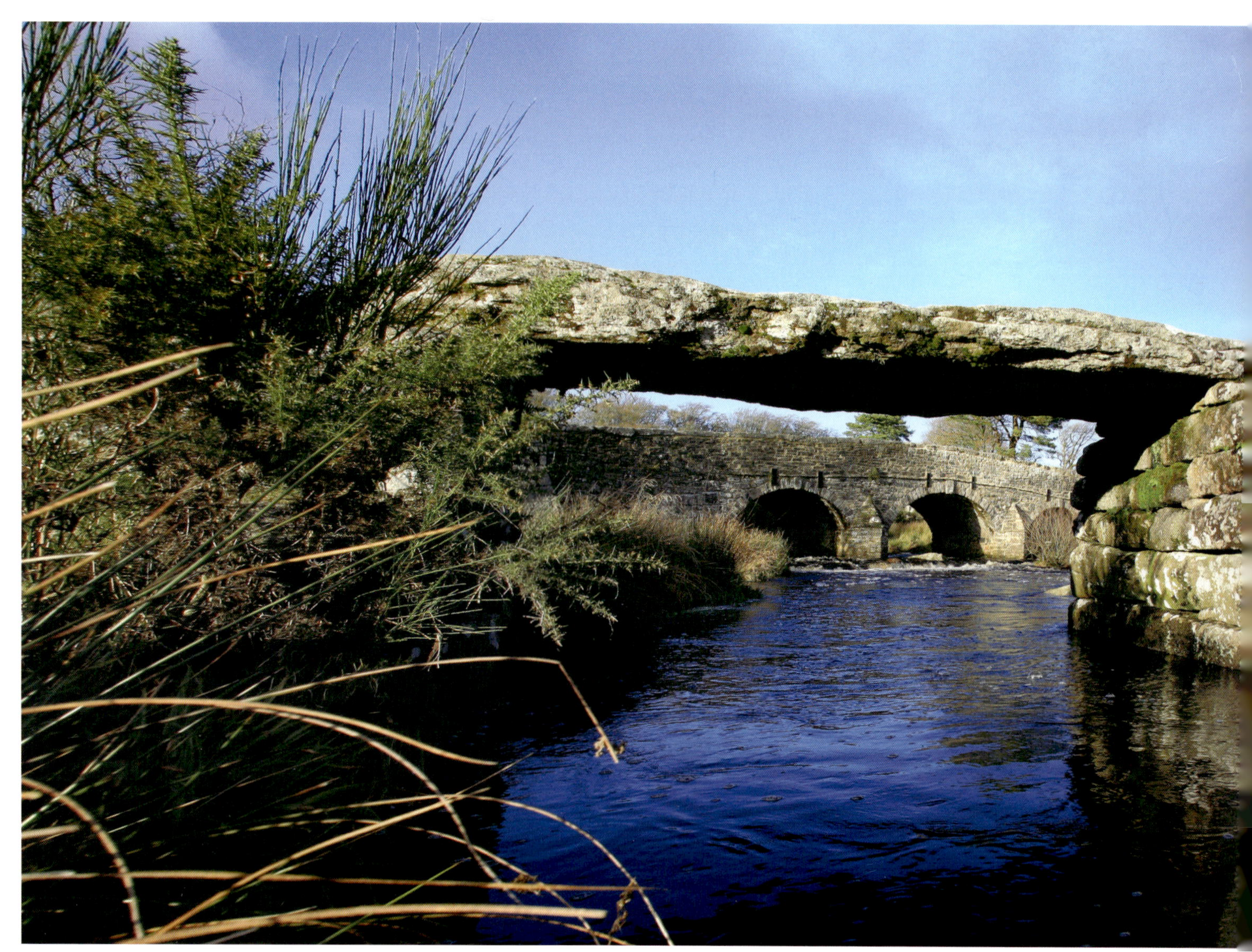

The best known and most accessible clapper bridge is at Postbridge.

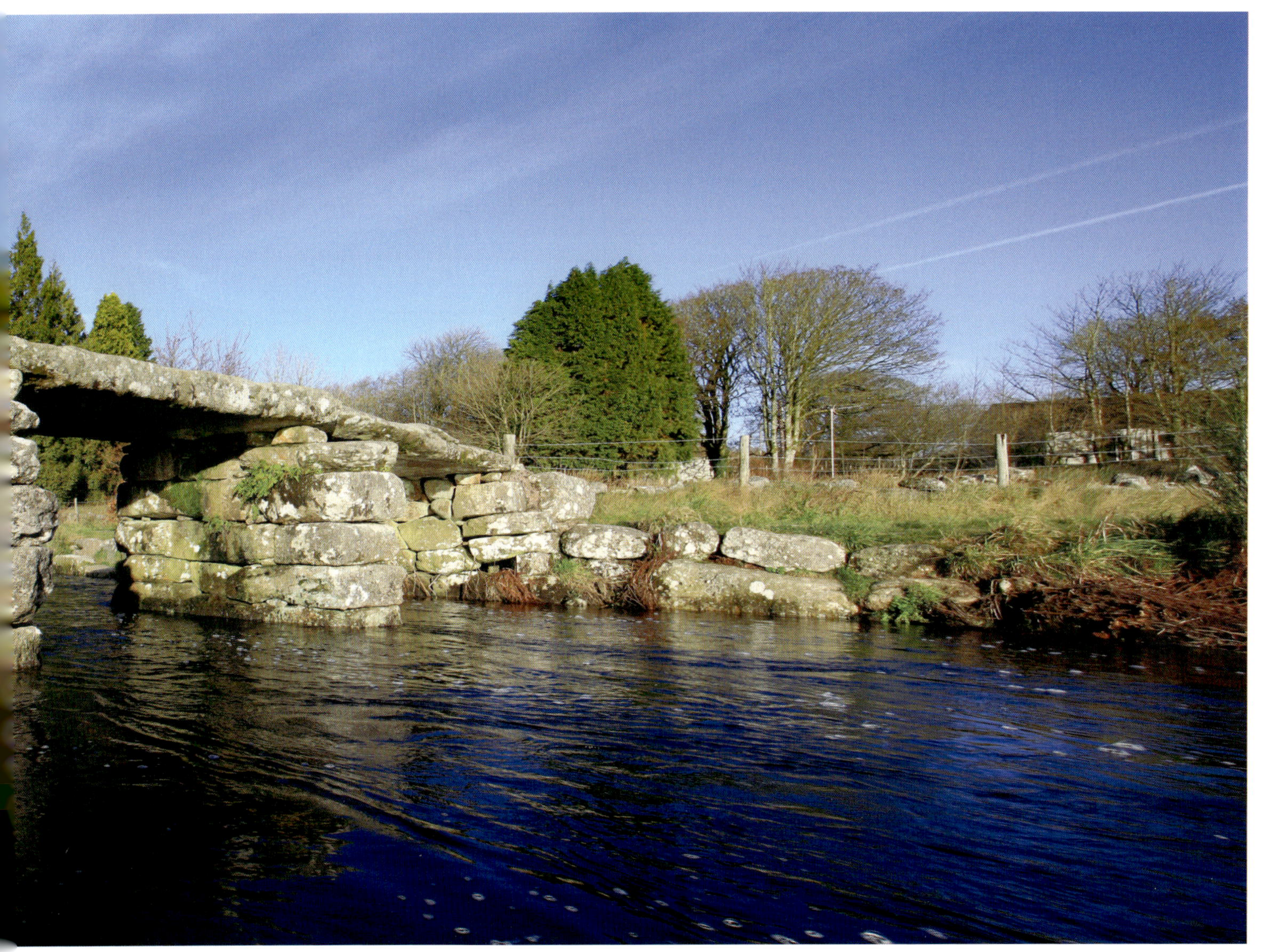

Such bridges are formed from large slabs of granite set across stone pillars. The name is thought to come from the Anglo-Saxon word, 'cleaca', meaning 'bridging the stepping stones'. The newer road bridge can be seen behind.

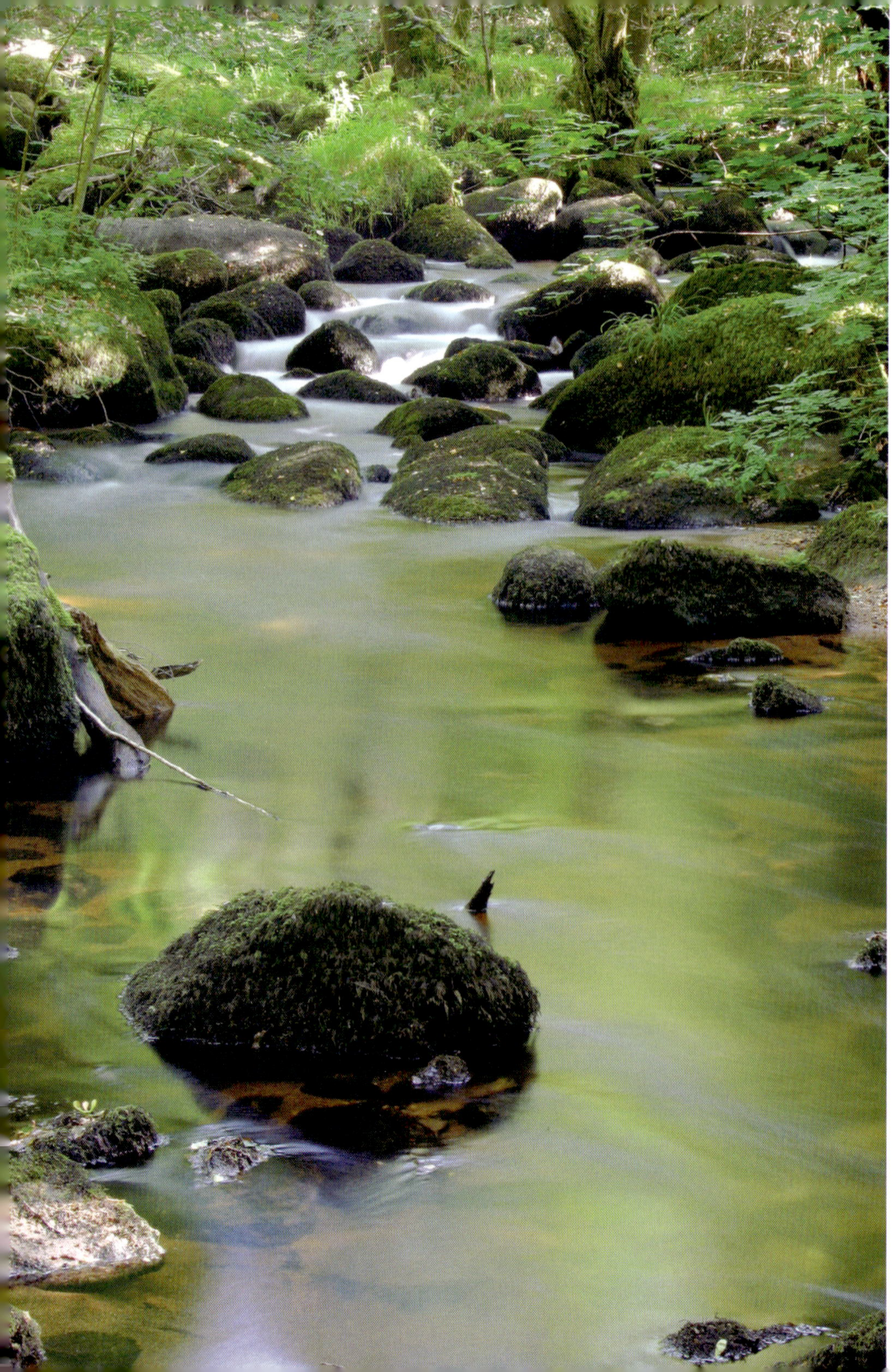

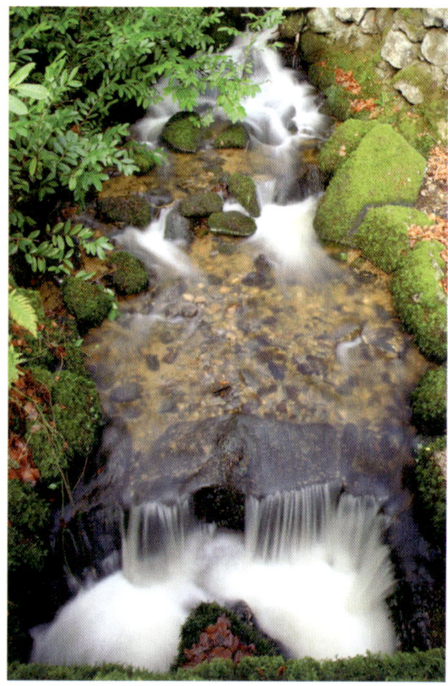

Waterfalls full of colour and character can often be found close to roads. This one (above) rushed into a well and under the road bridge.

Stream in summer at Lustleigh Cleave.

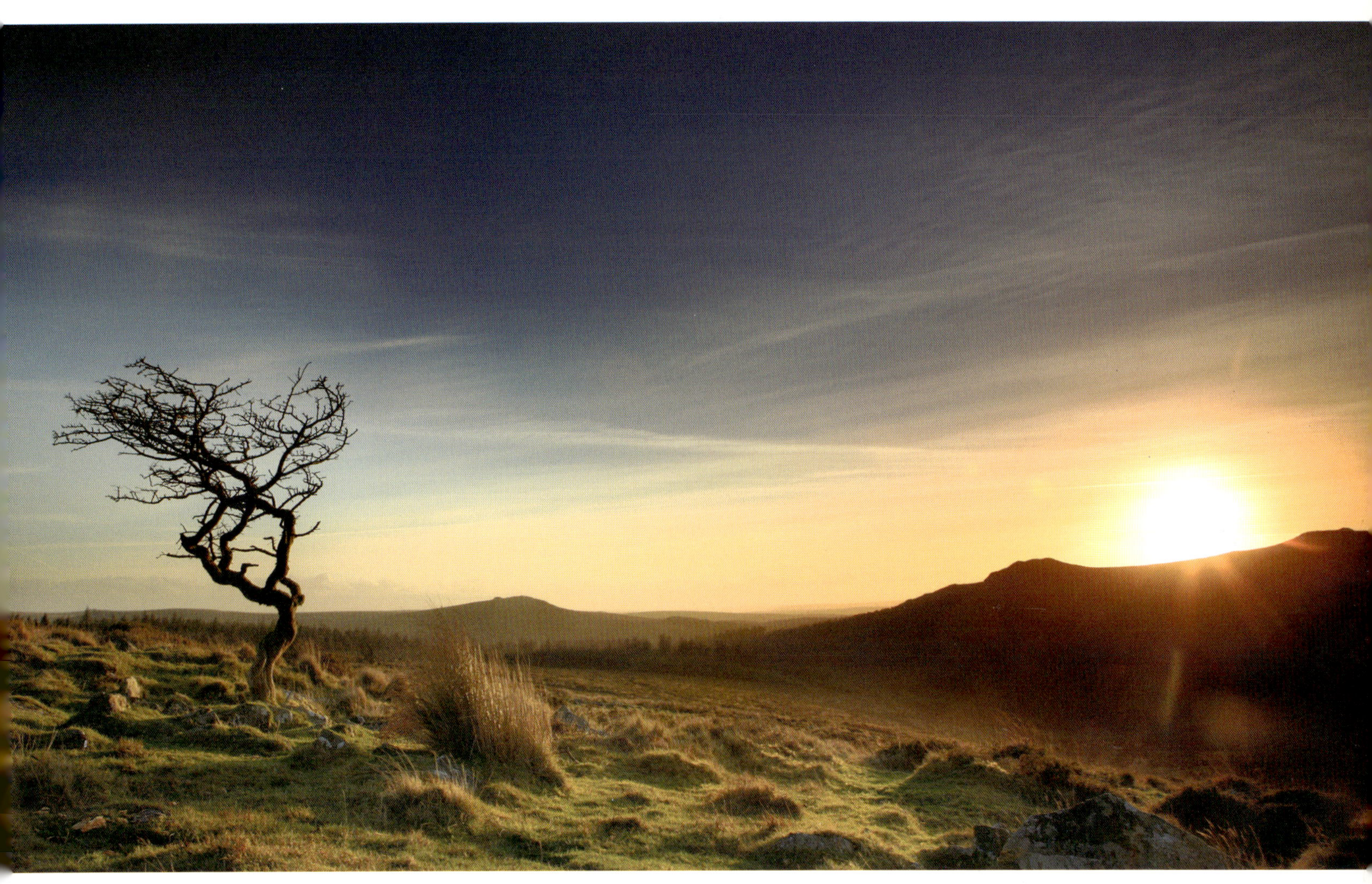

This sunset near Black Tor took my breath away.

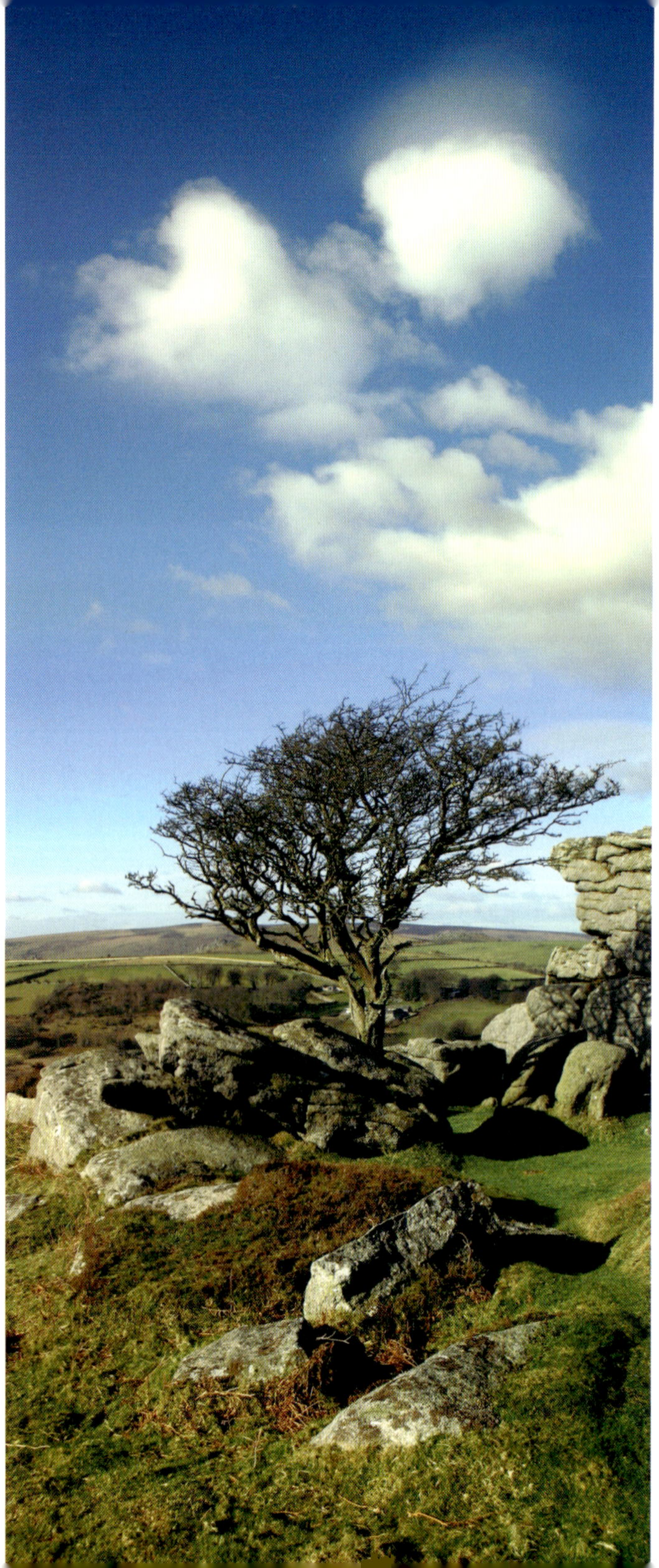

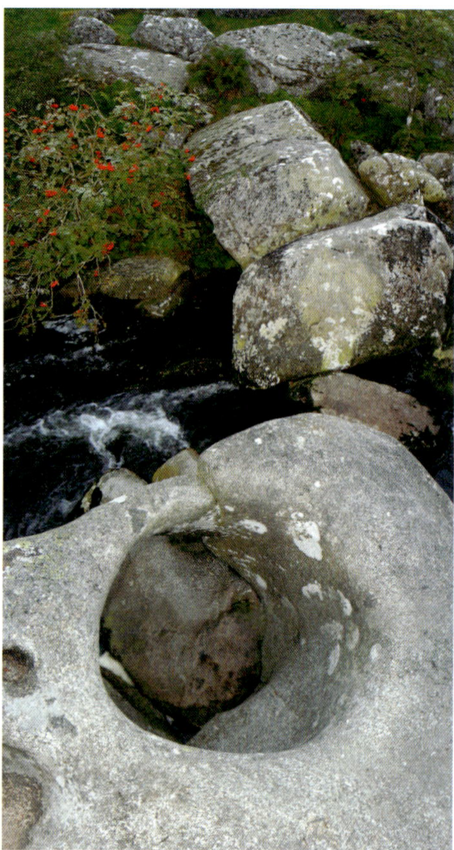

The Tolmen Stone sits in the North Teign river near Scorhill Circle. The stone has a one-metre diameter hole worn in it by river erosion. Ancient stories connected to the stone include the curing of rickets and rheumatism by passing the sufferer through the hole.

A weathered tree sits proud on top of the moor near Haytor.

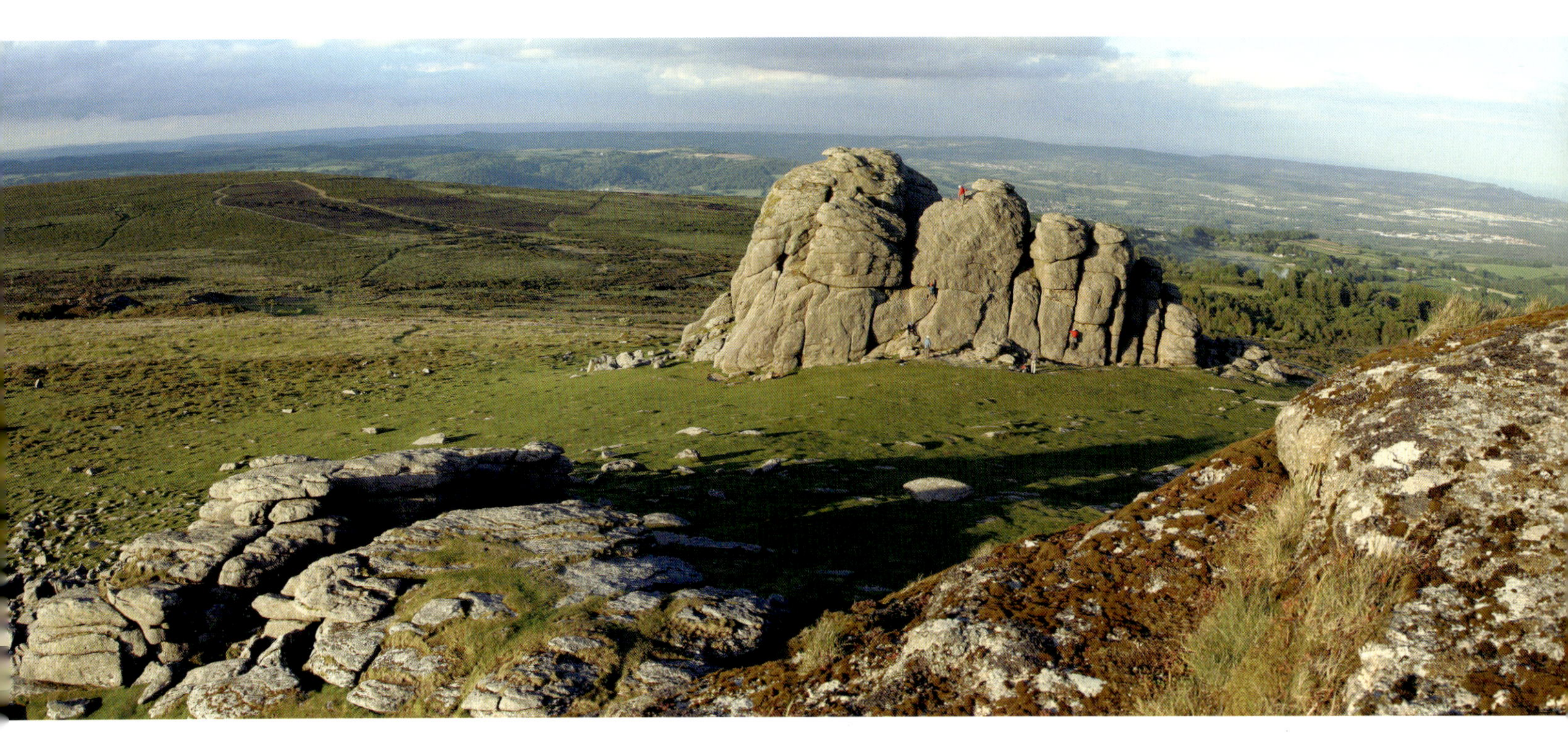

The moor attracts thousands of visitors and the Tors are popular with with walkers and climbers.
I watched these on Haytor for some time as the sun slowly set behind me.

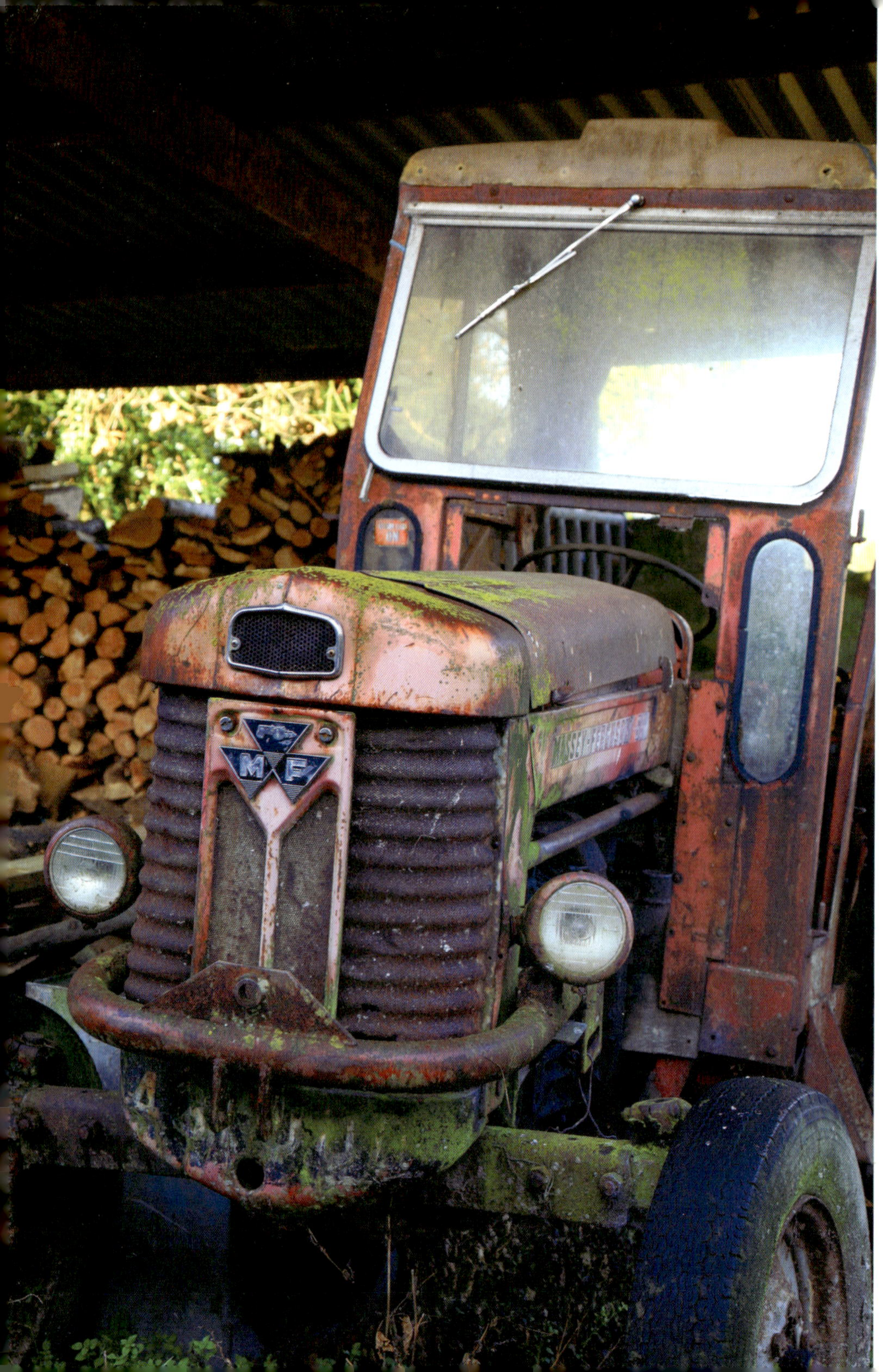

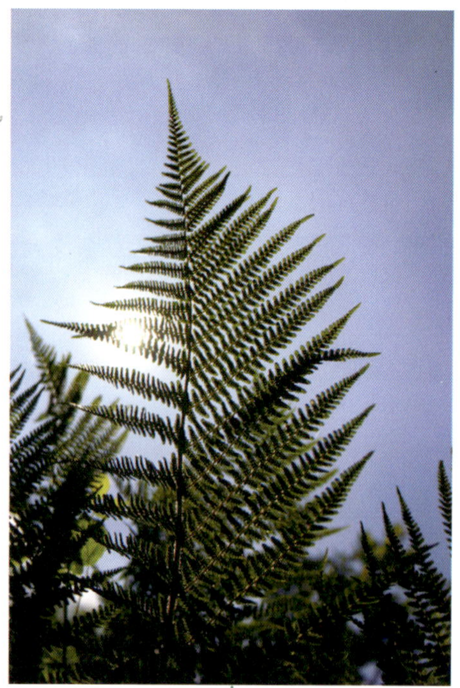

A fern filters the summer sun.

An old tractor sits worn and battered from years of toil on a farm near Chagford.

Thick moss adorns a stone wall
in the forest near Dartmeet.

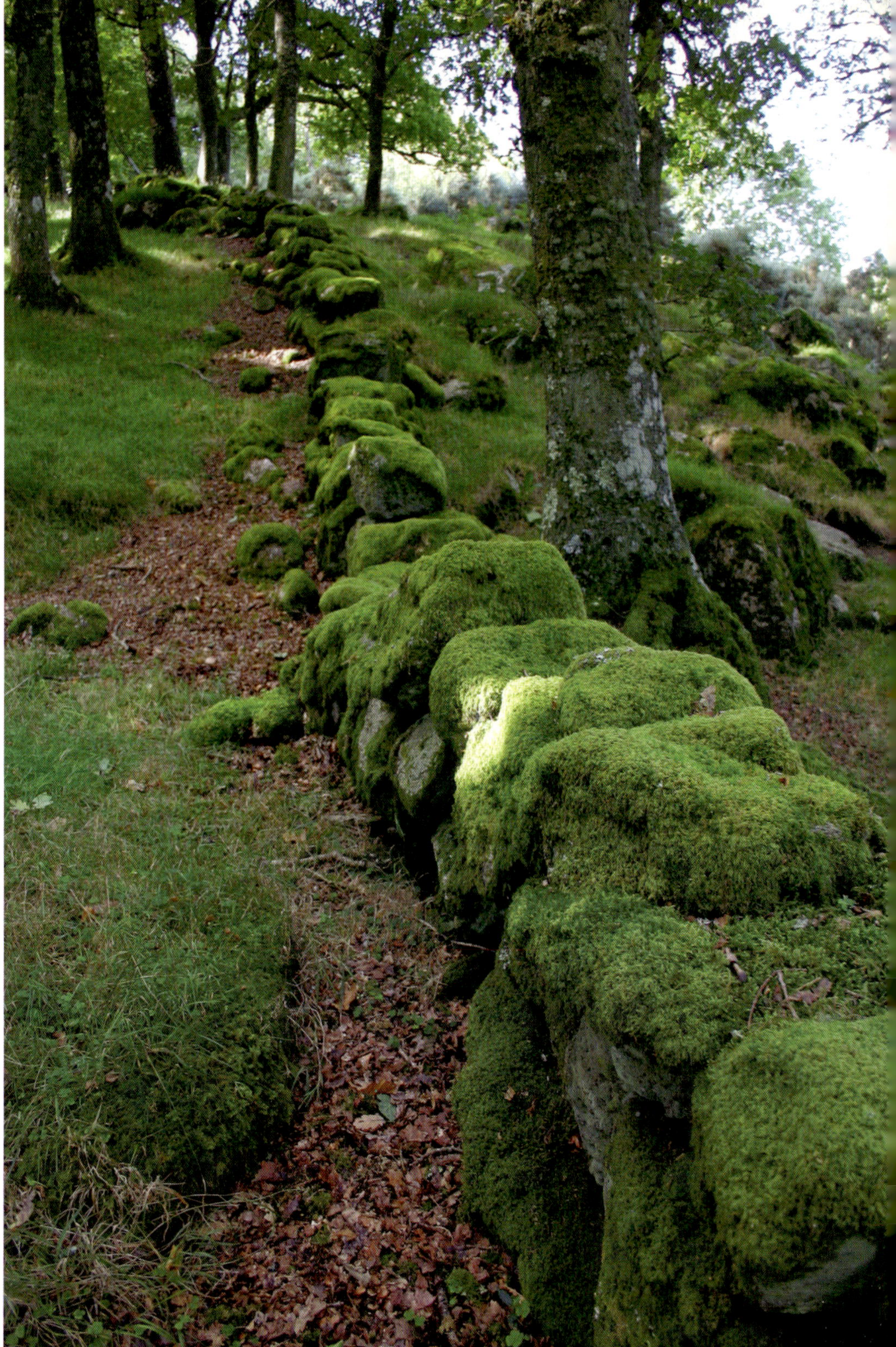

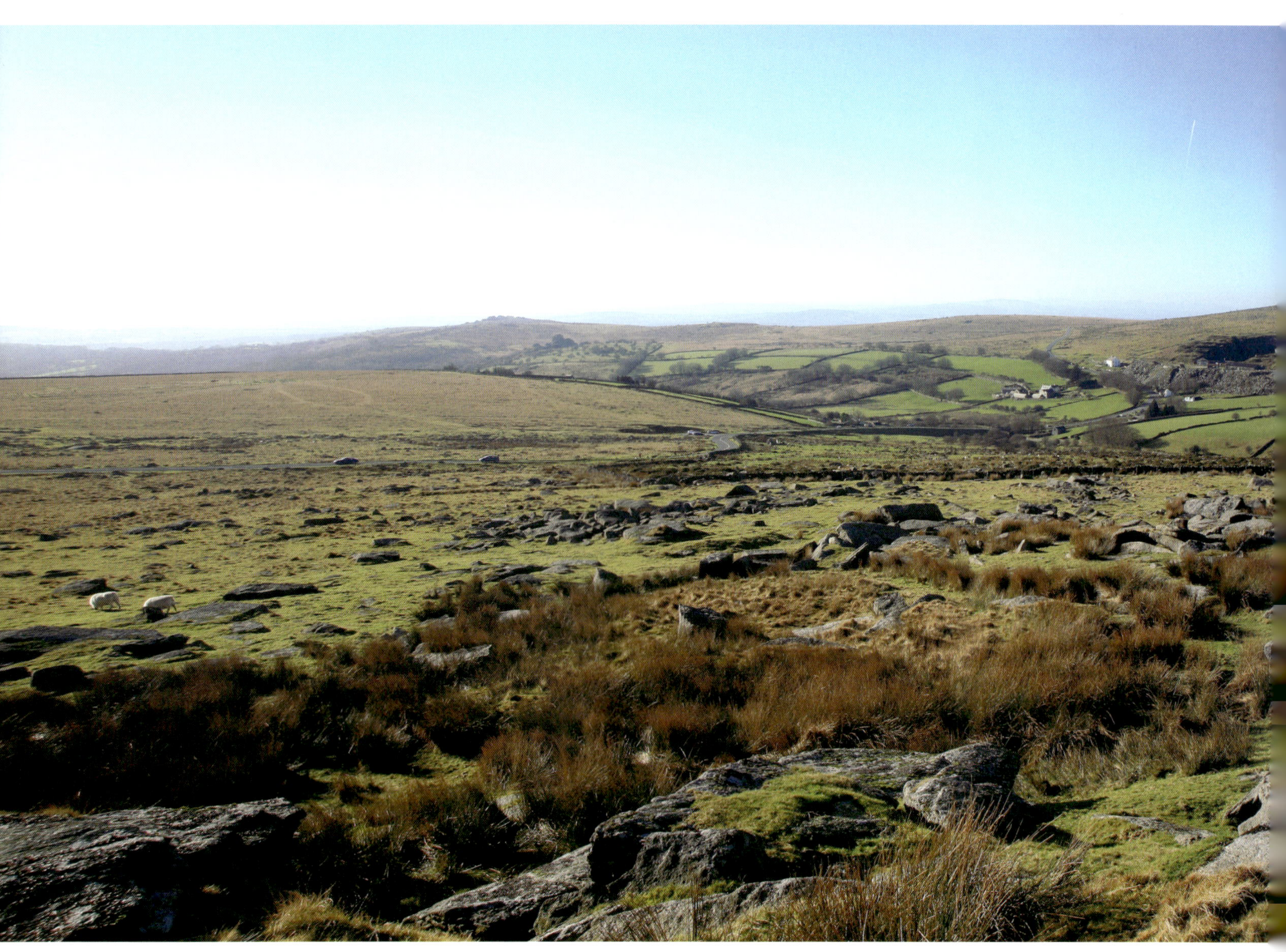

A panoramic view looking west near Merrivale on a beautifully clear day.

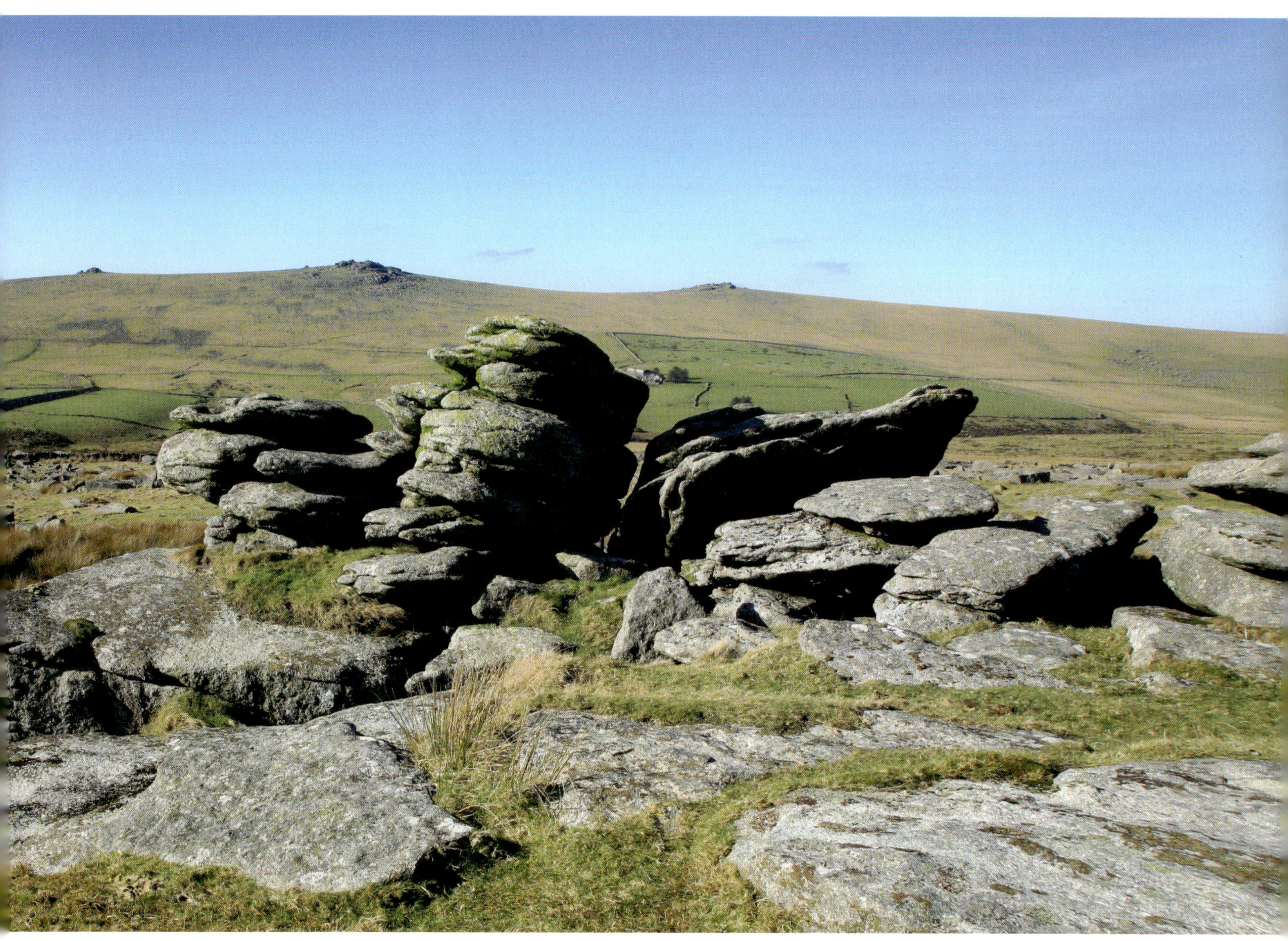

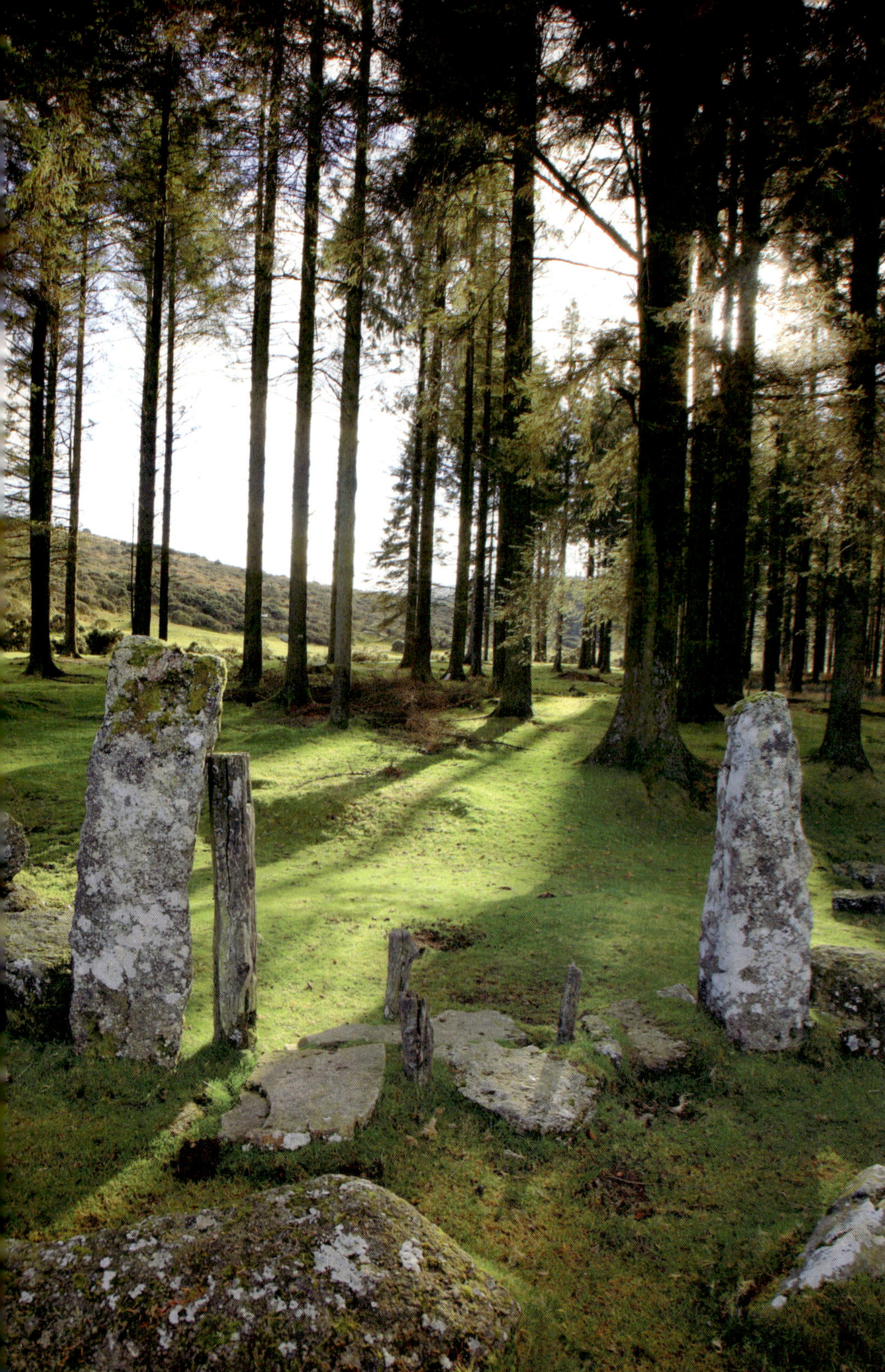

Gate posts on the moor were traditonally made of granite. This well-preserved pair stand near Bellever Bridge leading into the forest. Such posts often had slots or holes cut into them into which horizontal bars were placed. Many are still in use and can be seen all over the Moor.

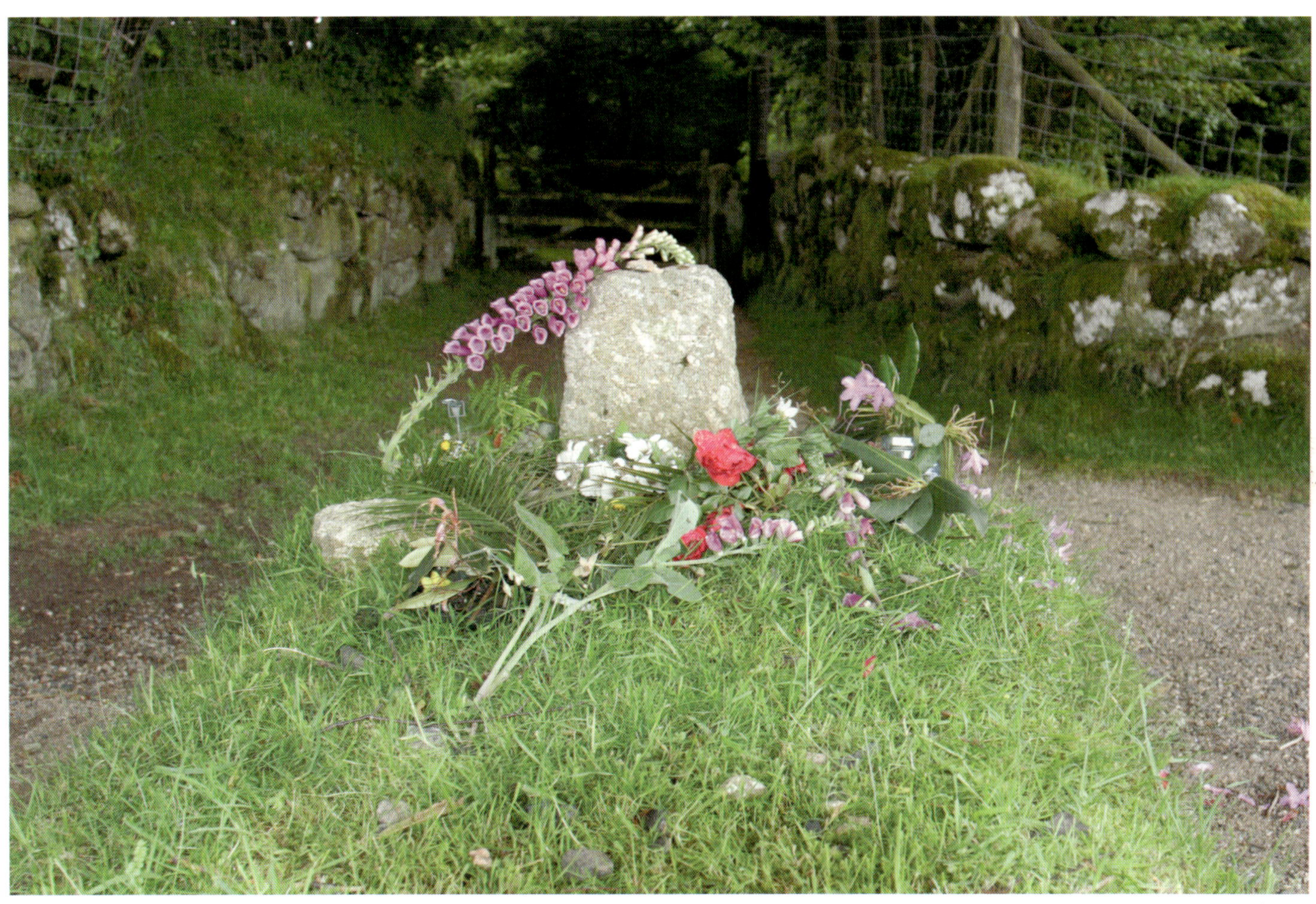

Kitty Jay's grave sits beside the road near Hound Tor. It is said to be the resting place of a young farm girl, spurned by her lover, who then hanged herself in a barn. Flowers mysteriously appear on the grave each day, supposedly put there by pixies, or some say a hooded figure!

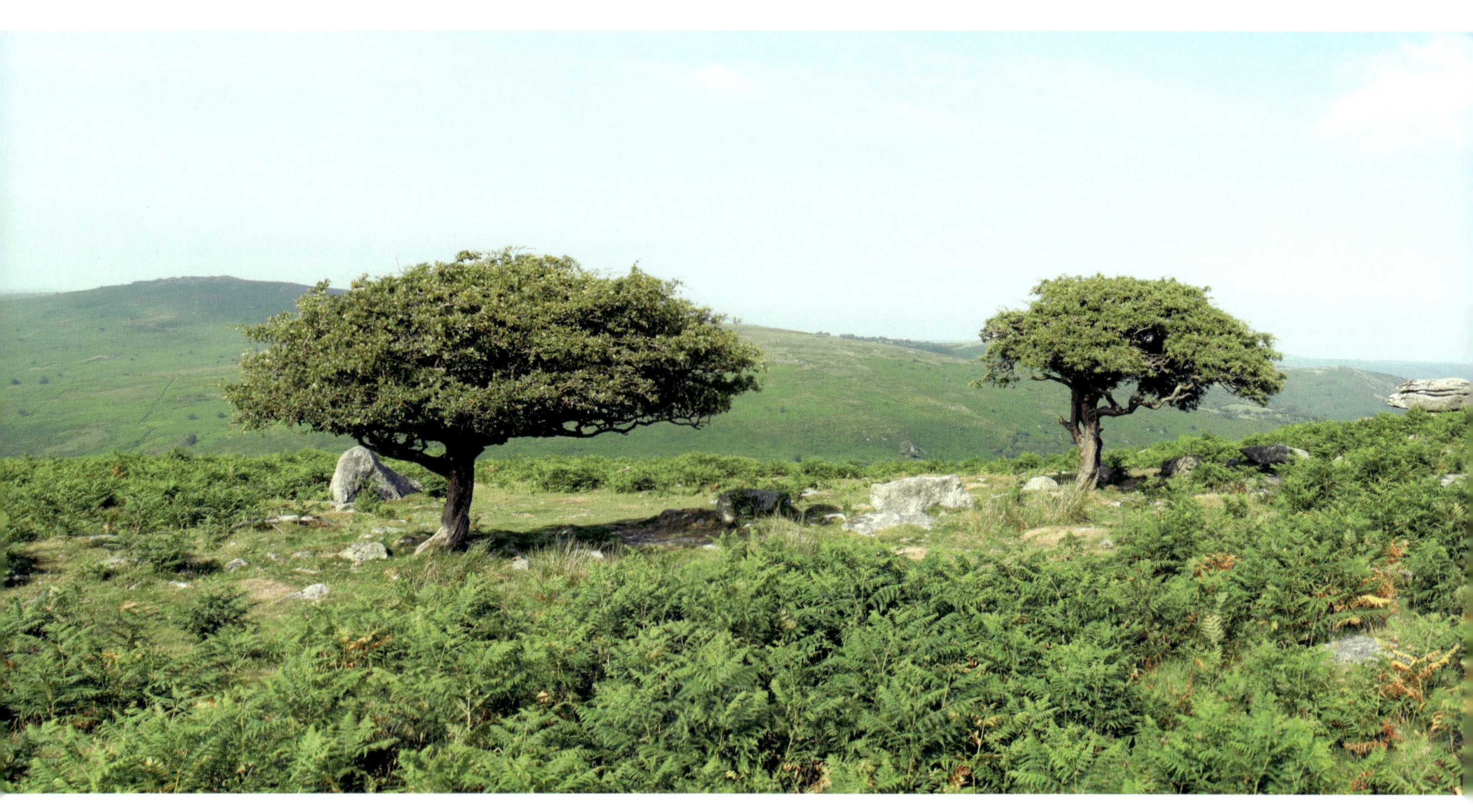

Combestone Tor panorama. This is one of the moor's most accessible Tors, and views of the open moor are fantastic from here.

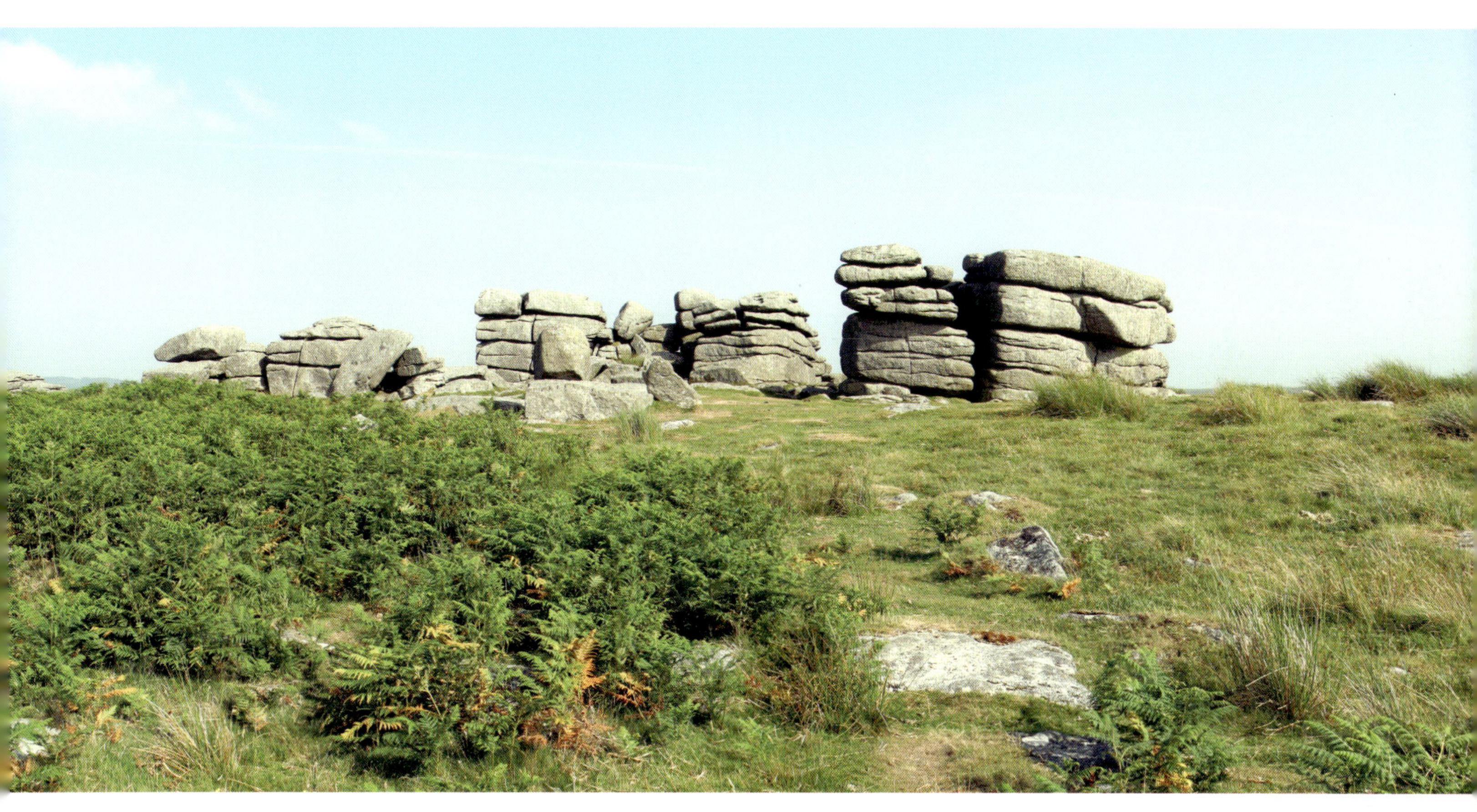

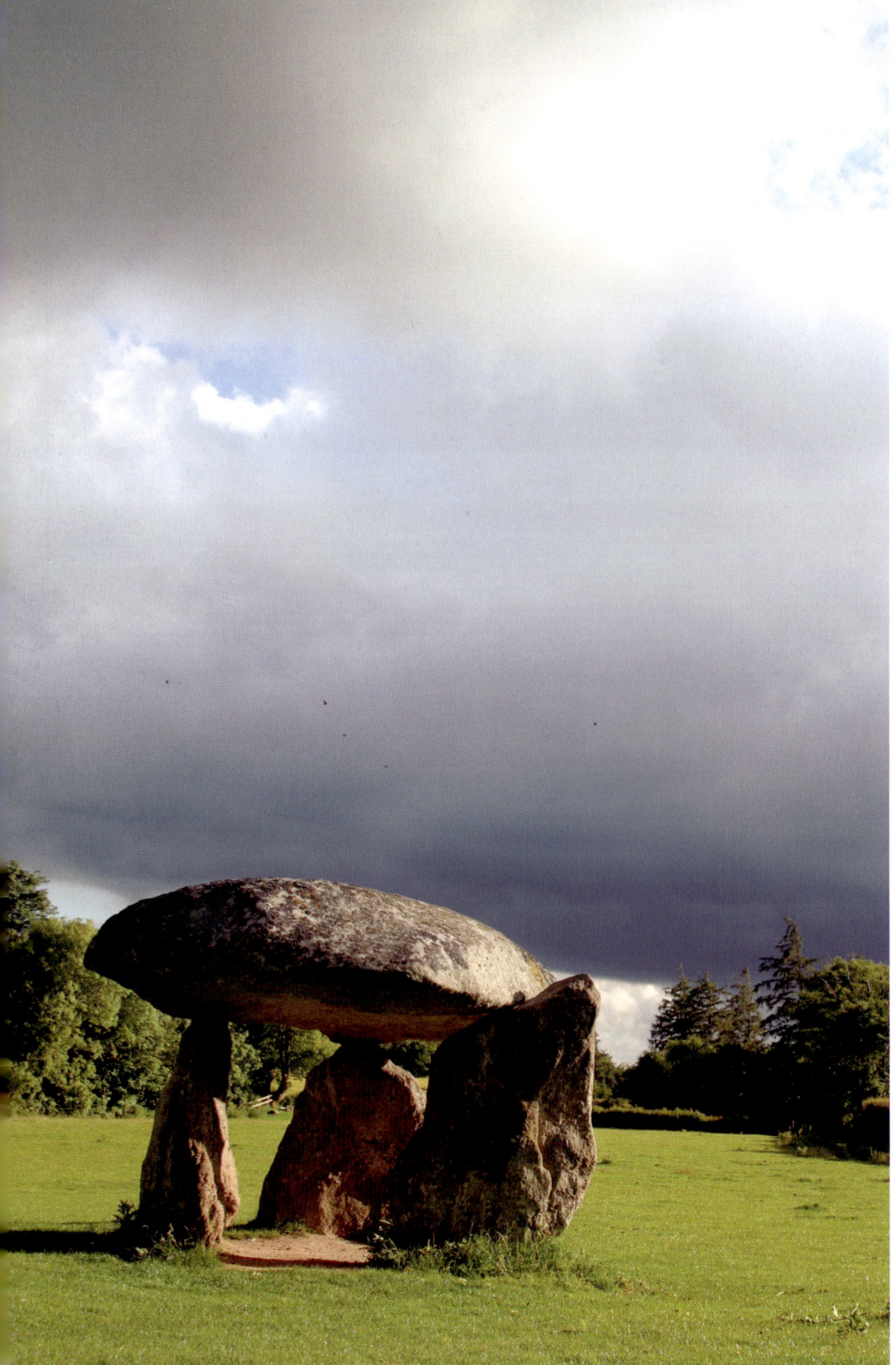

Spinster's Rock is an ancient Dolmen and would originally have been covered with earth as a burial chamber.

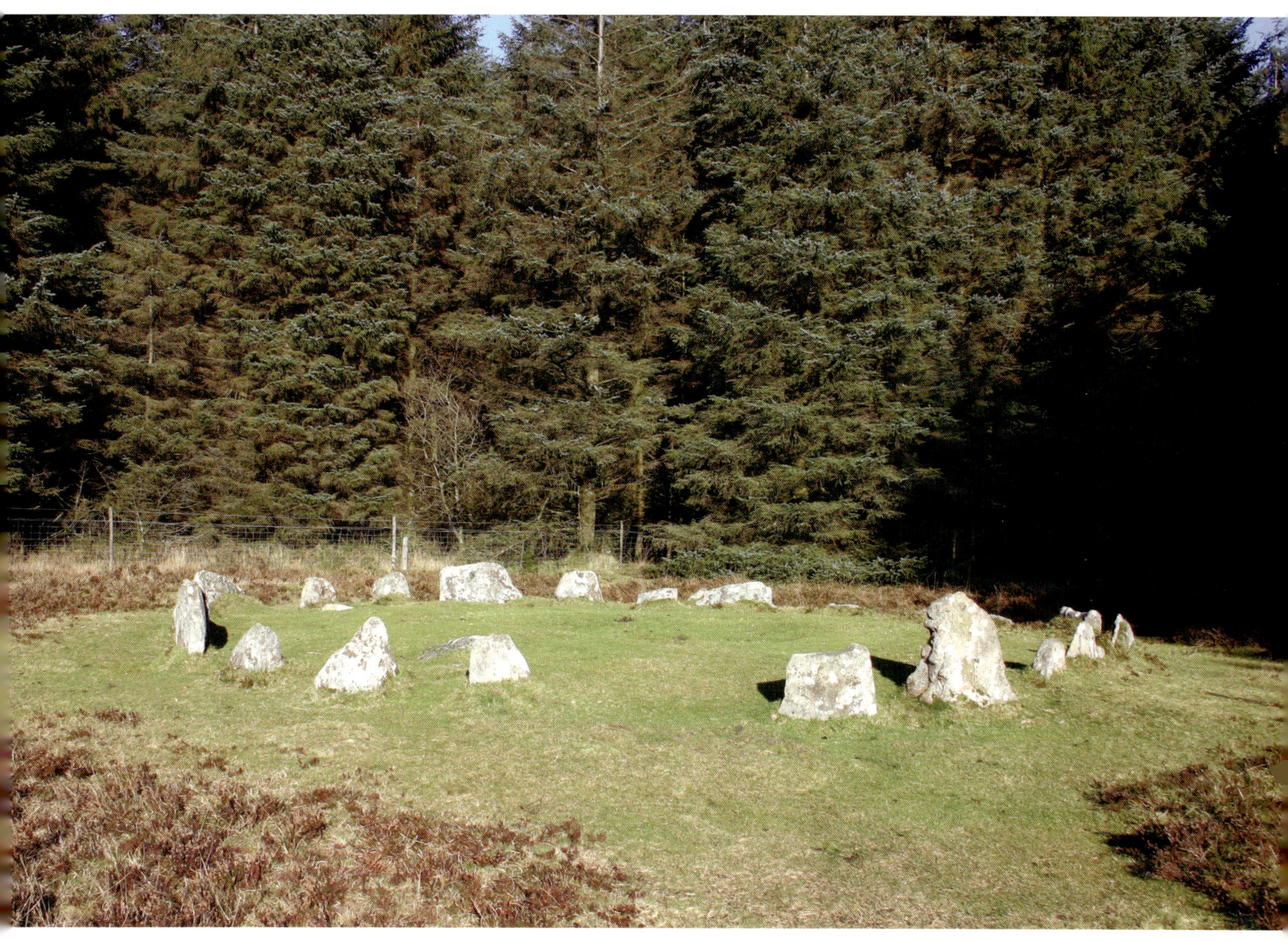

A ring cairn at Soussons Common.

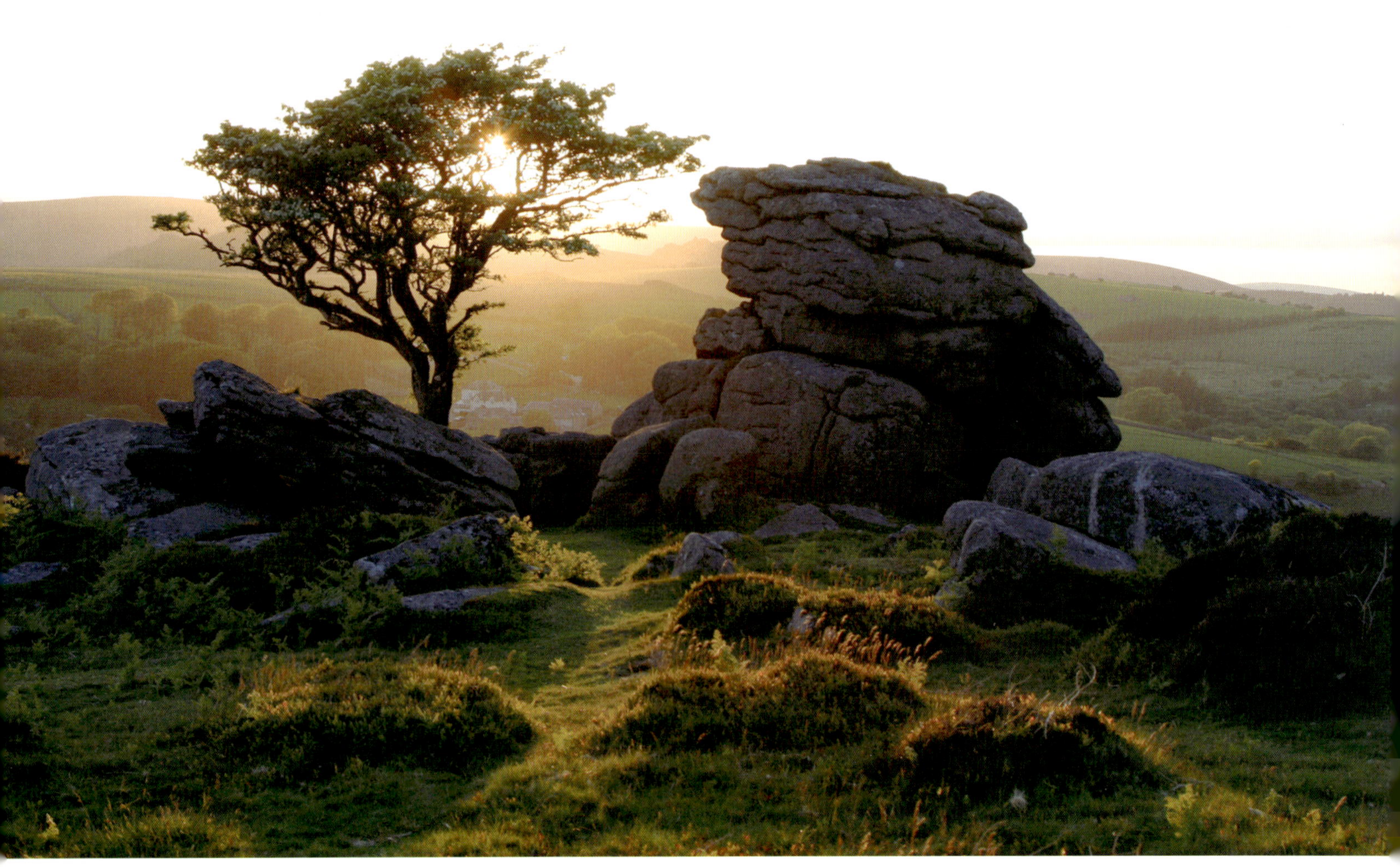

Sunset near Staple Tor.

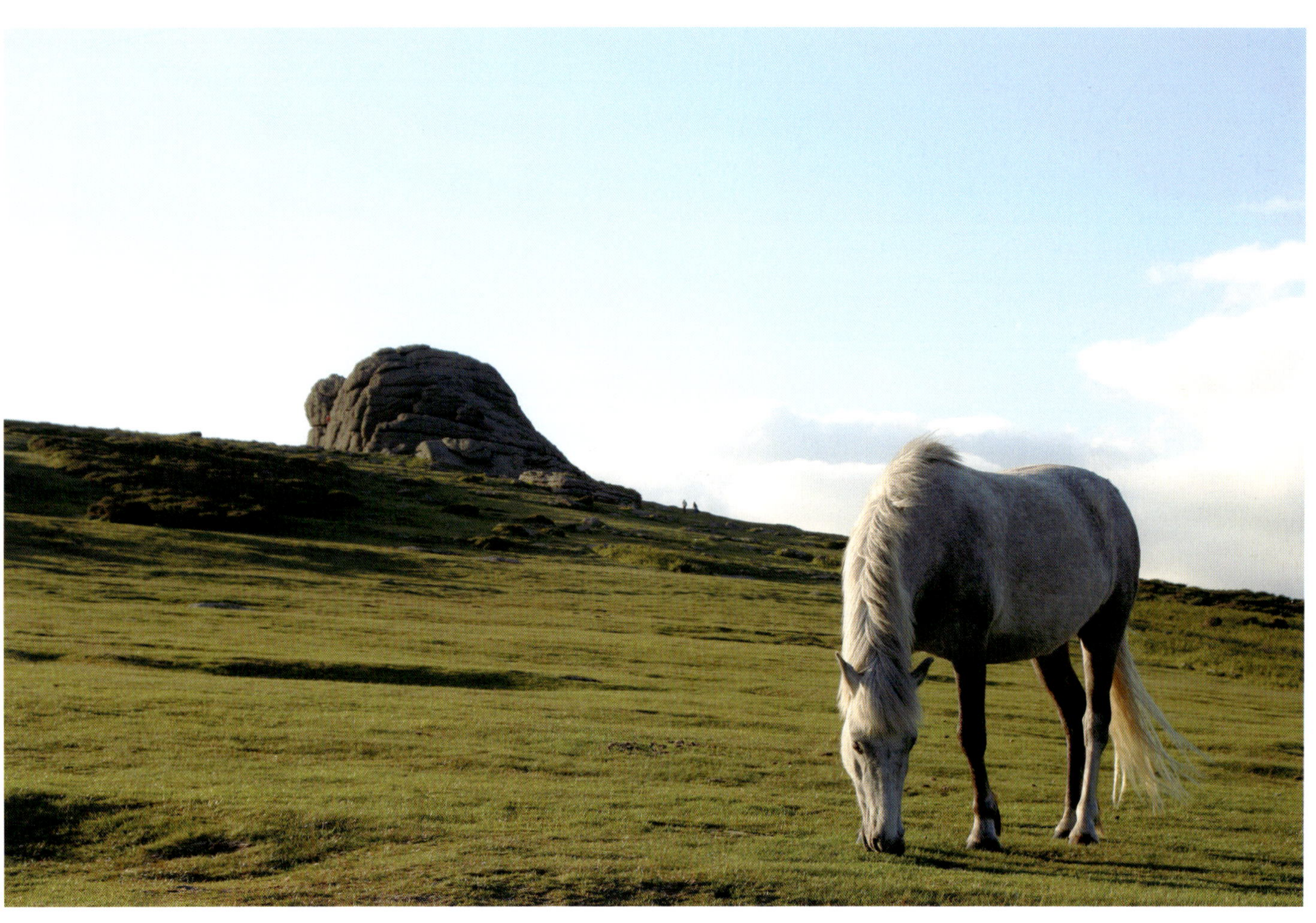

A Dartmoor pony grazes near Haytor in the late evening sun.

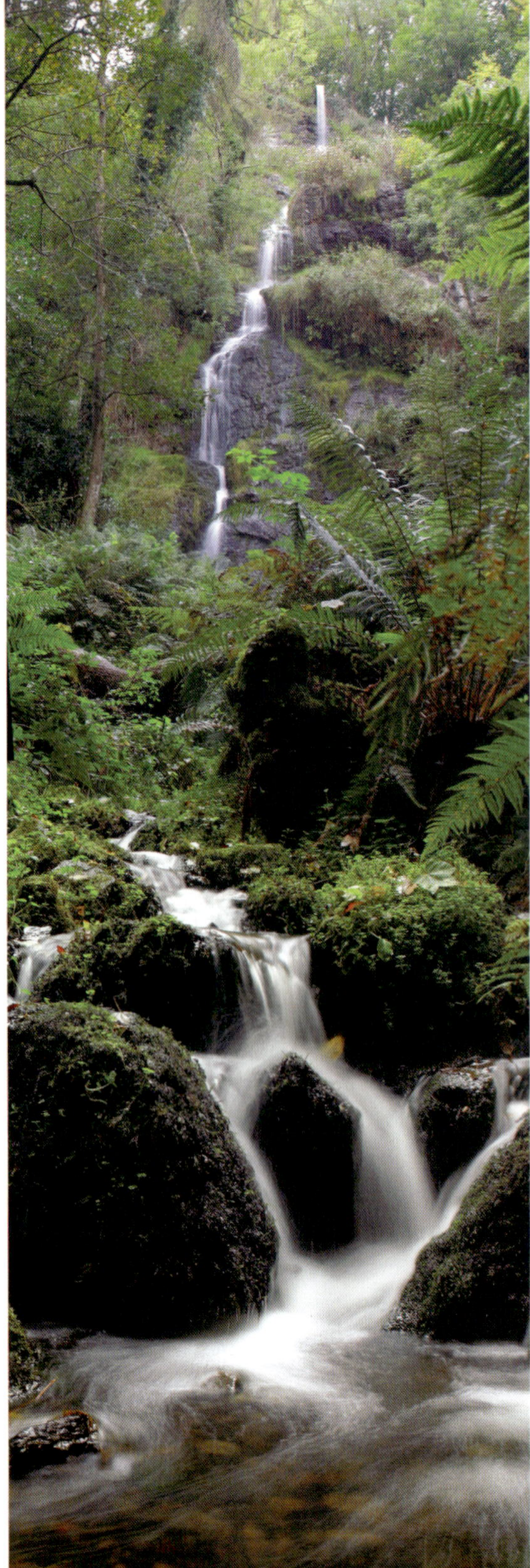

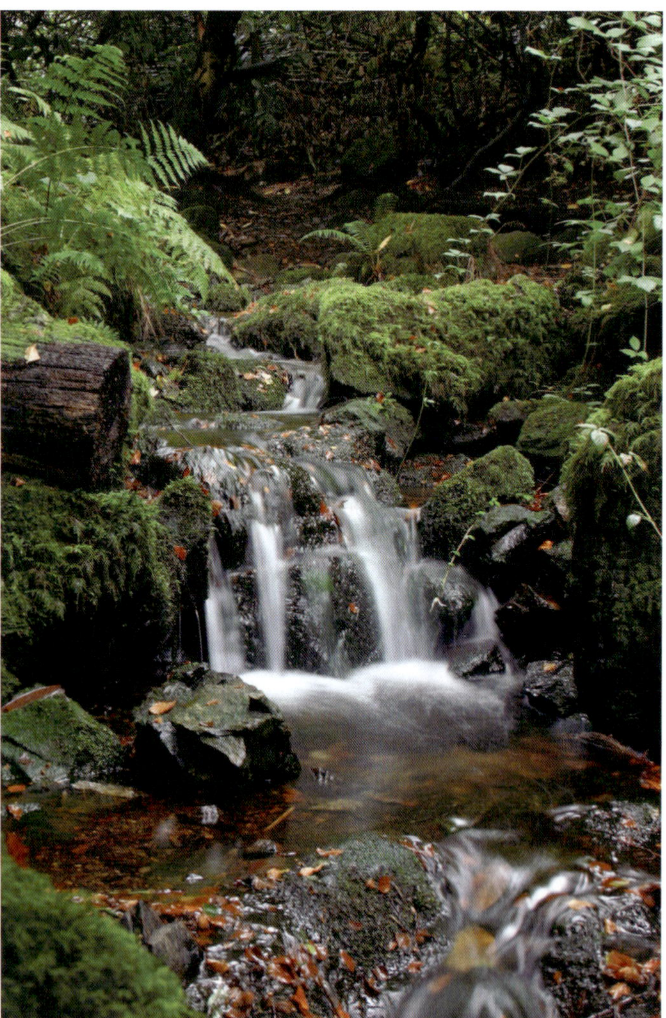

A beautiful fall in miniature.

Lady Exmouth Fall (left), the tallest waterfall in England at 220 feet.

Dartmoor hosts many ancient oaks. This one, deep in a woodland, was completely covered in an inch-thick coat of moss.

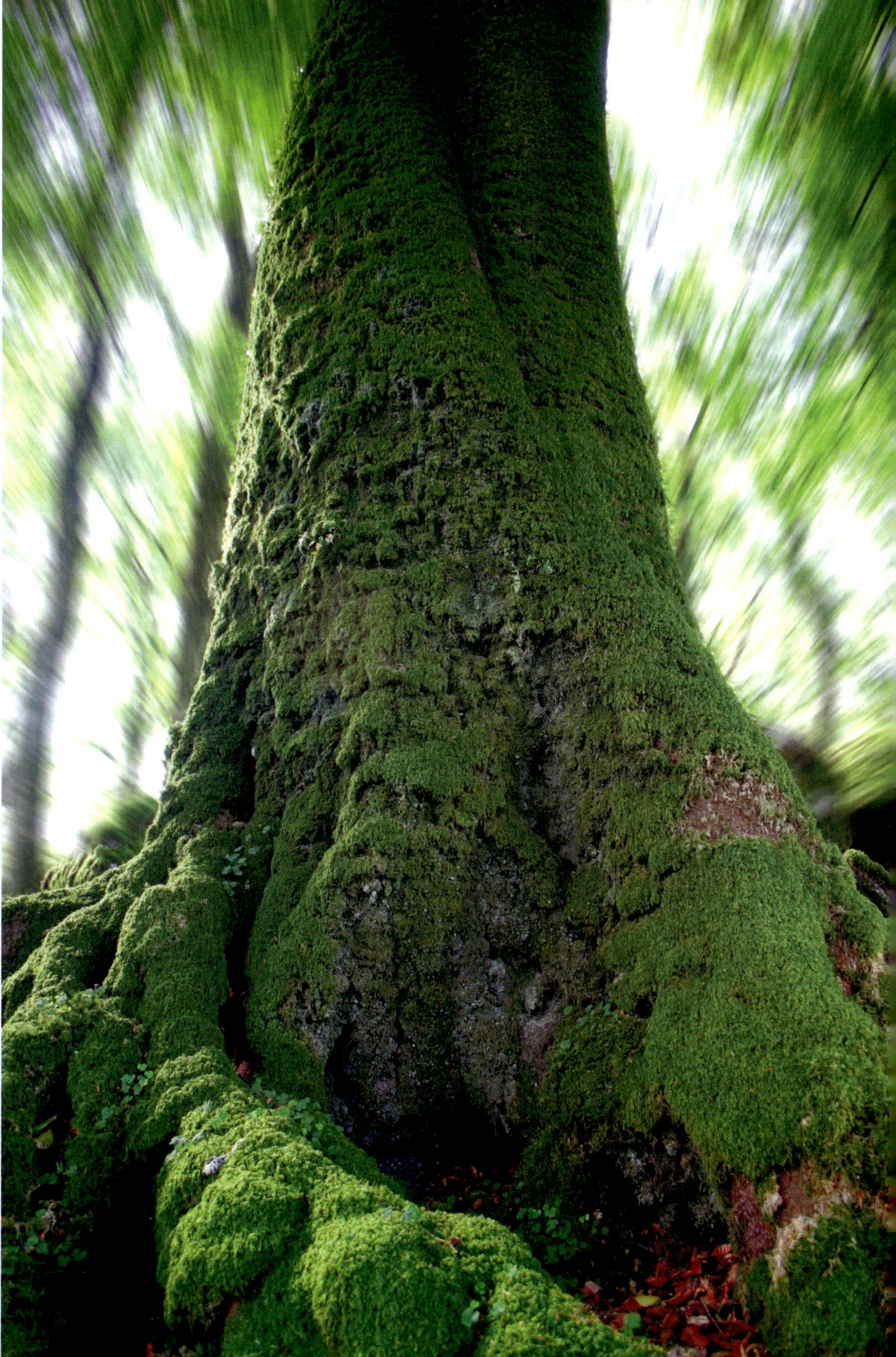

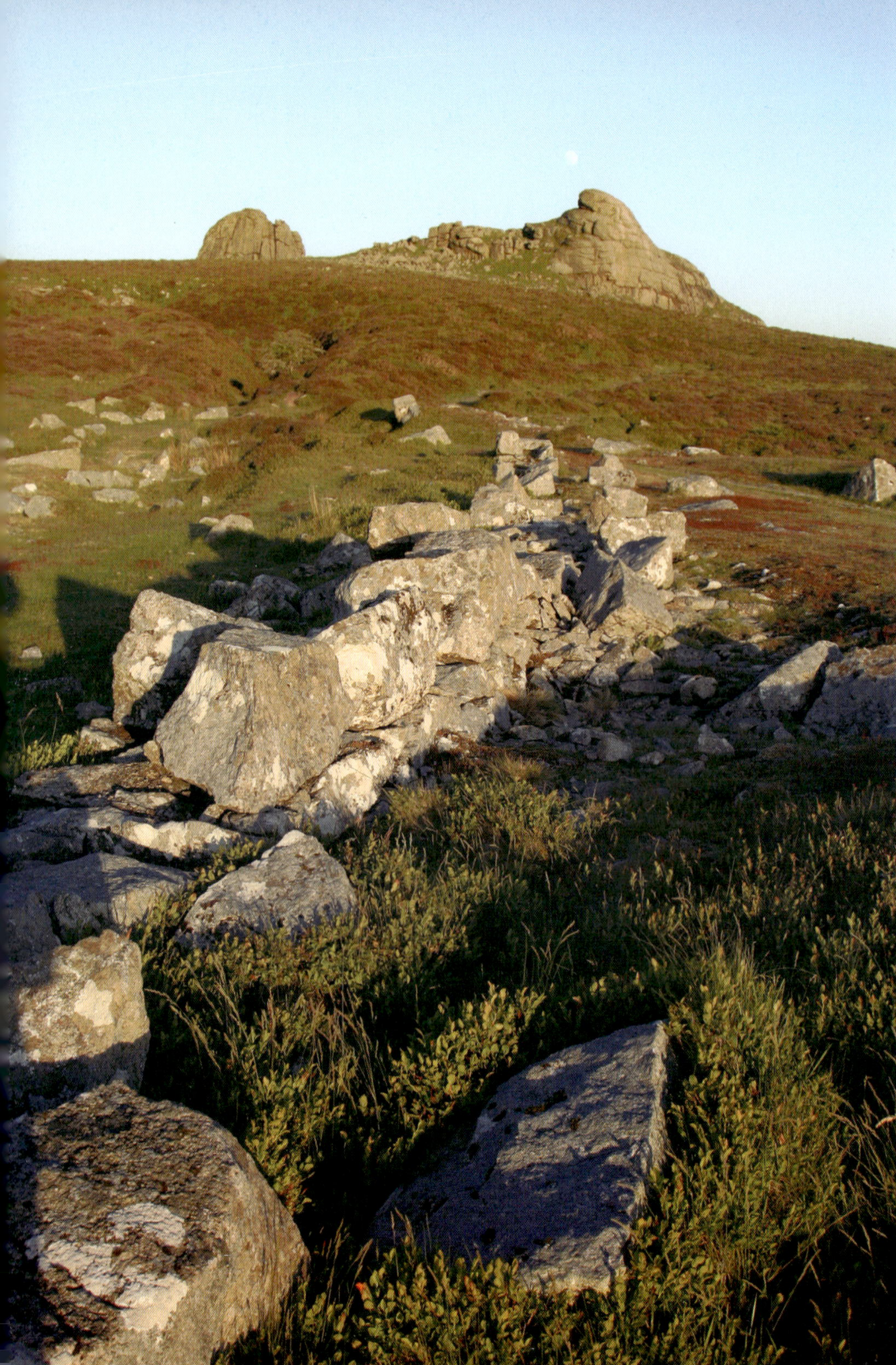

Moonrise over Haytor.

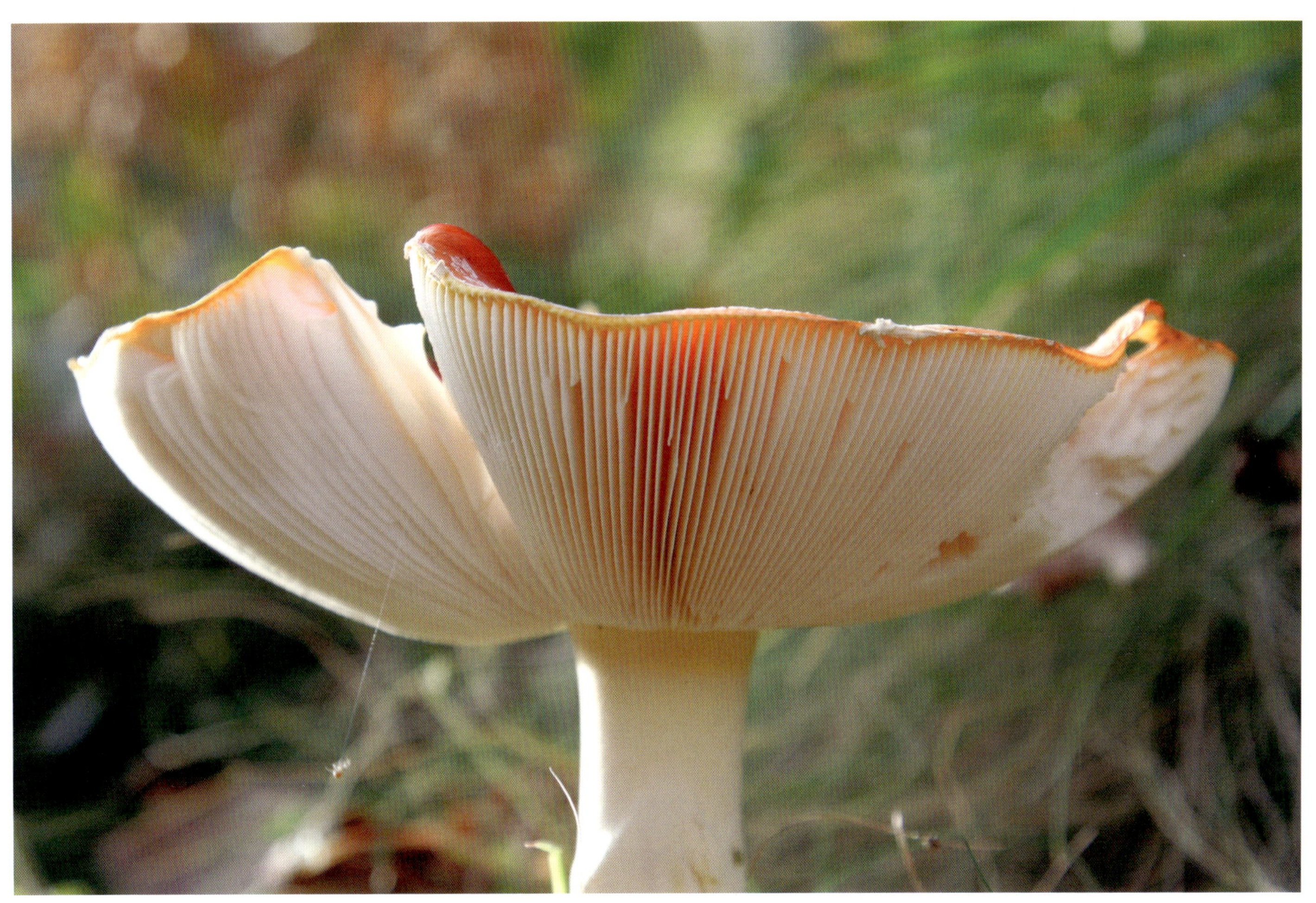

A fungus attracts a tiny spider that scurries quickly along a narrow thread.

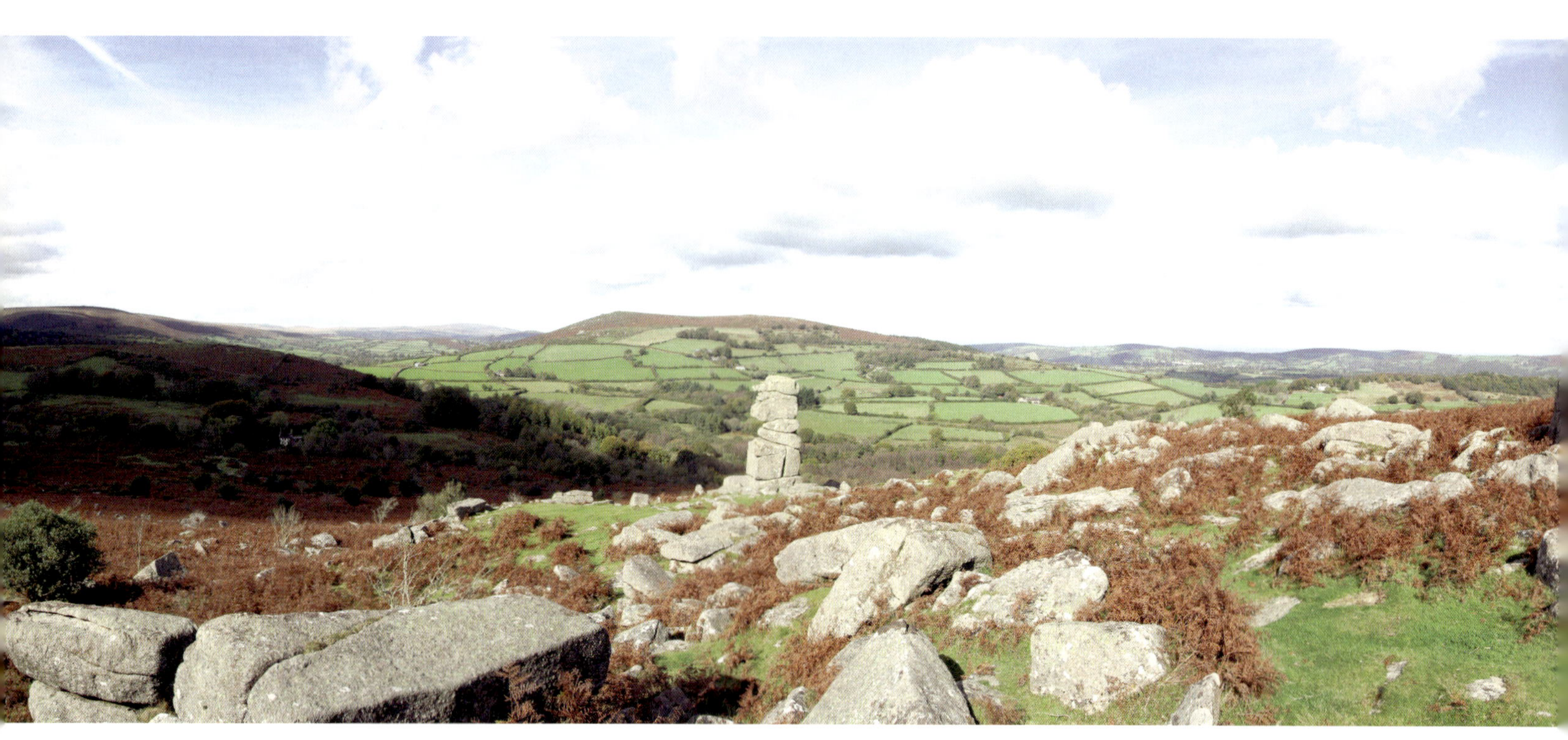

Panorama at Bowerman's Nose.

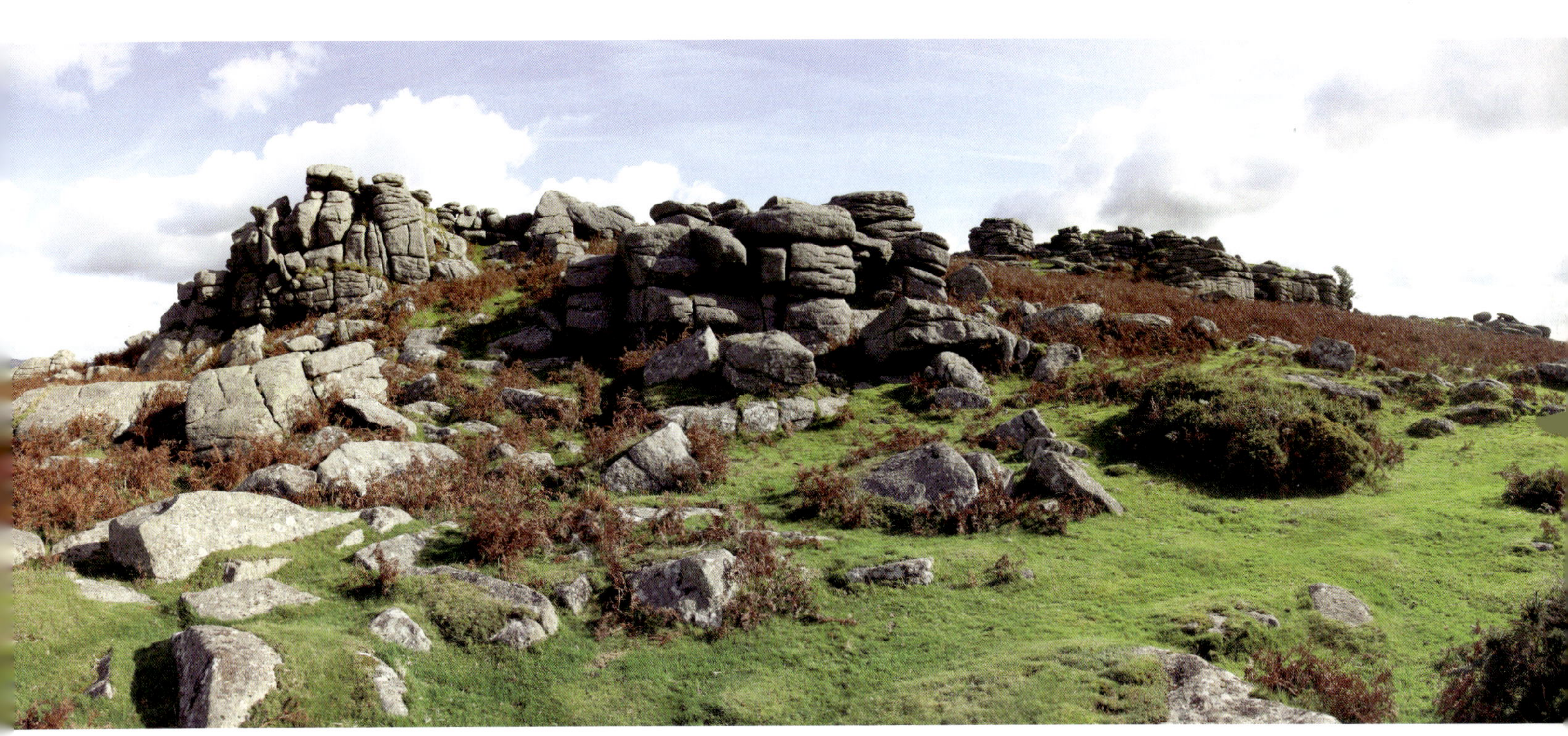

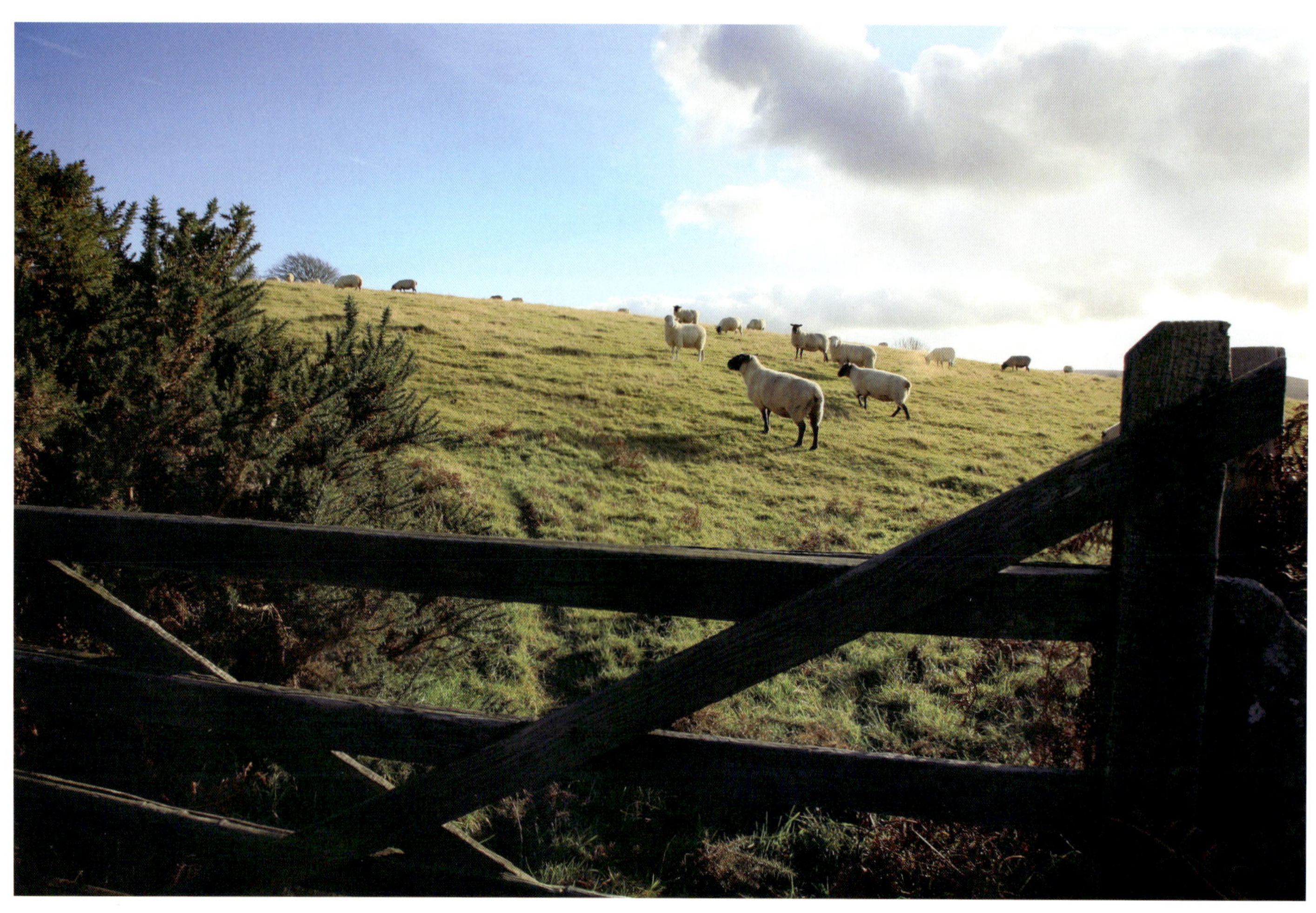

Late afternoon near Chagford.

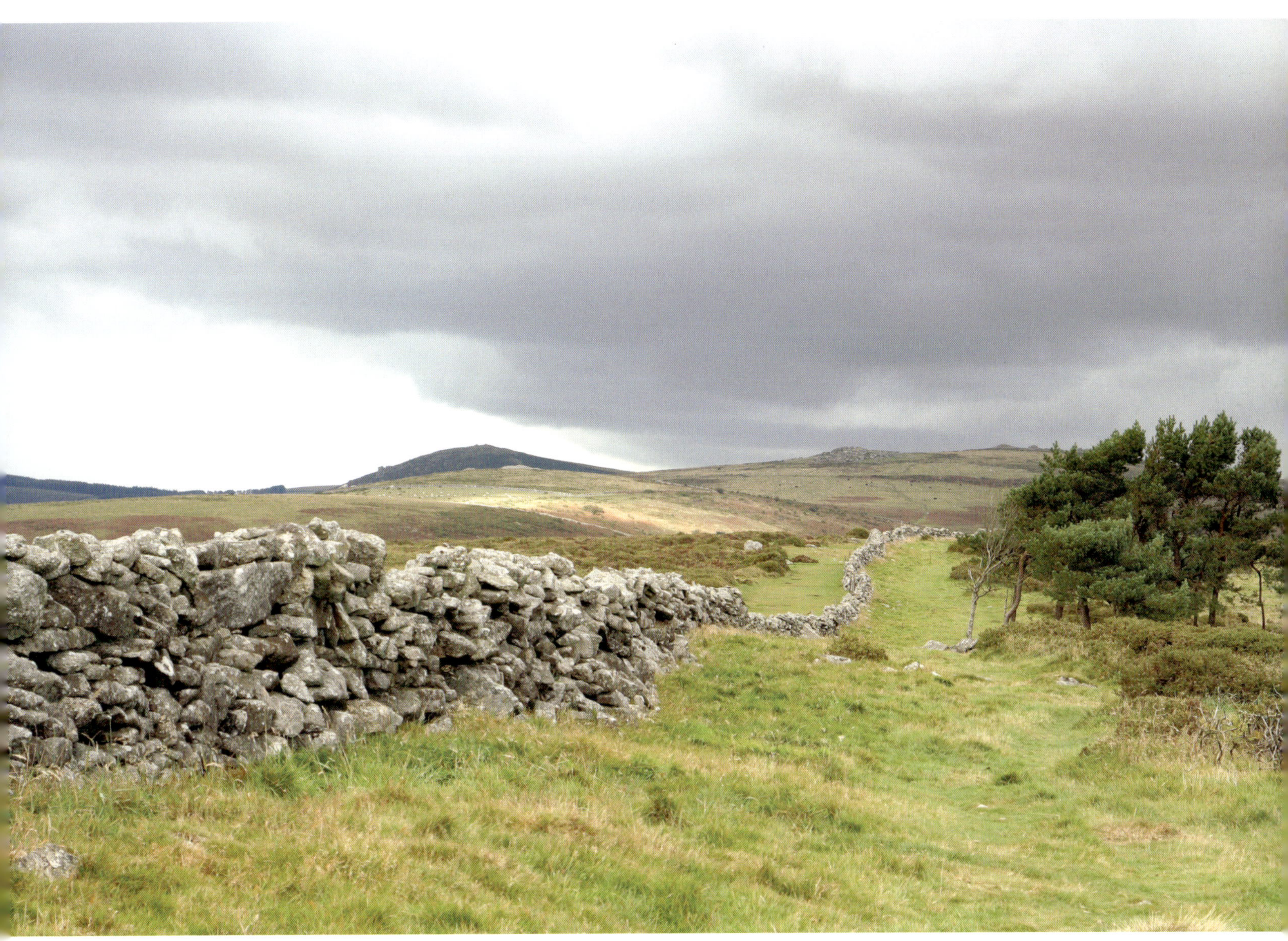

A weathered stone wall stretches into the distance, with threatening cloud overhead.

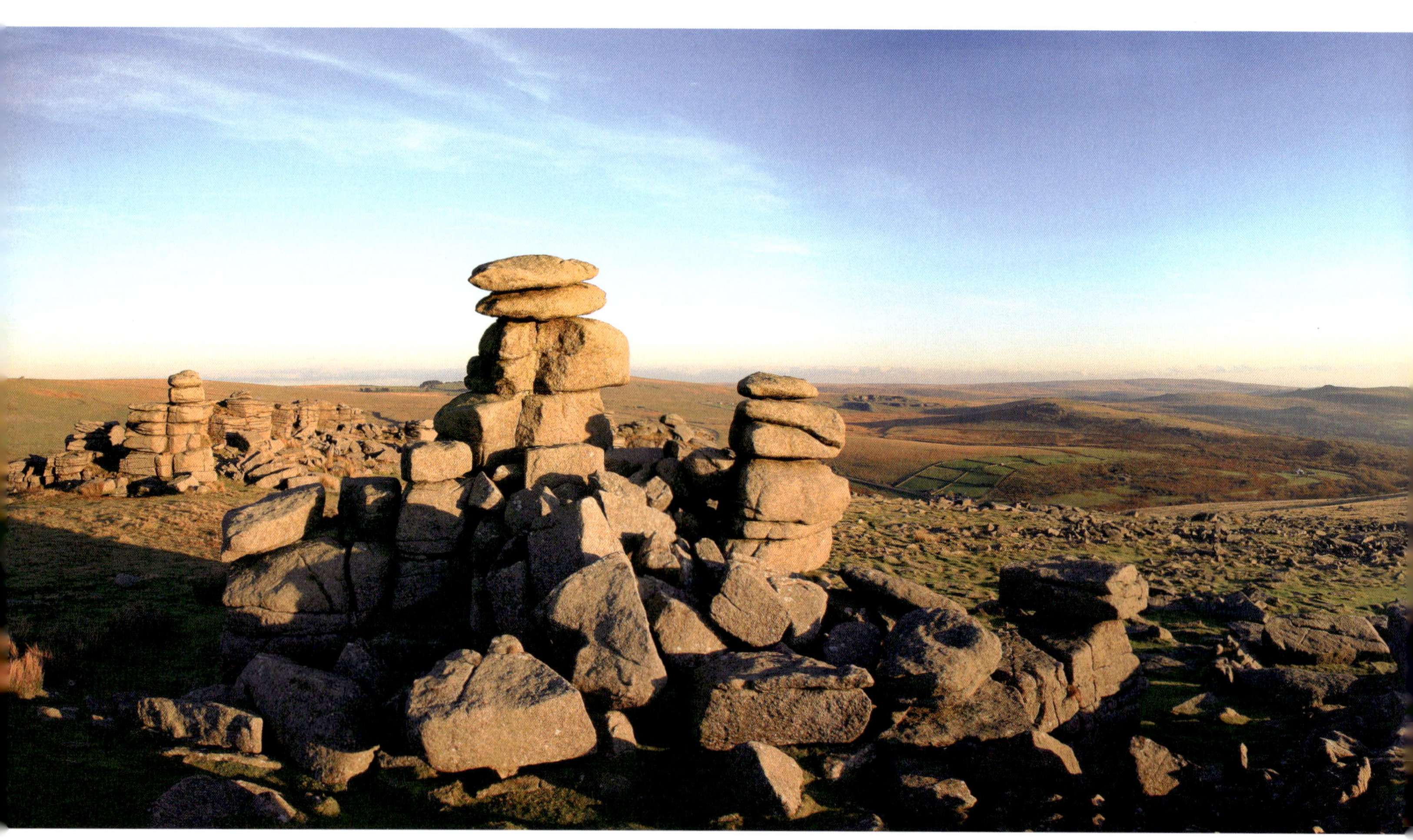

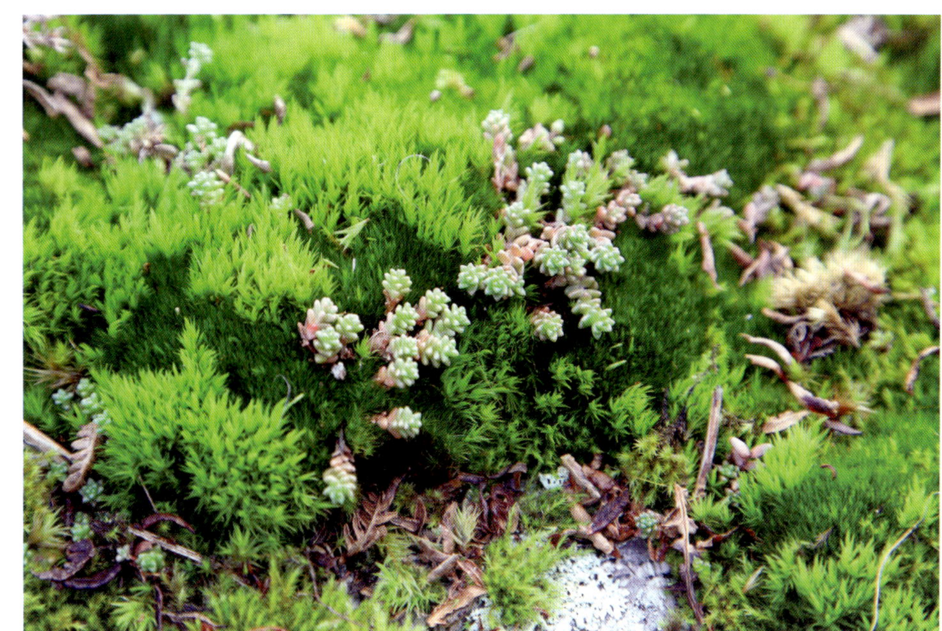

Rich growth on rocks near Chinkwell Tor.

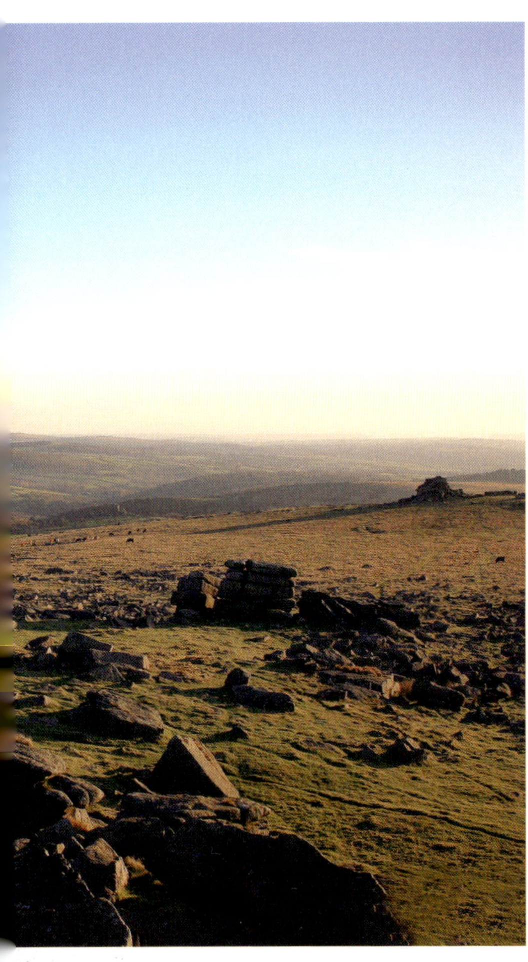

Late evening light at Staple Tor near Merrivale.

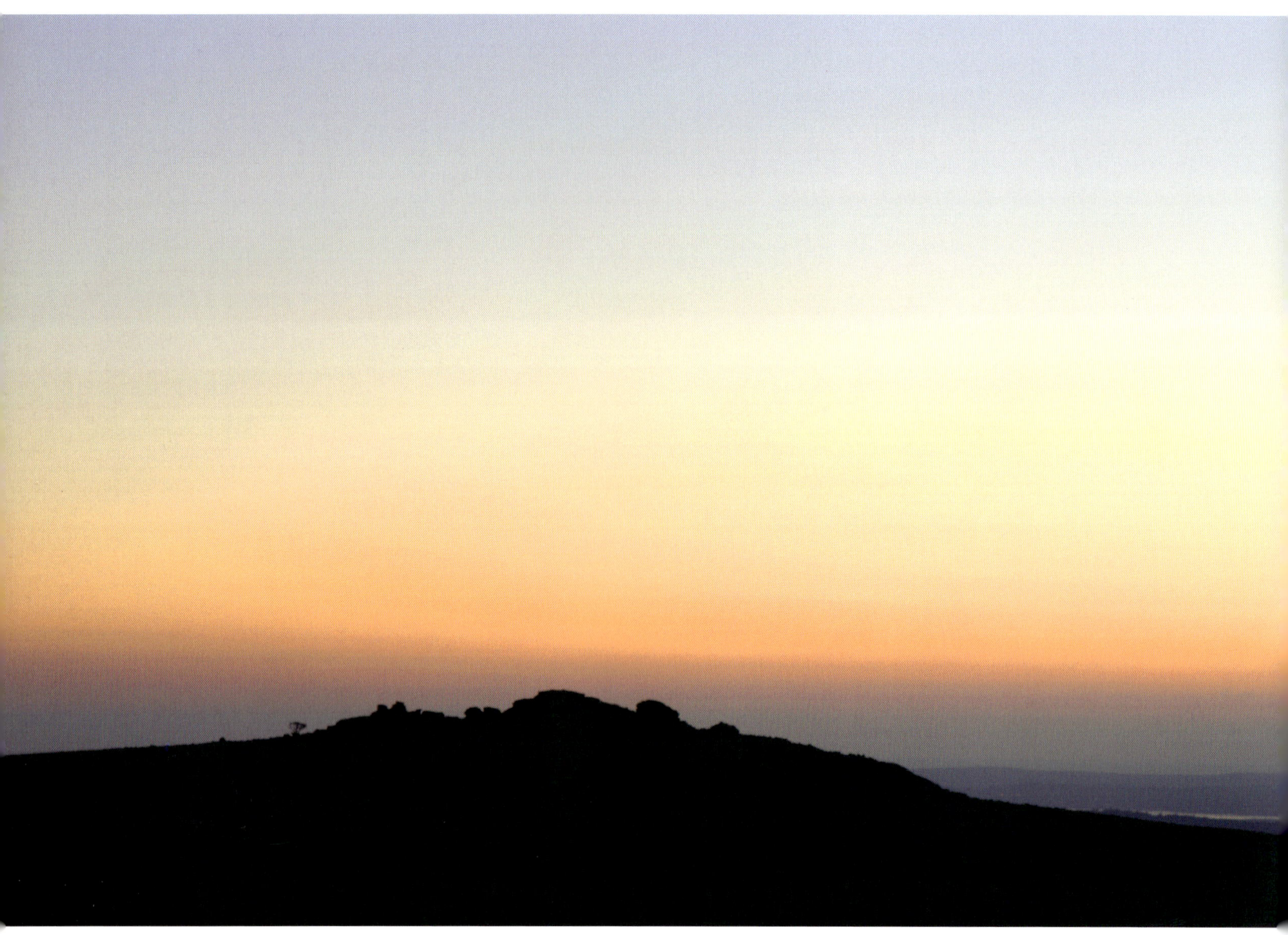

Sunset often creates the most magical atmosphere. This beautiful colour and tone was at sunset over Feather Tor.

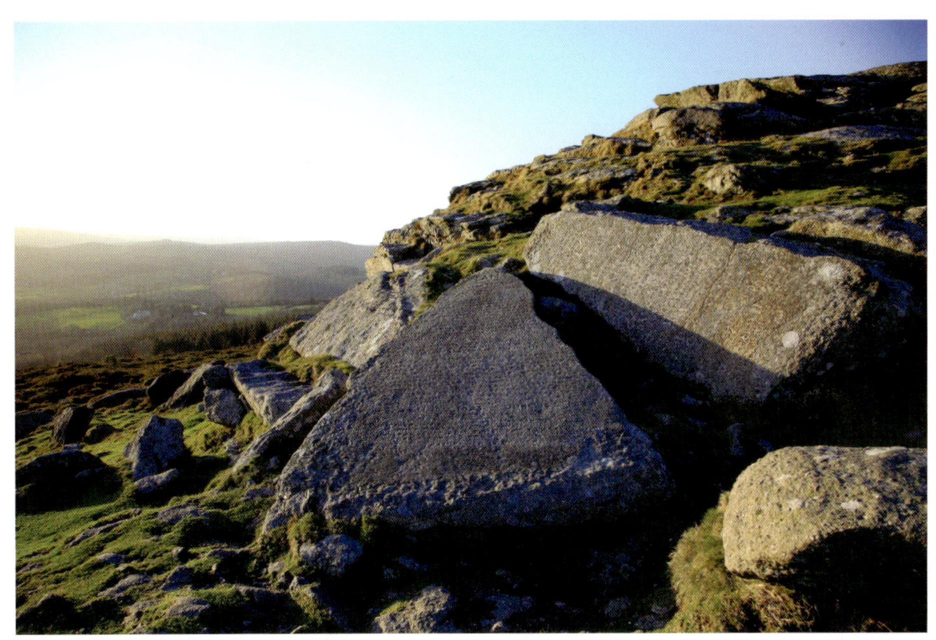

The Ten Commandment stones at Buckland Beacon. The beacon, standing at 1253ft, was the site of a fire beacon, used as early-warning in times of war. The Commandments were carved into the dressed stones by the sculptor W. A. Clement in 1928.

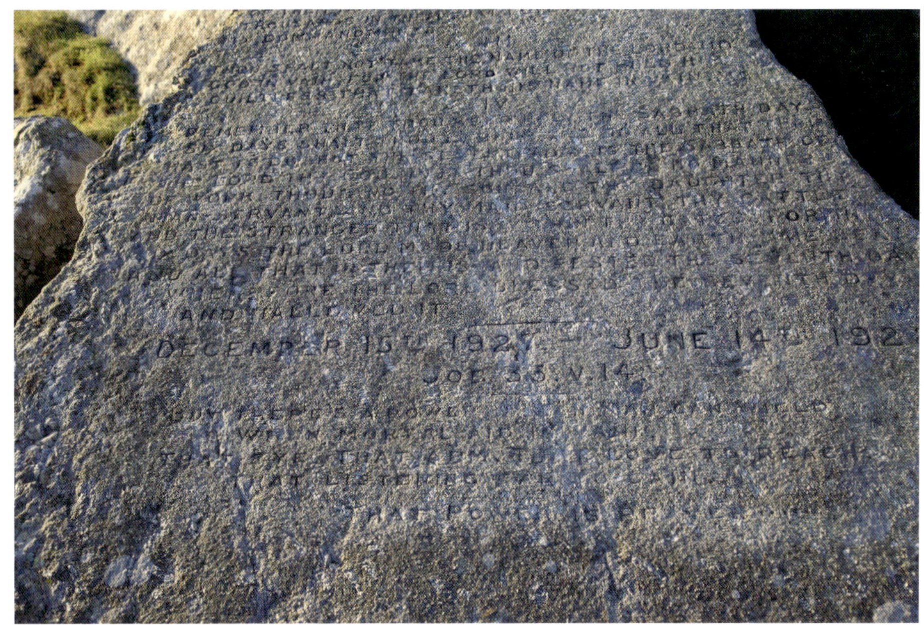

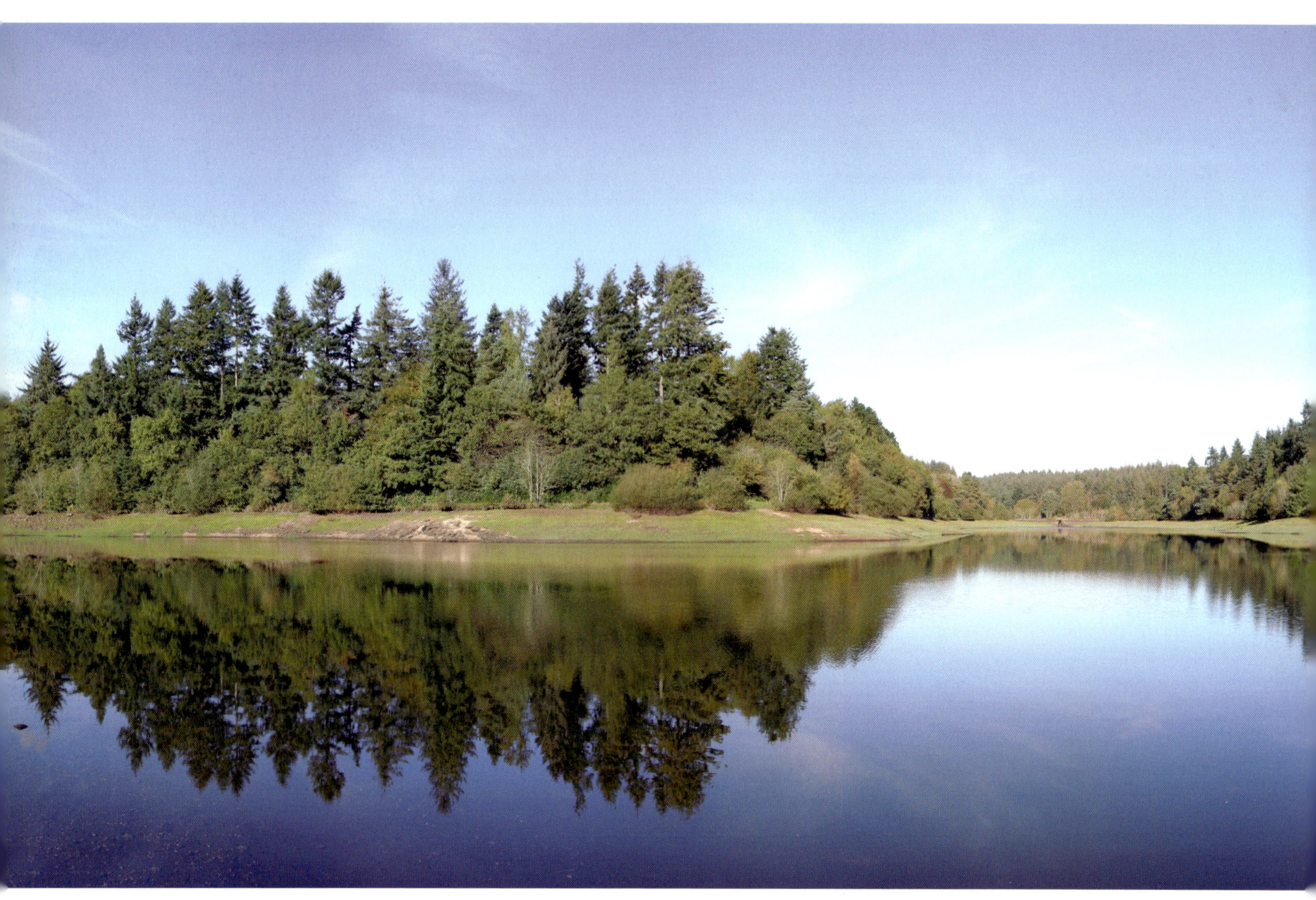

Panorama of Tottiford reservoir.

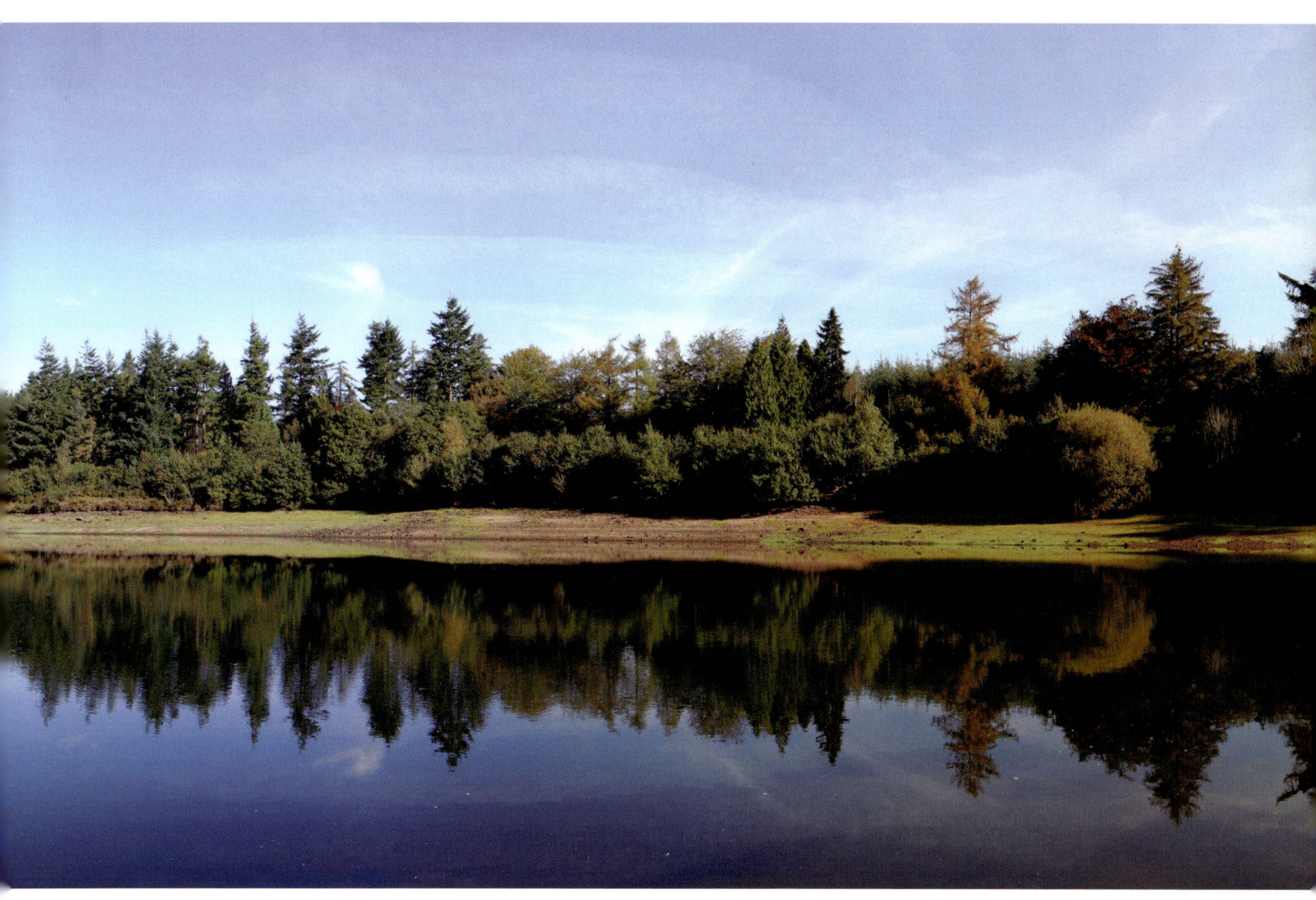

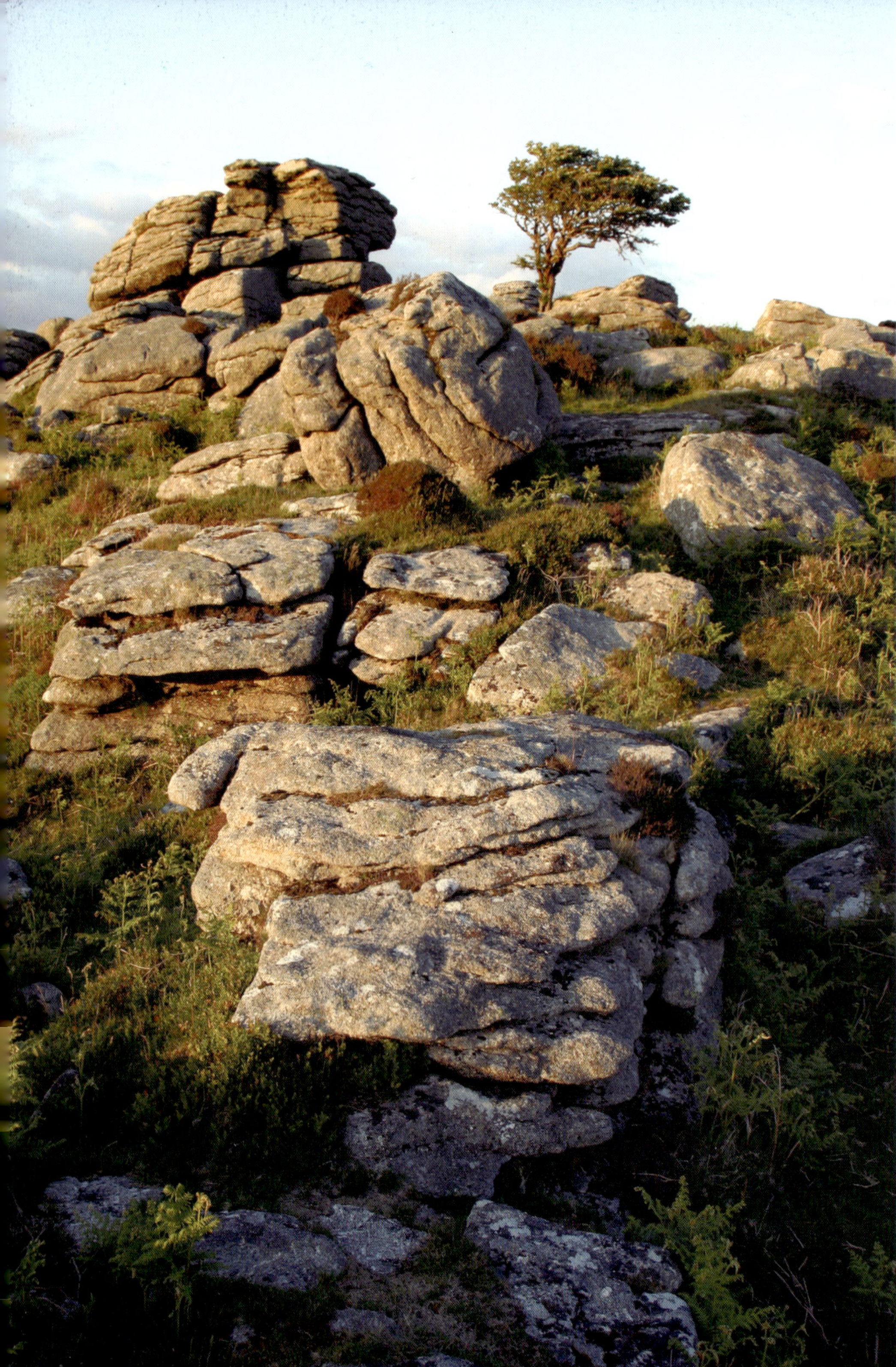

Granite and a lone tree in the evening light.

Opposite:
Wheal Betsy – the leaning tower of Dartmoor. This was the engine house for the mine that operated here from 1740 until 1877. It produced over 53 000 ounces of silver and over 4000 tons of lead.

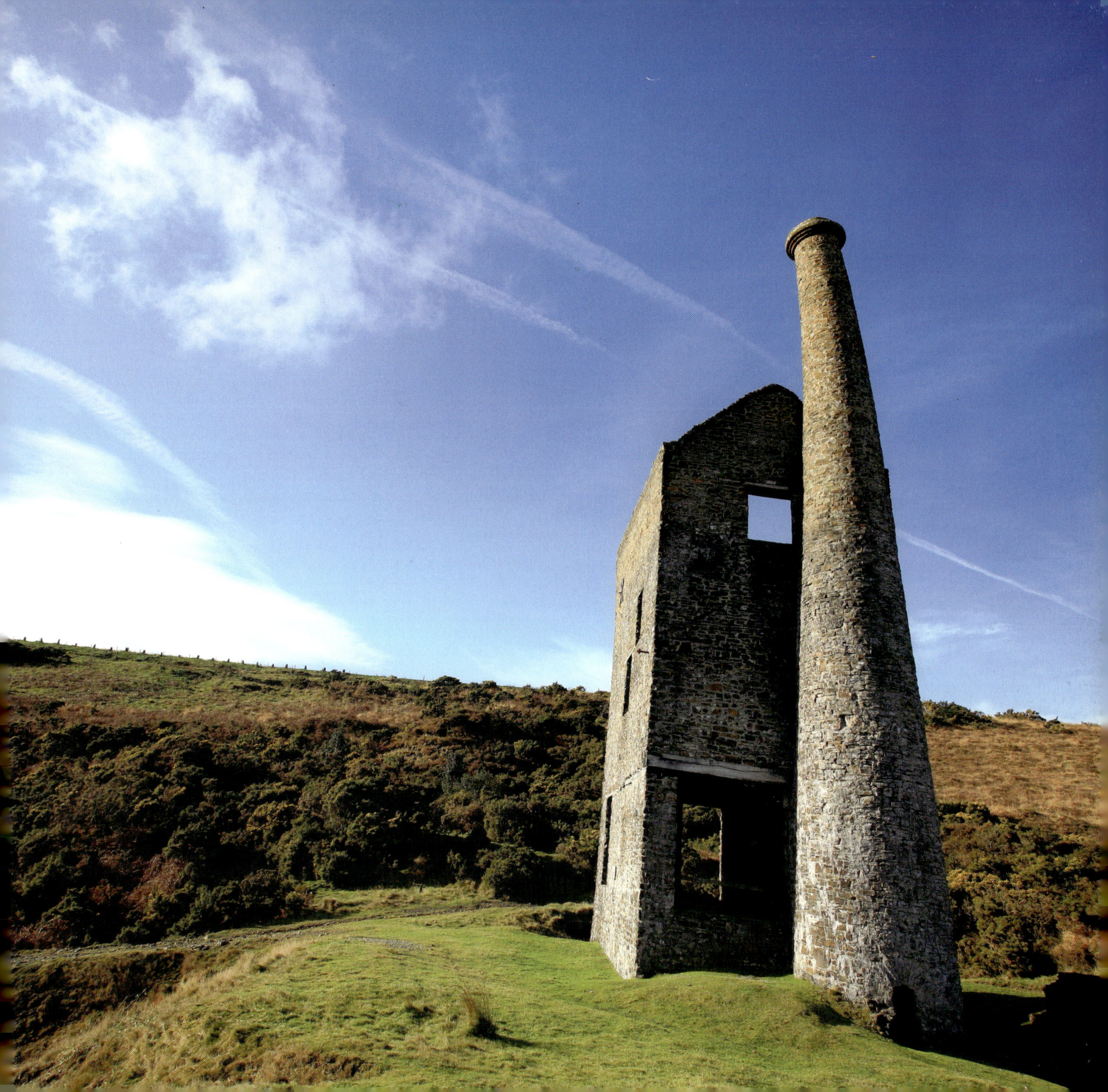

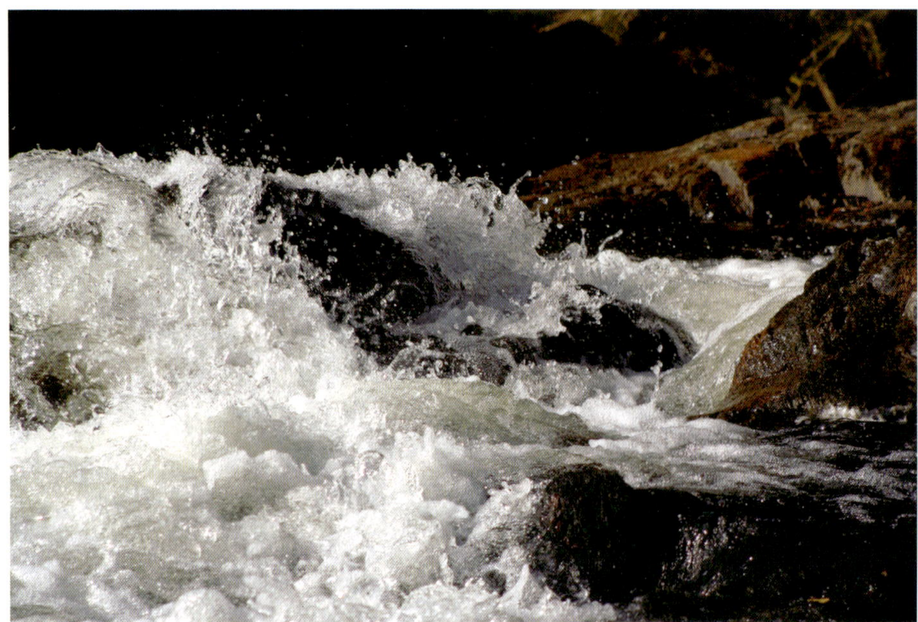

Cascading water at Holne Chase.

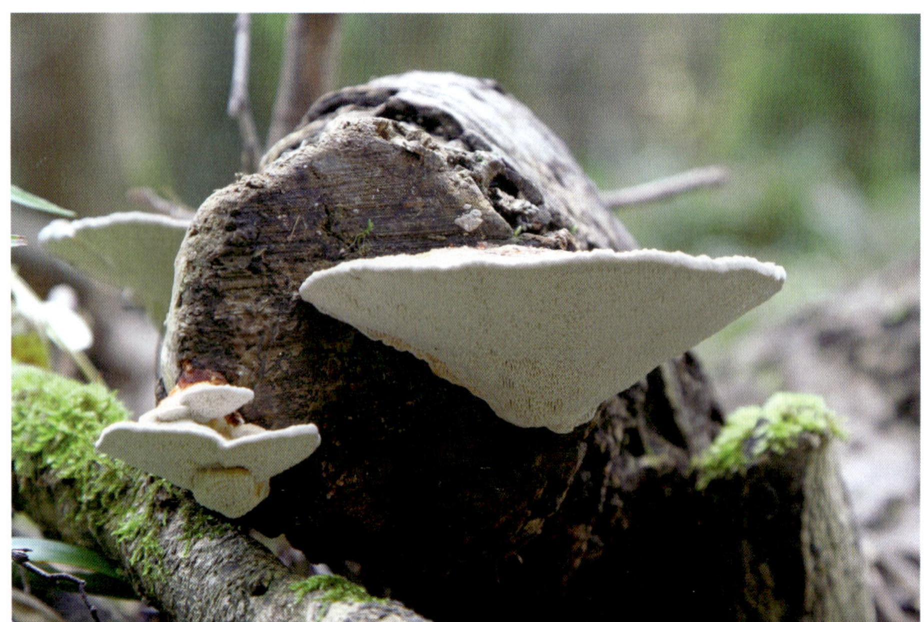

Fungi on a log in Hannicombe Wood near the River Teign.

A foxglove sits tall in the spring sunshine.

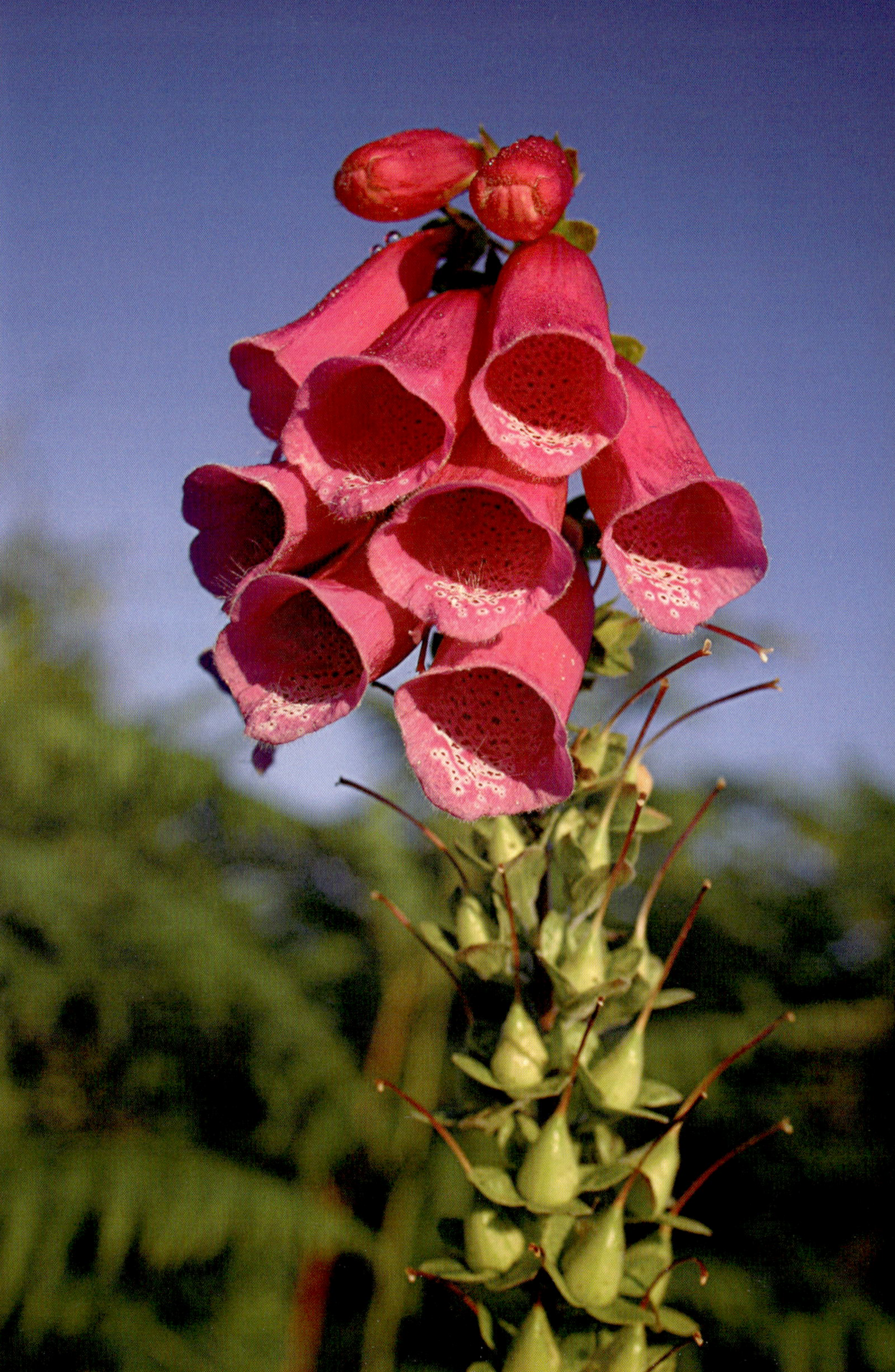

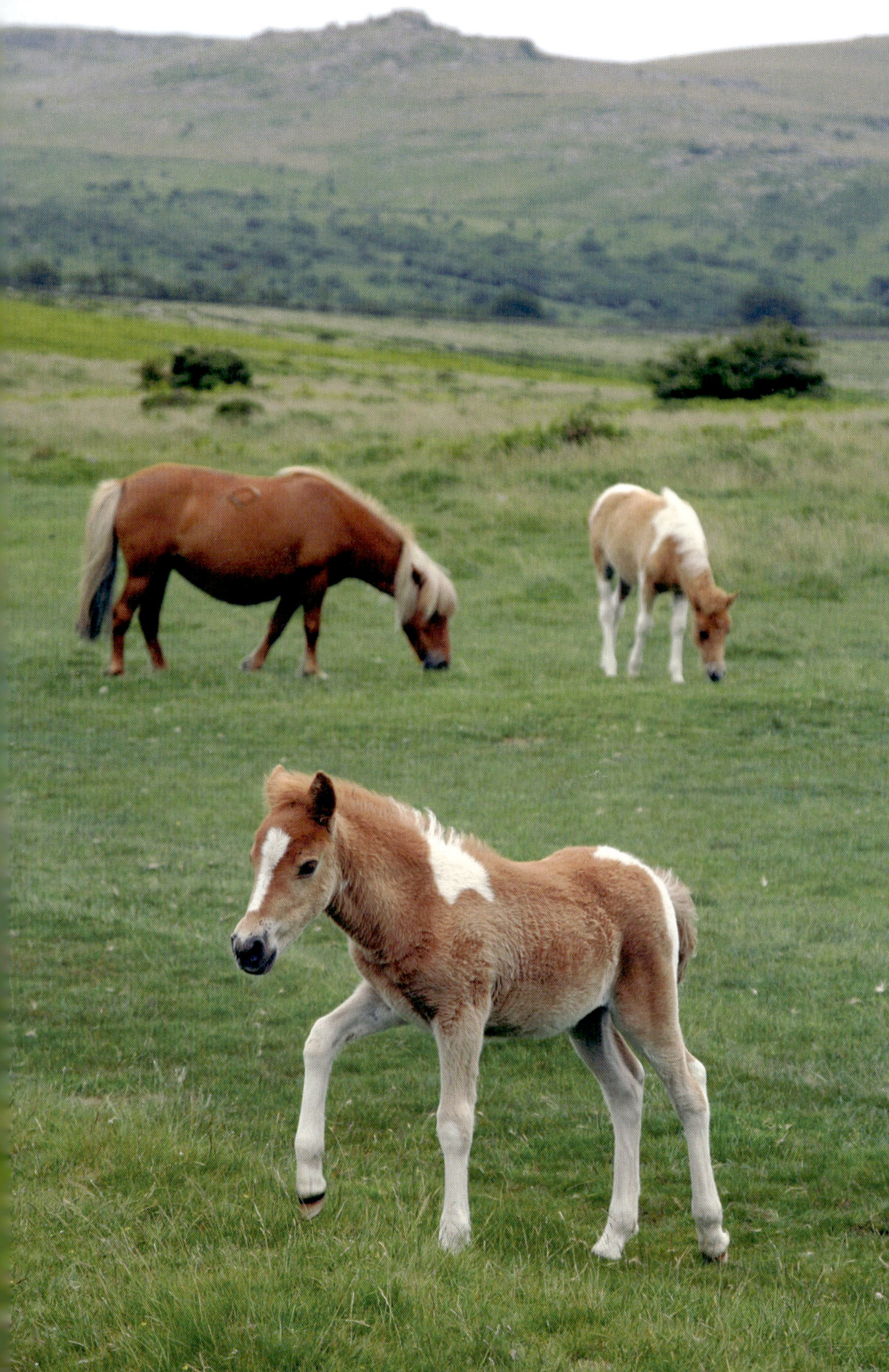

A foal near Staple Tor in late spring.

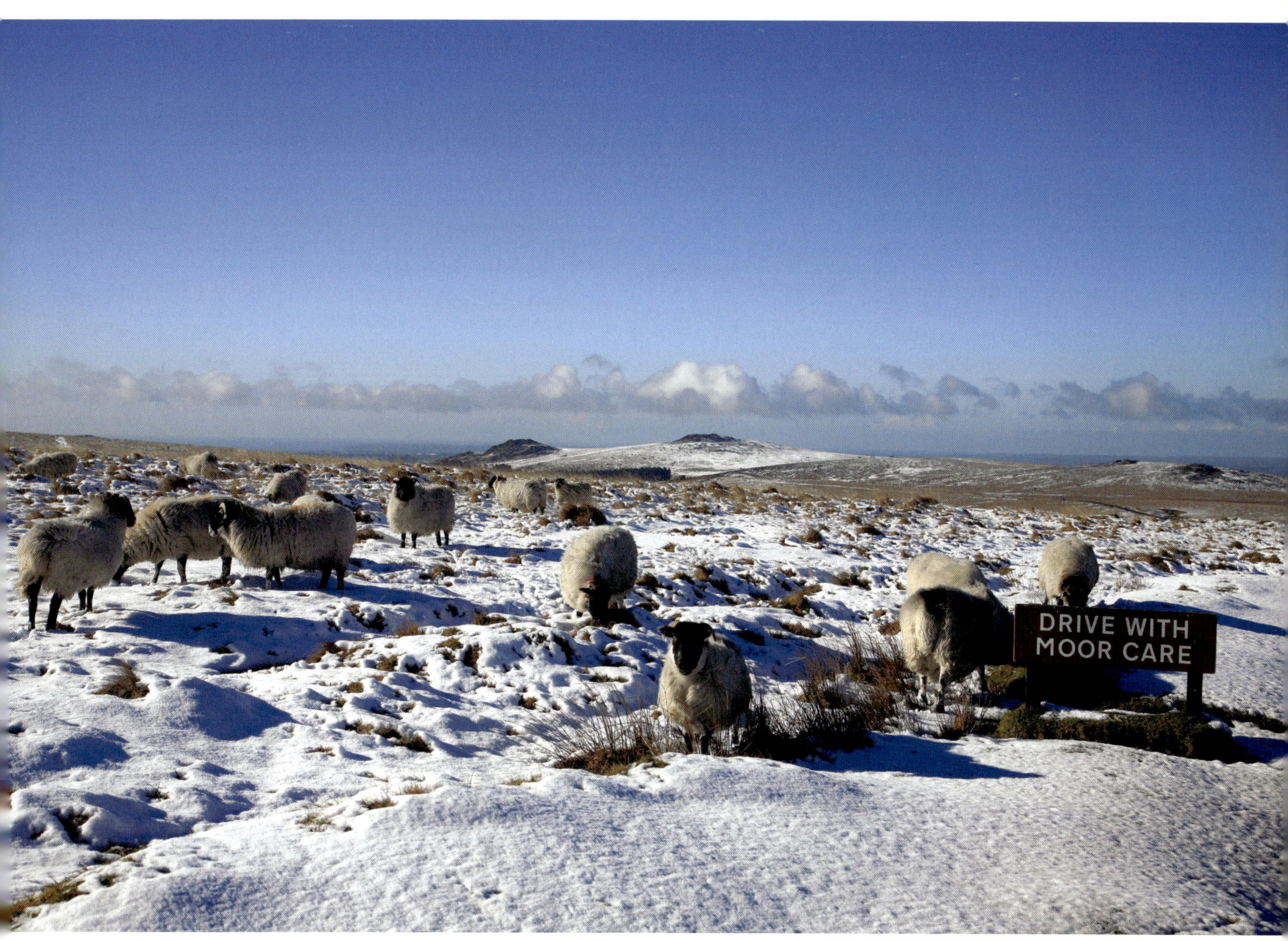

Sheep graze in the snow outside Princetown.

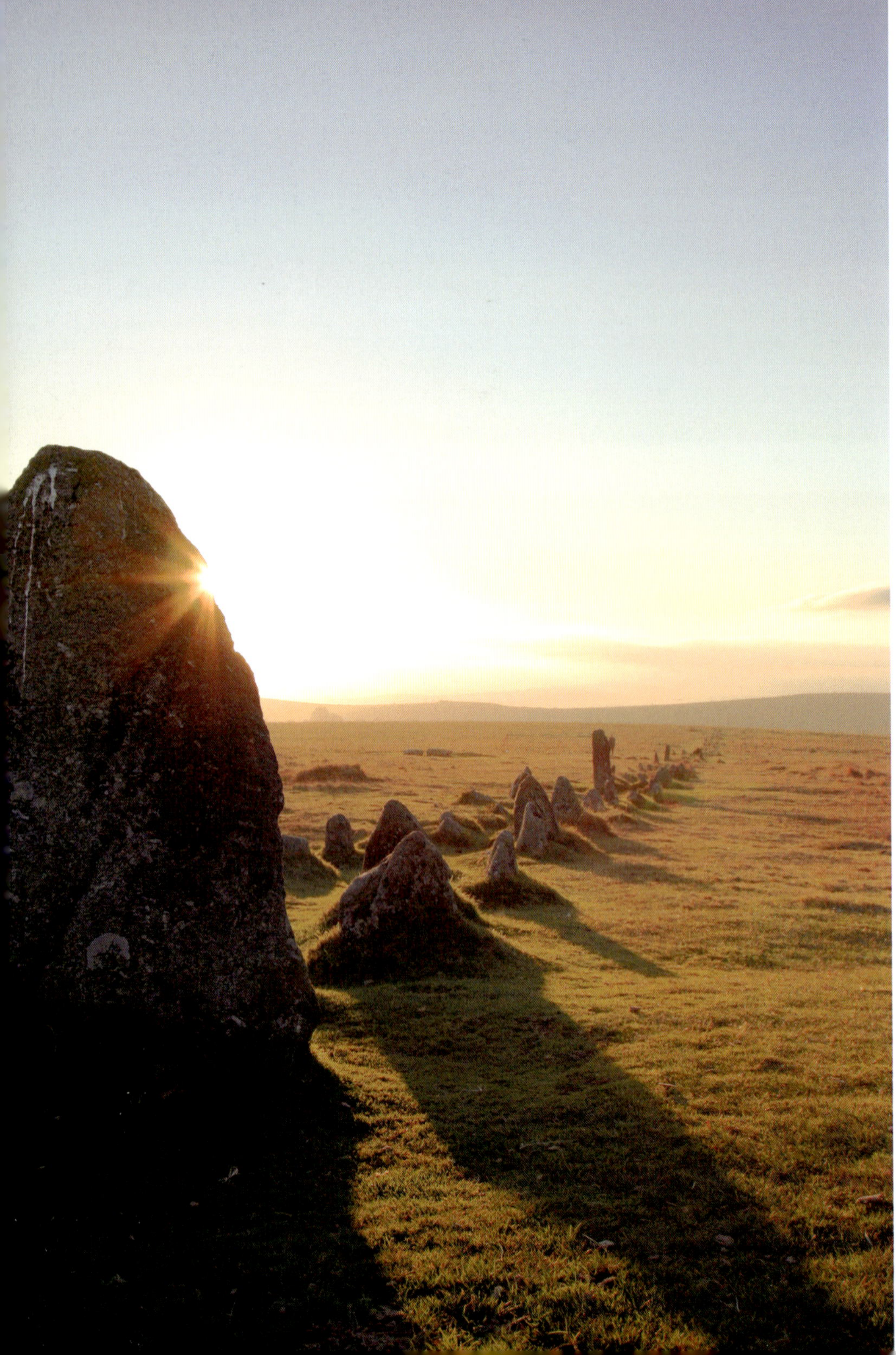

Merrivale Stone row at sunset.
There are over 60 such stone rows on Dartmoor. This group comprises three rows – the longest being 264 metres, containing over 200 stones.

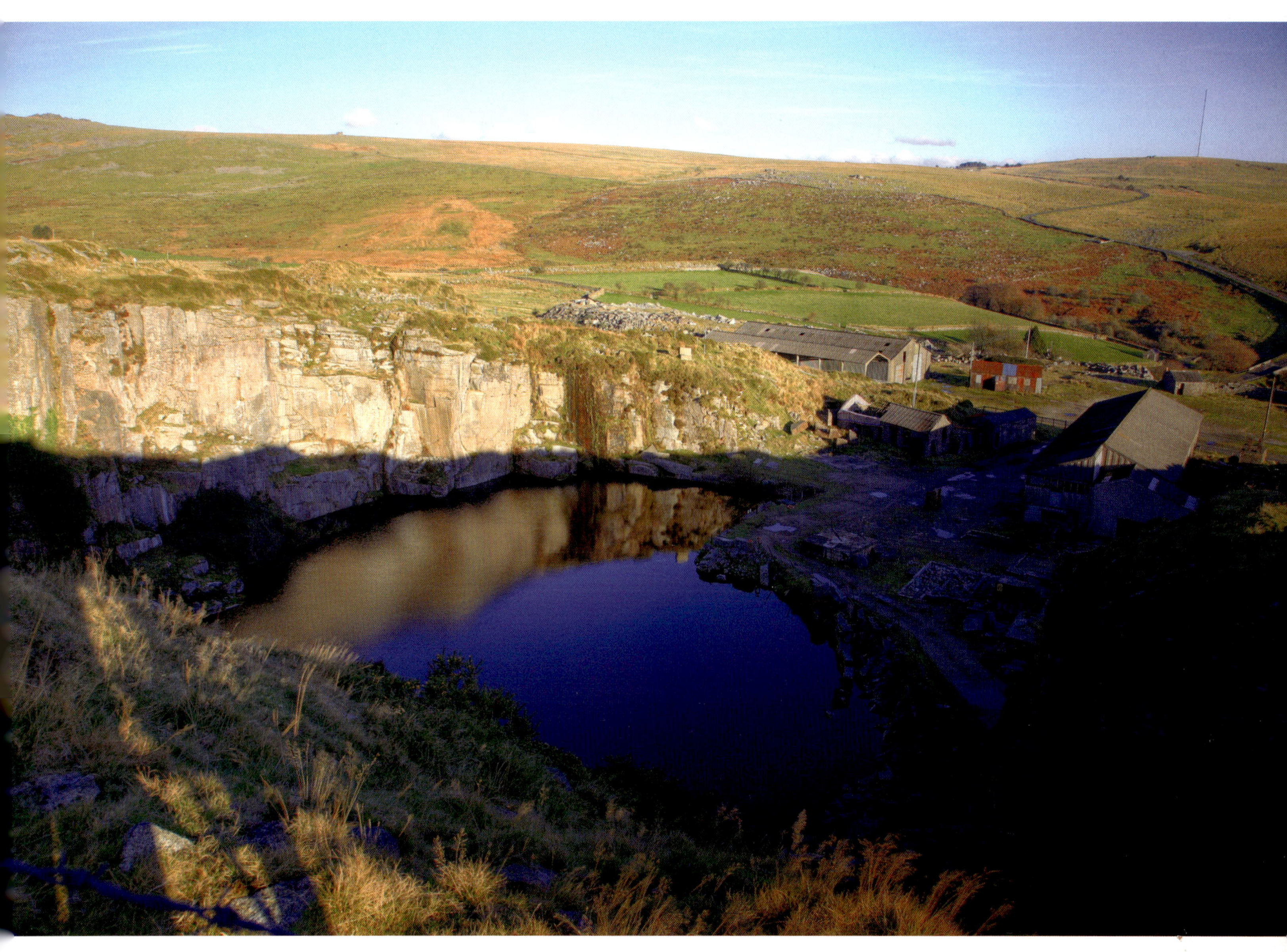

Merrivale is also the site of the now disused Merrivale Quarry.
It produced granite and operated from 1876 until it closed in 1997.

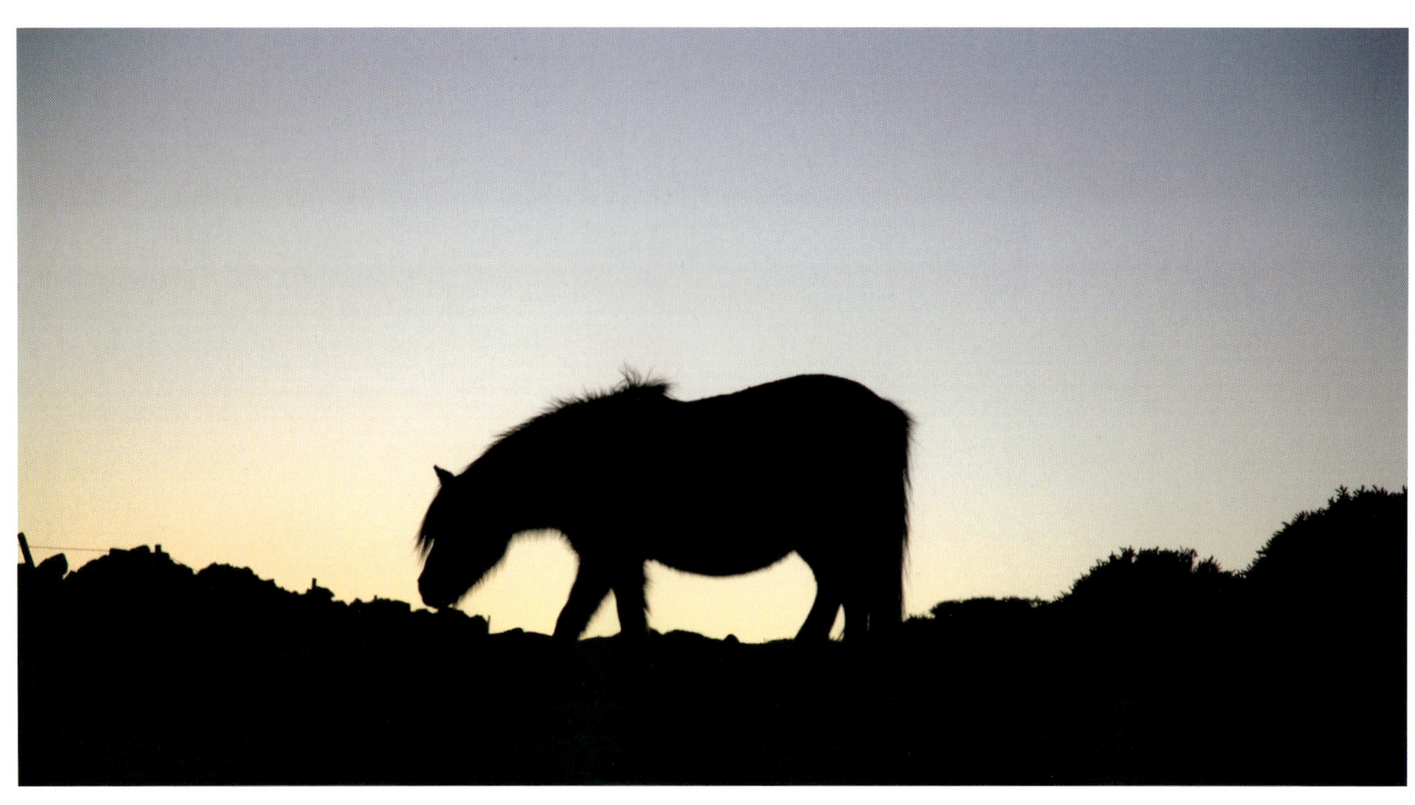

A lone pony grazes at sunset. The animals are normally found in small herds but no others were seen nearby.

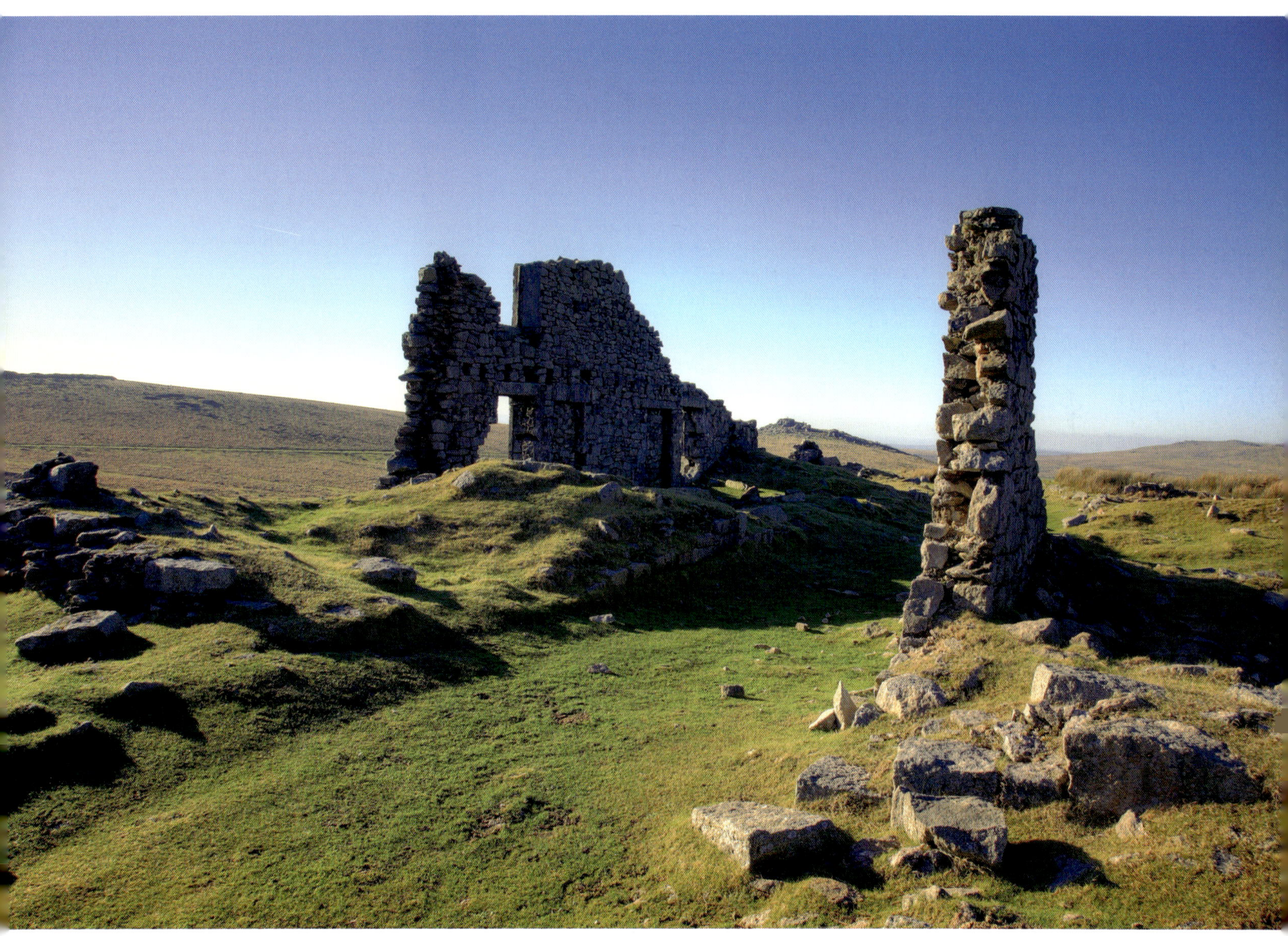

An atmospheric image among the ruins at Foggintor quarry, with King's Tor visible between the ruined walls.

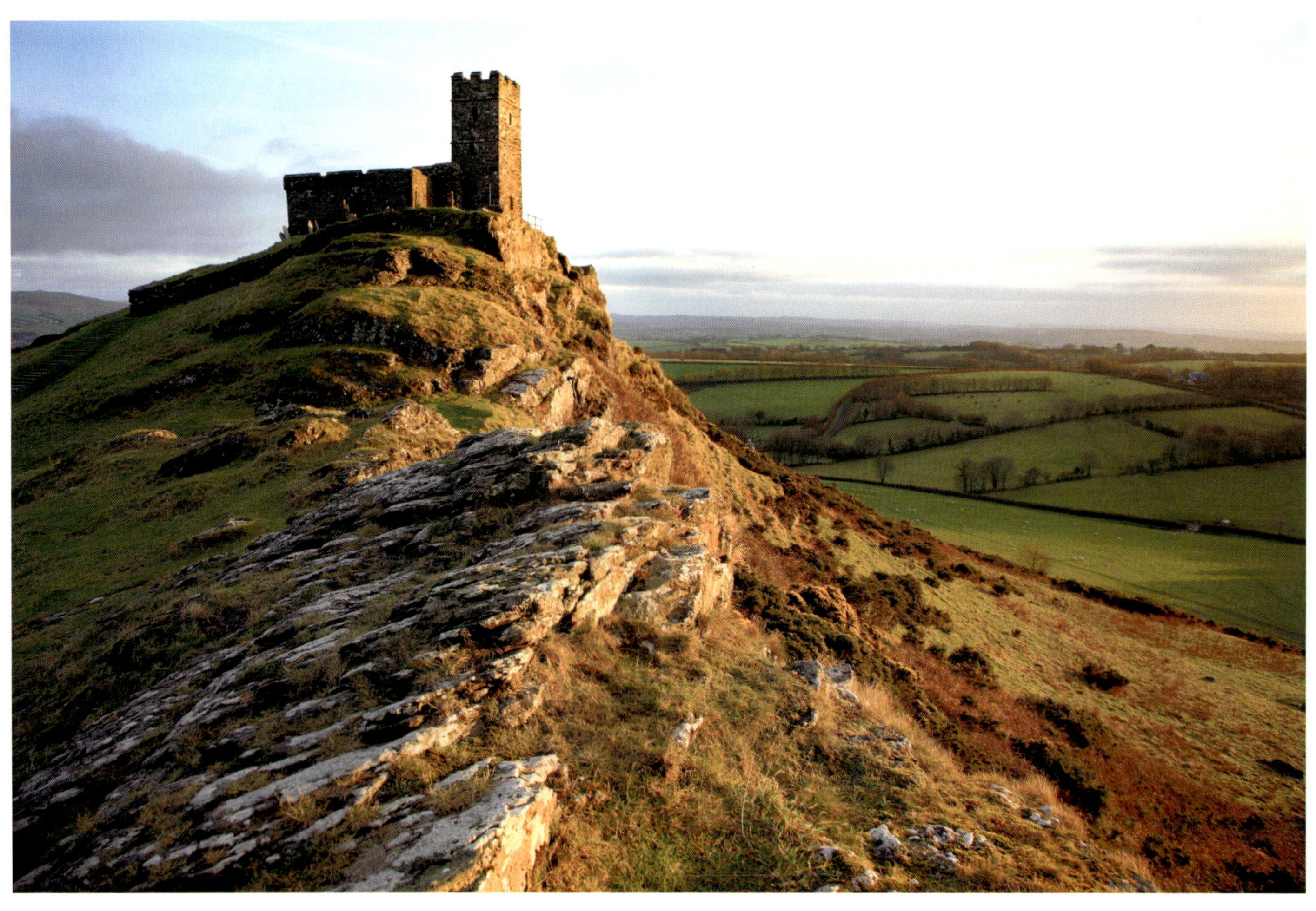

Patience was rewarded with this glorious sunset that illuminated the side of Brentor church and the rock outcrop upon which it rests. The church sits at 1130ft and dates back to the 13th century.

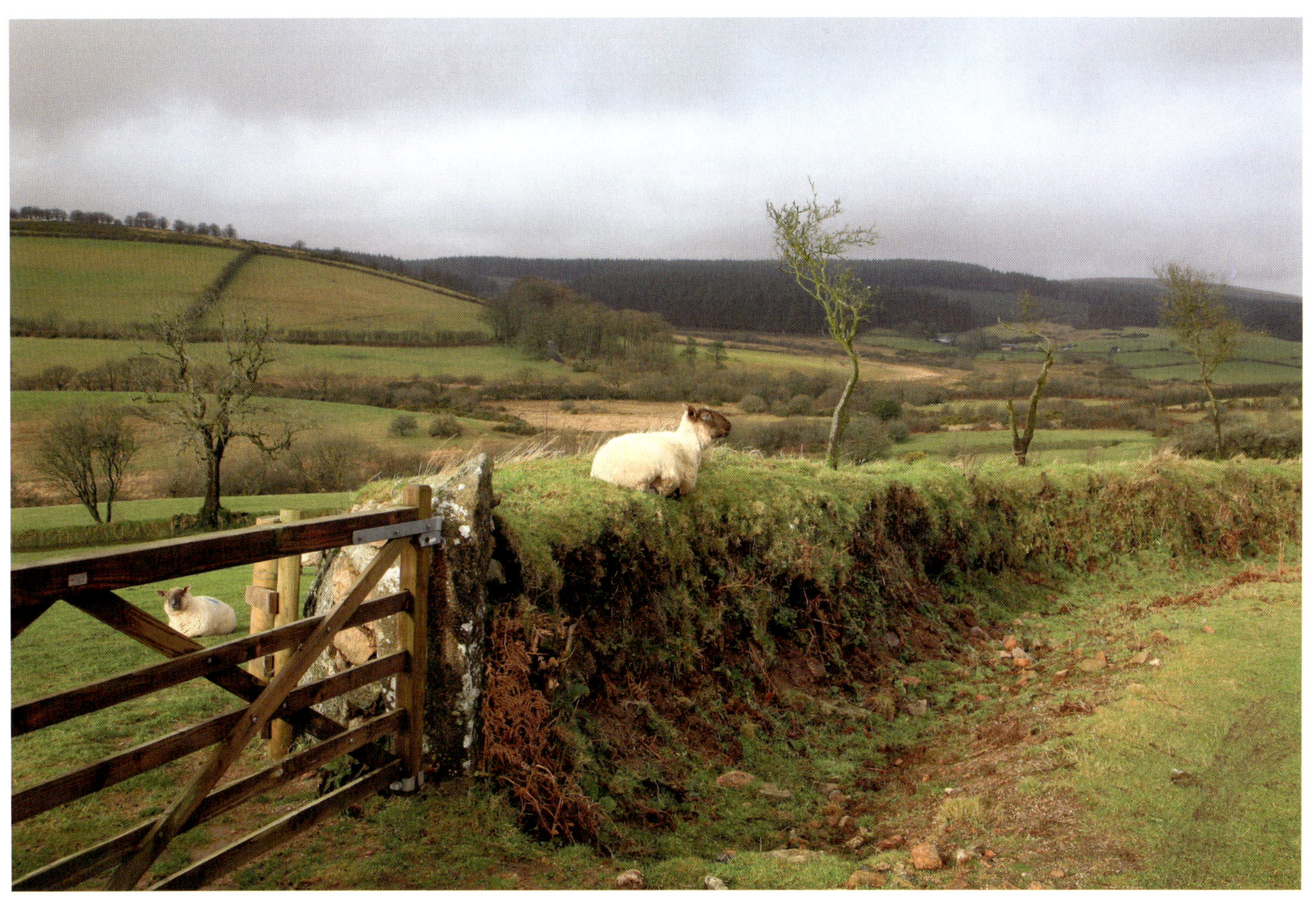

A sheep calls from the top of a moss-covered wall on a blustery winter's day.

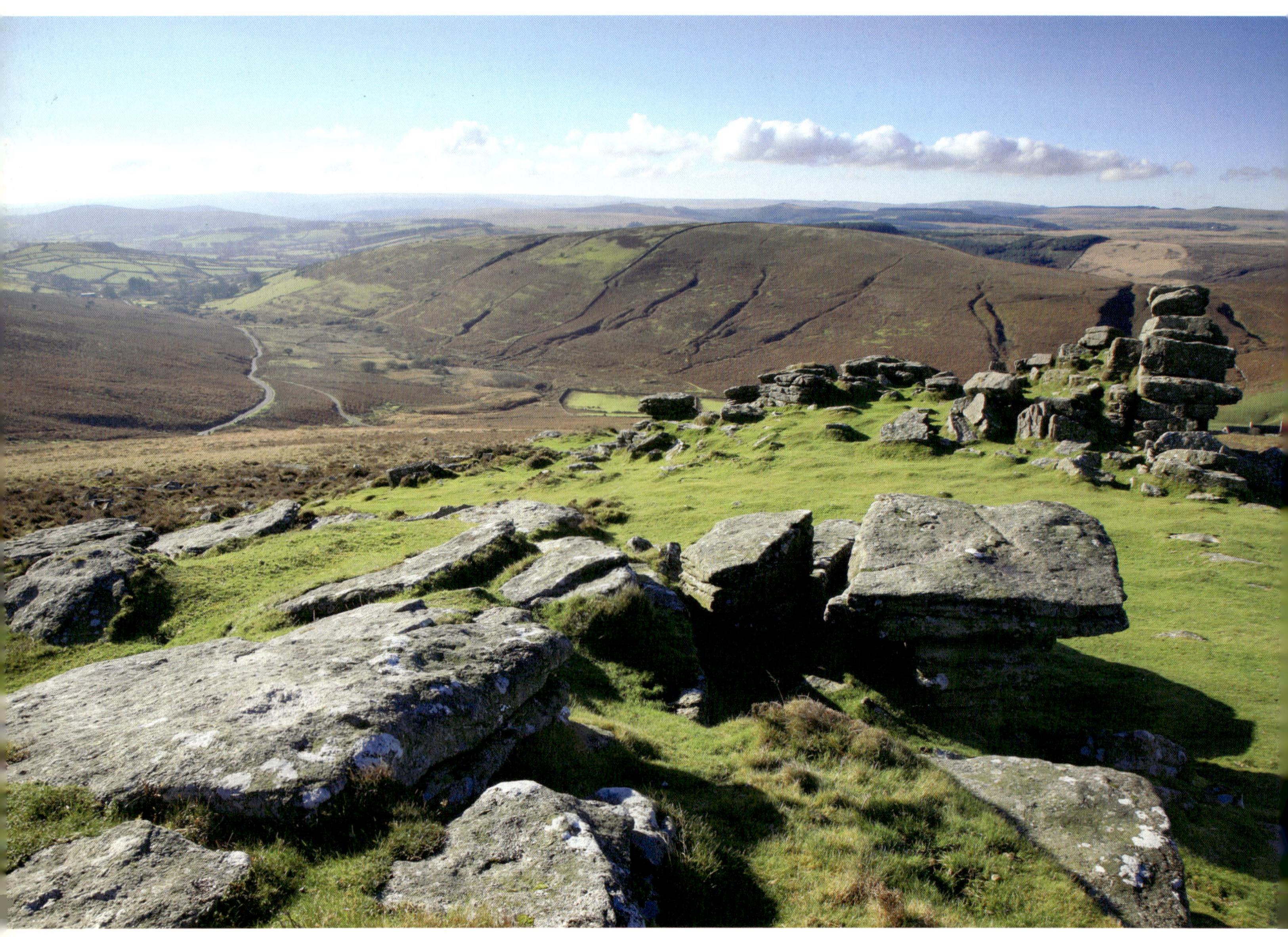

A beautiful day, looking across the moor from the top of Hookney Tor.

Dartmoor waterfall.

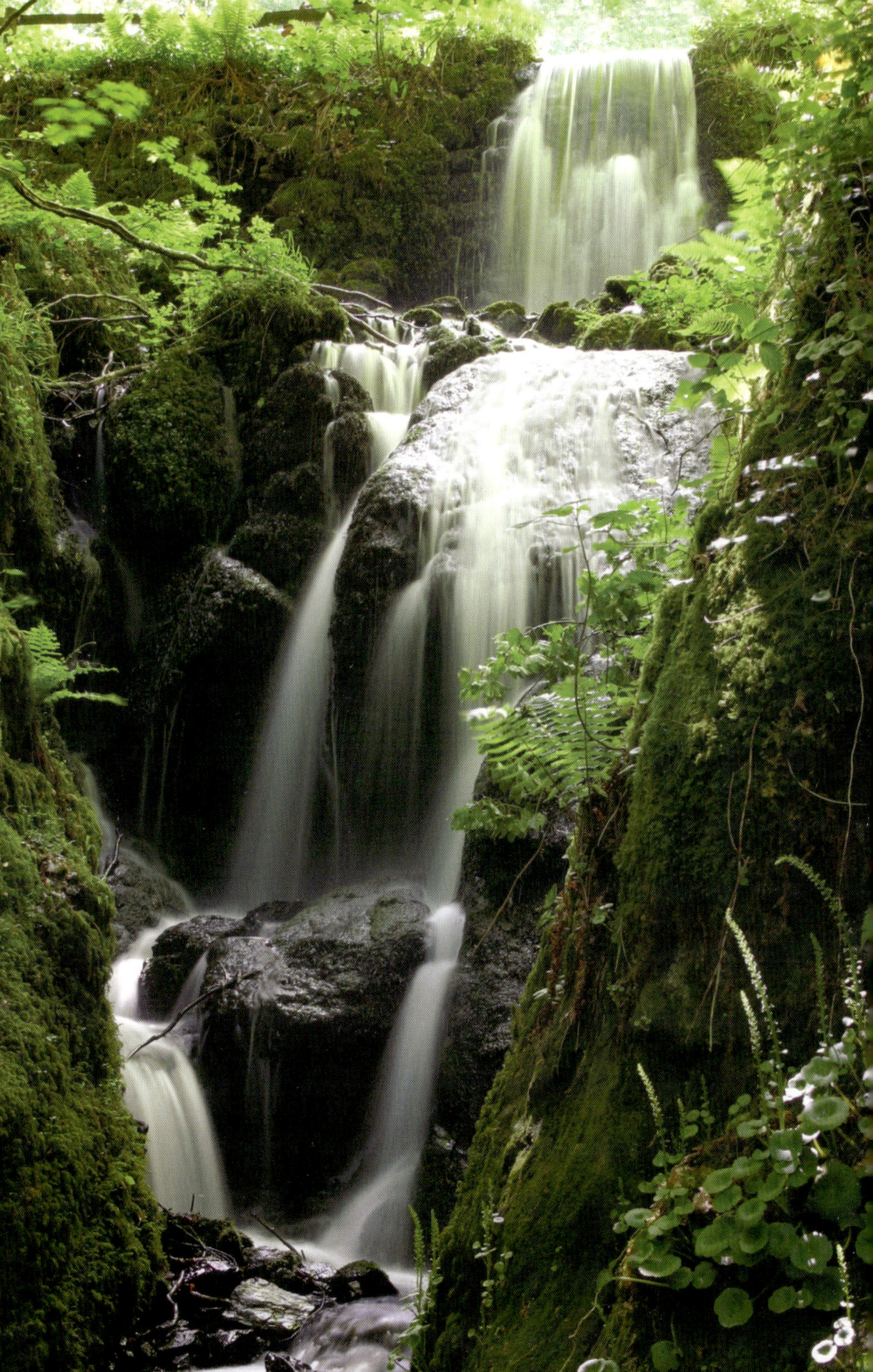

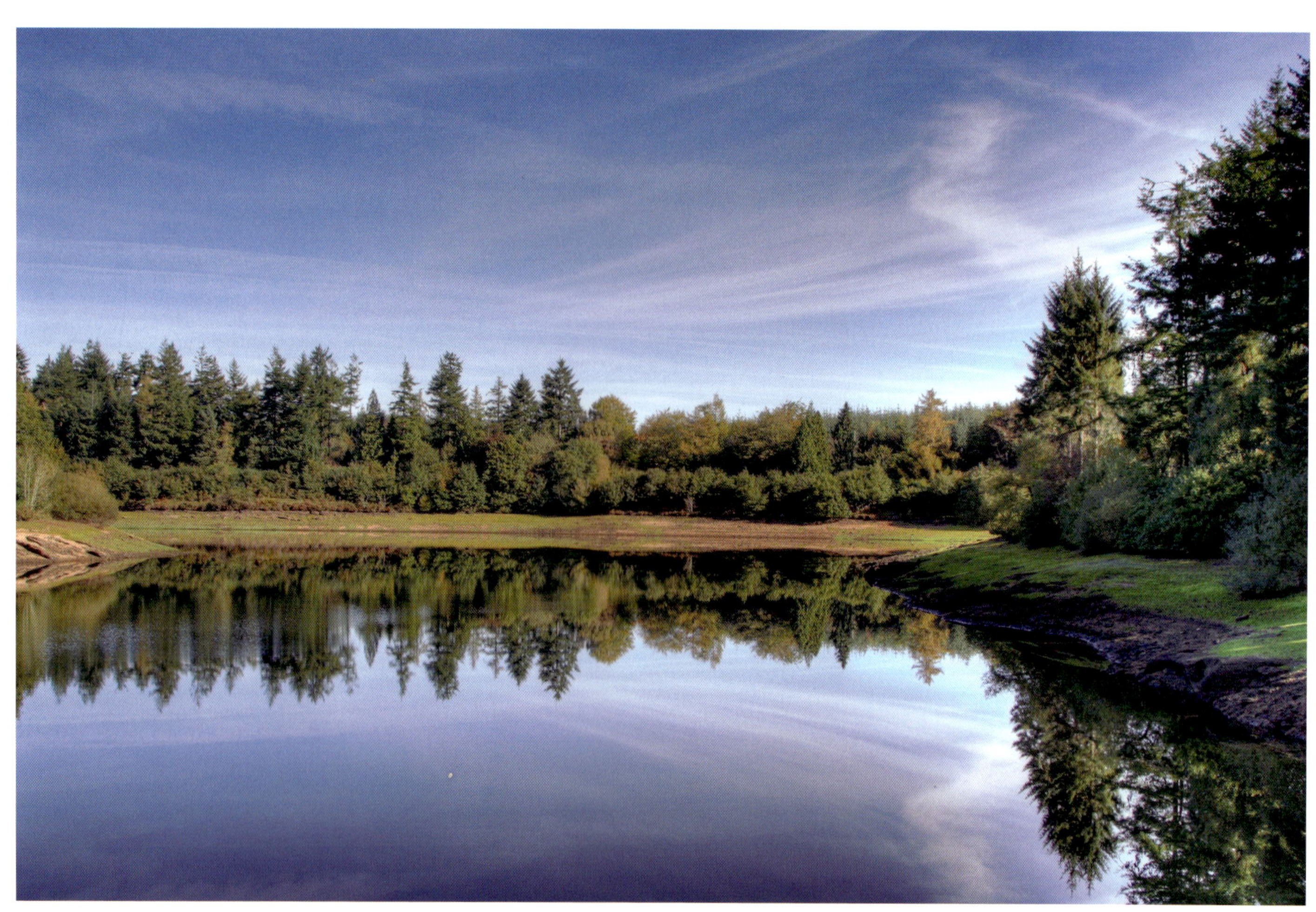

Colourful autumn reflections.

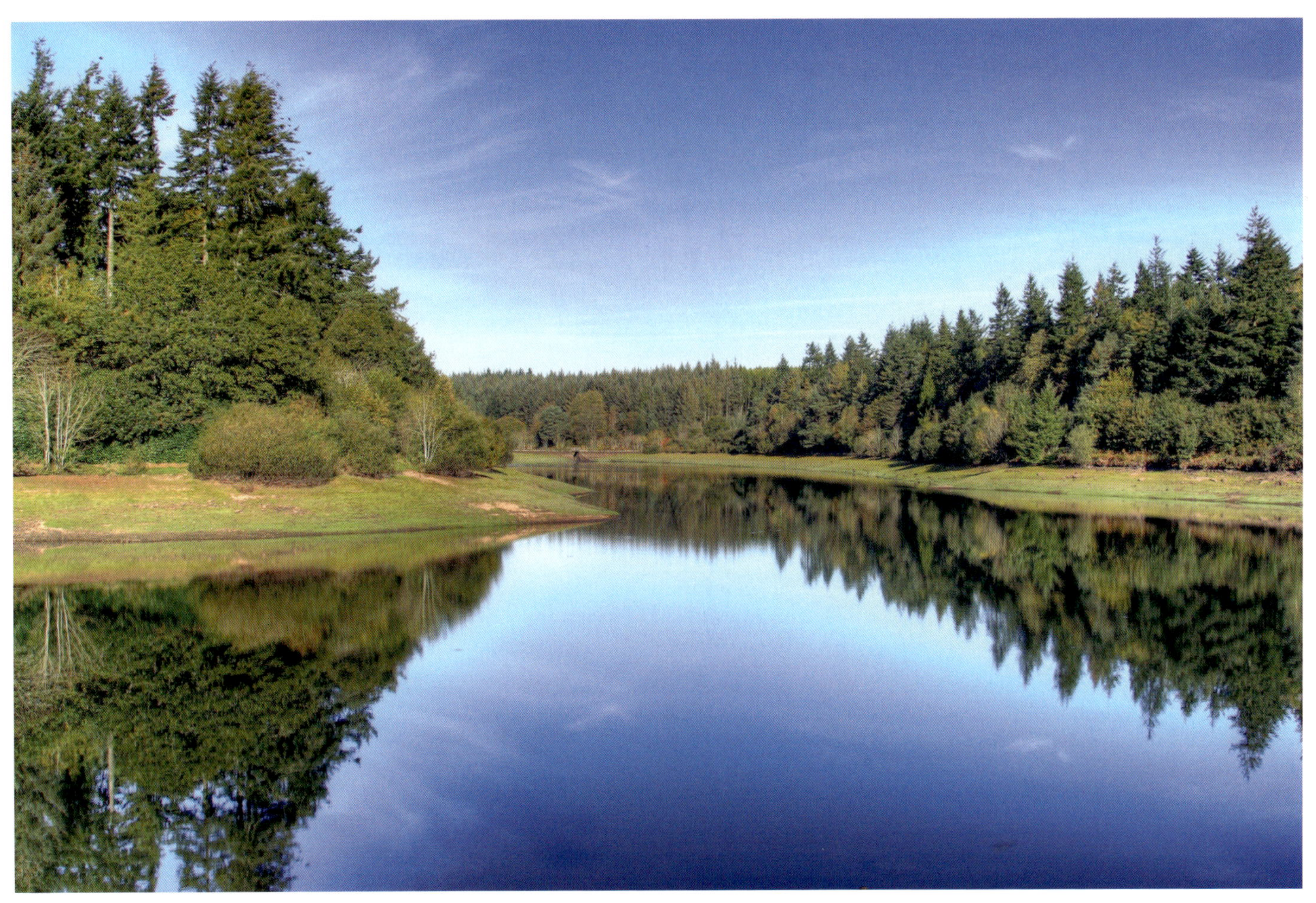

A mirror view.

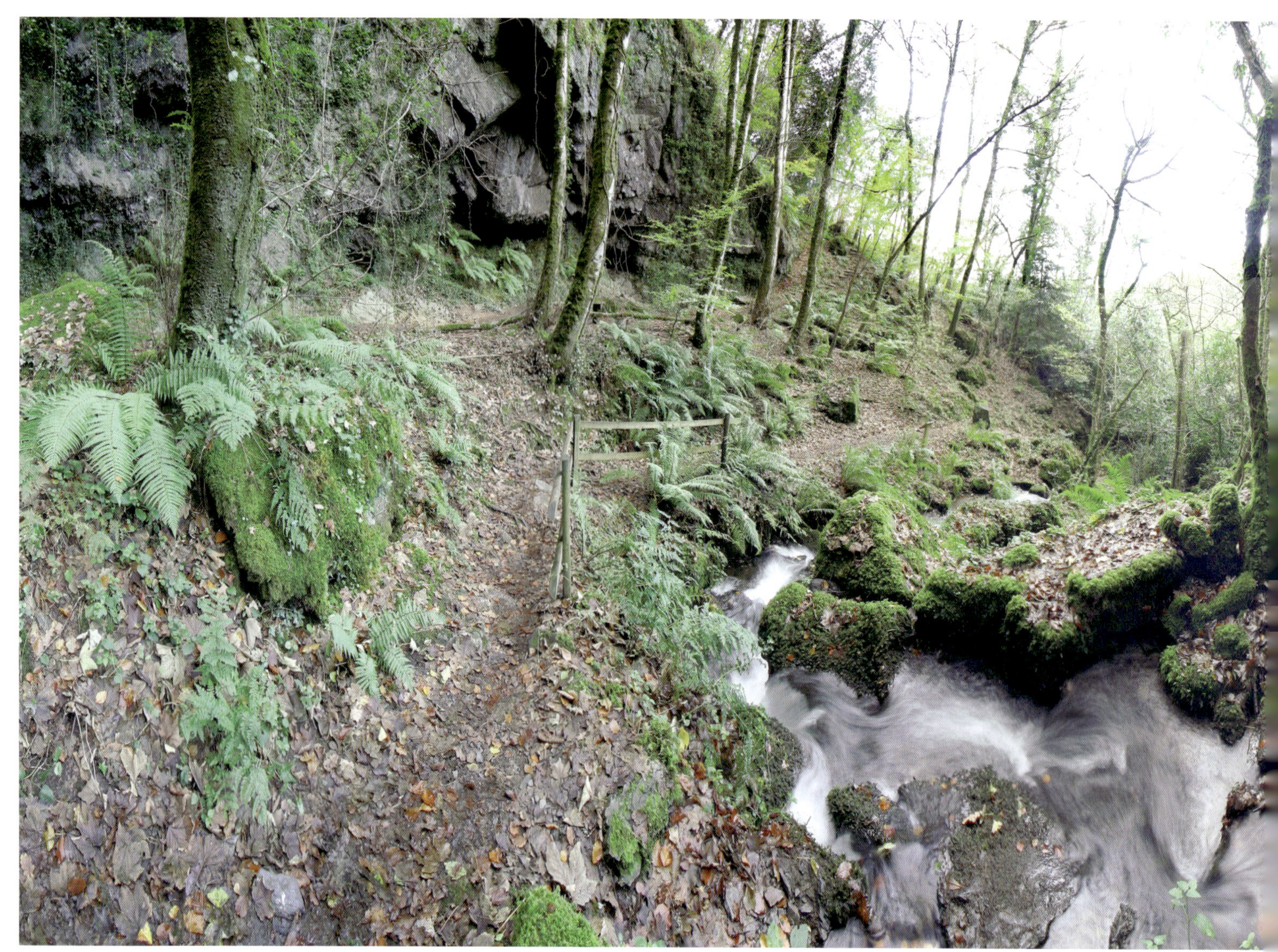

Panorama of a 'Secret Garden'.

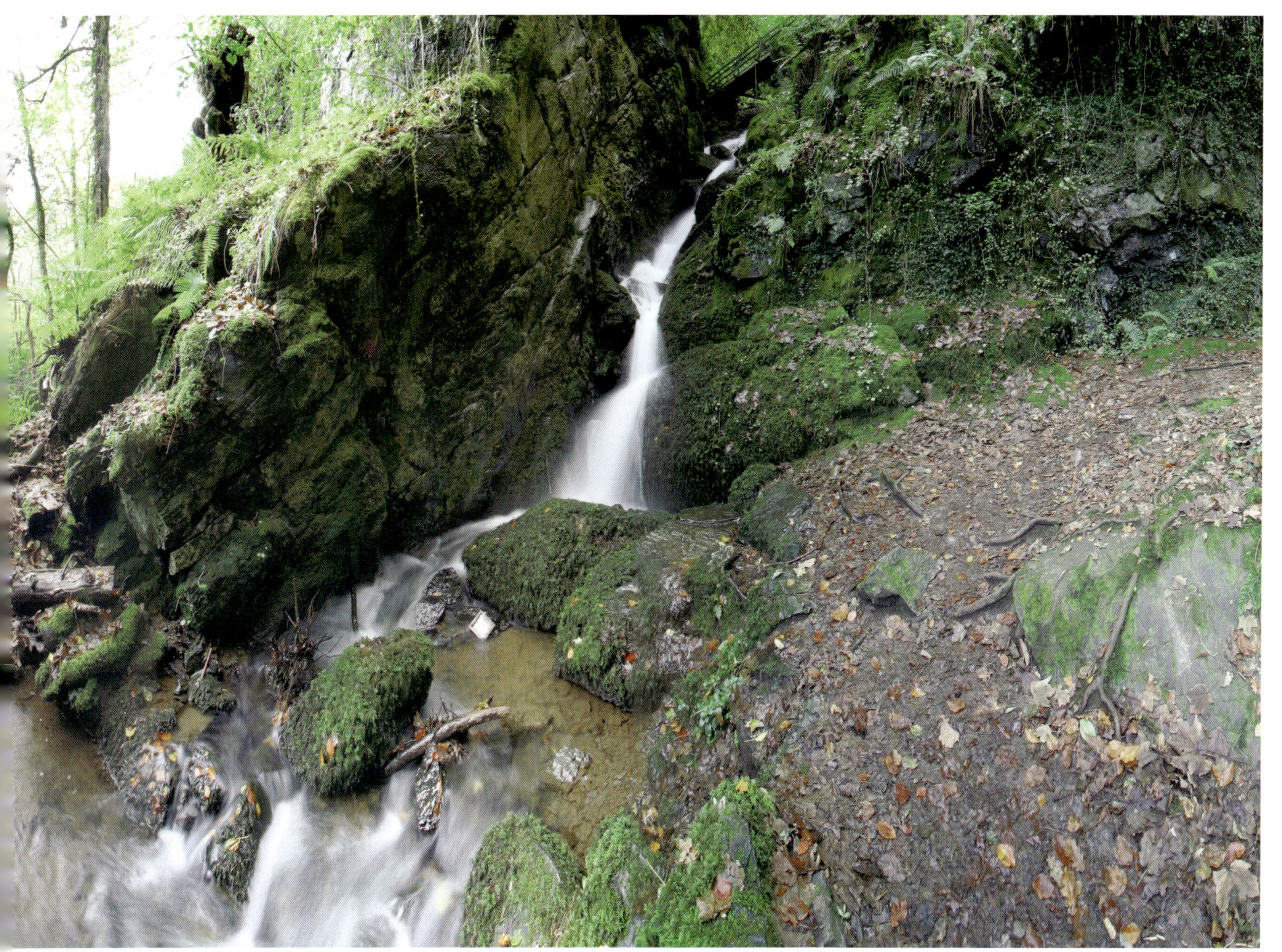

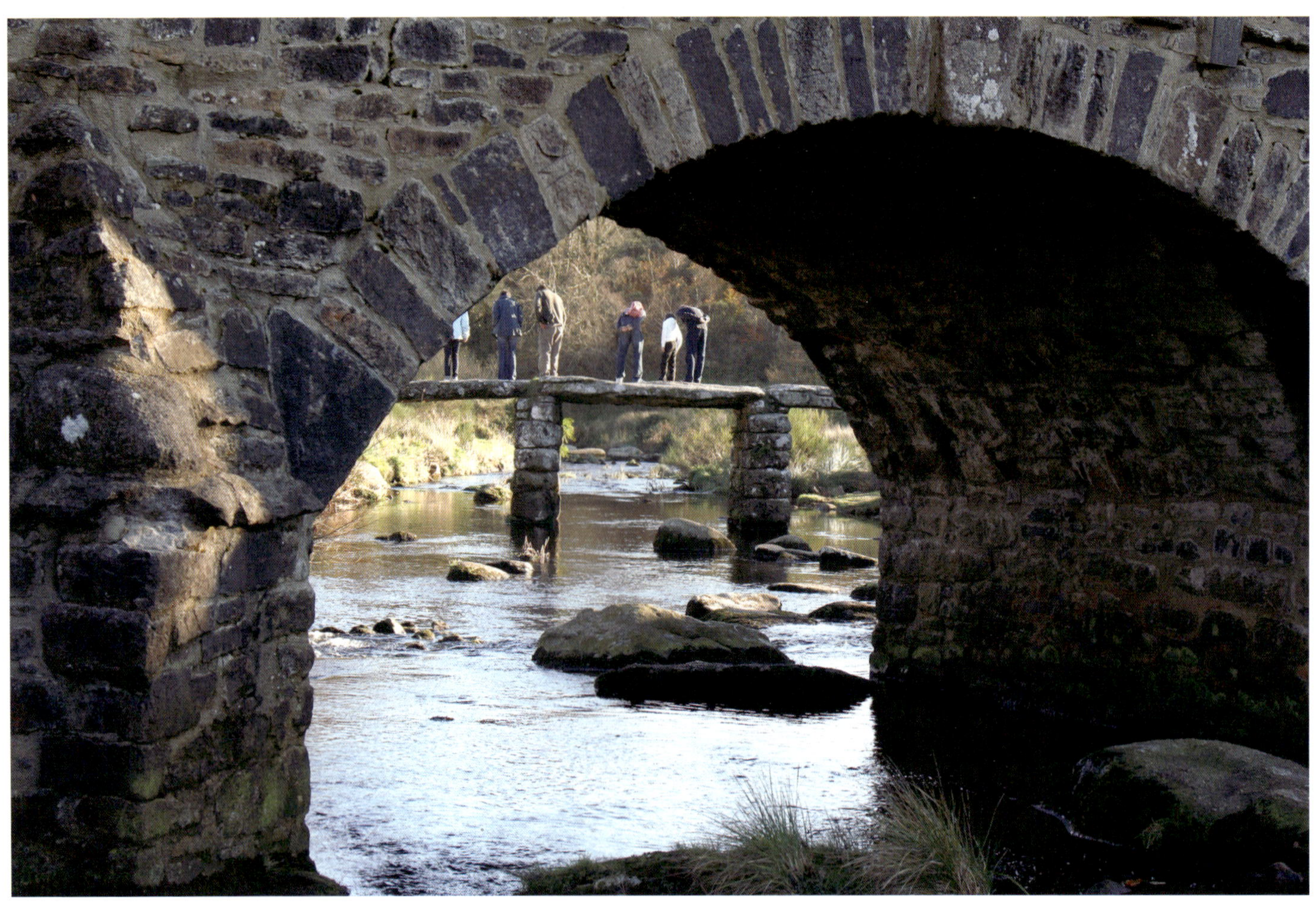

Exploring at Postbridge in the late afternoon sun.

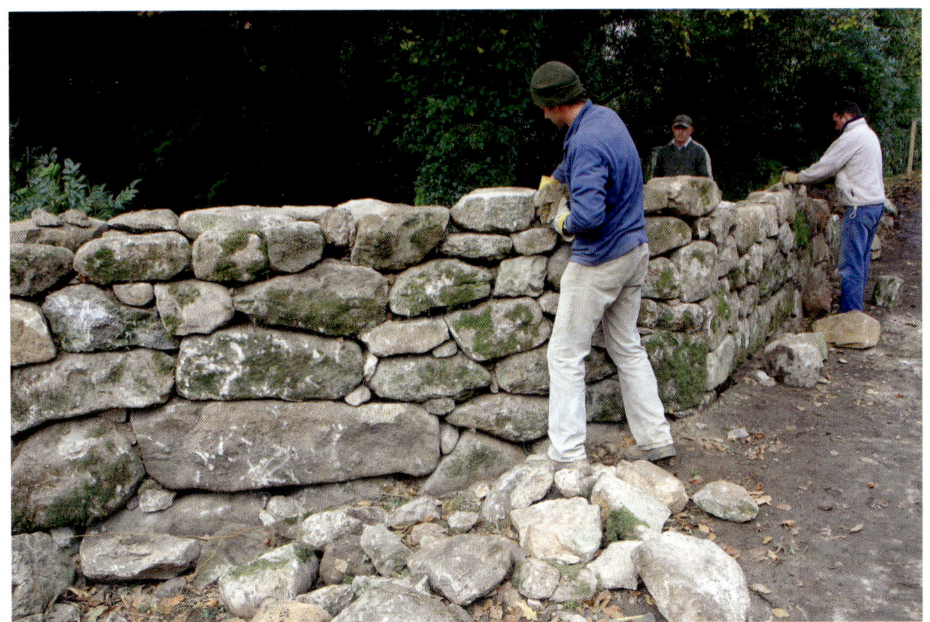

Vince Pipe, Peter Druett and Mike Smerdon – Dartmoor stone wallers. I watched them work for a while and it truly is a great skill.

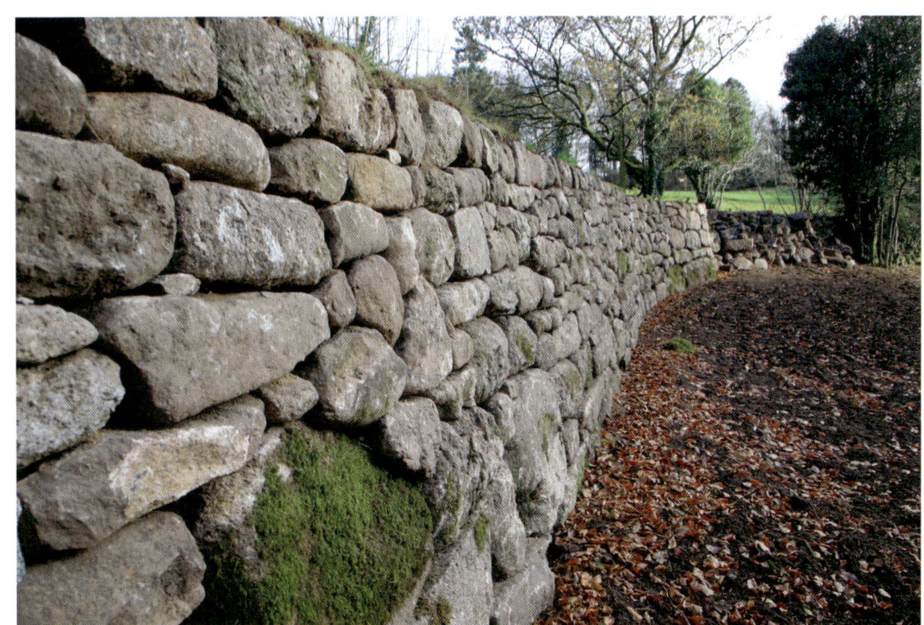

A finished granite wall that will last many decades.

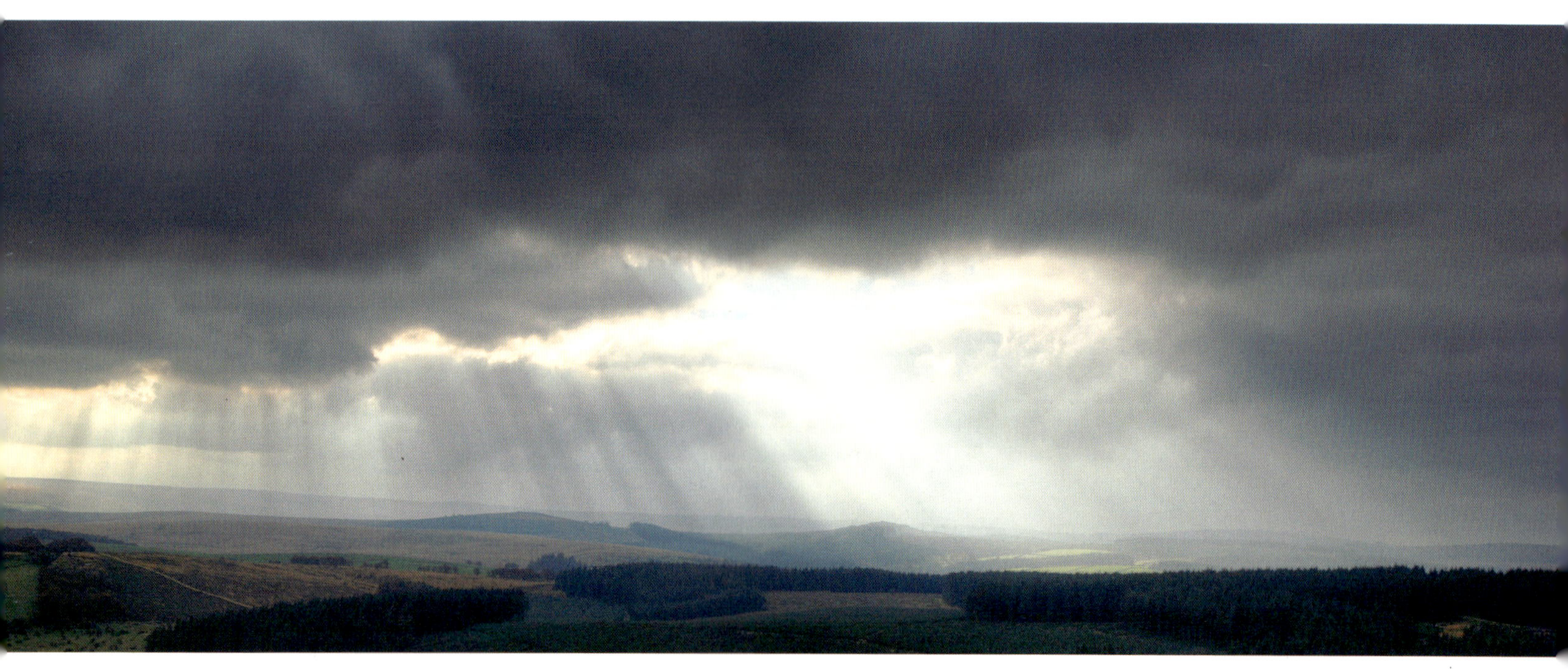

Shafts of light break through the cloud and illuminate the distant Tors looking from above Challacombe.

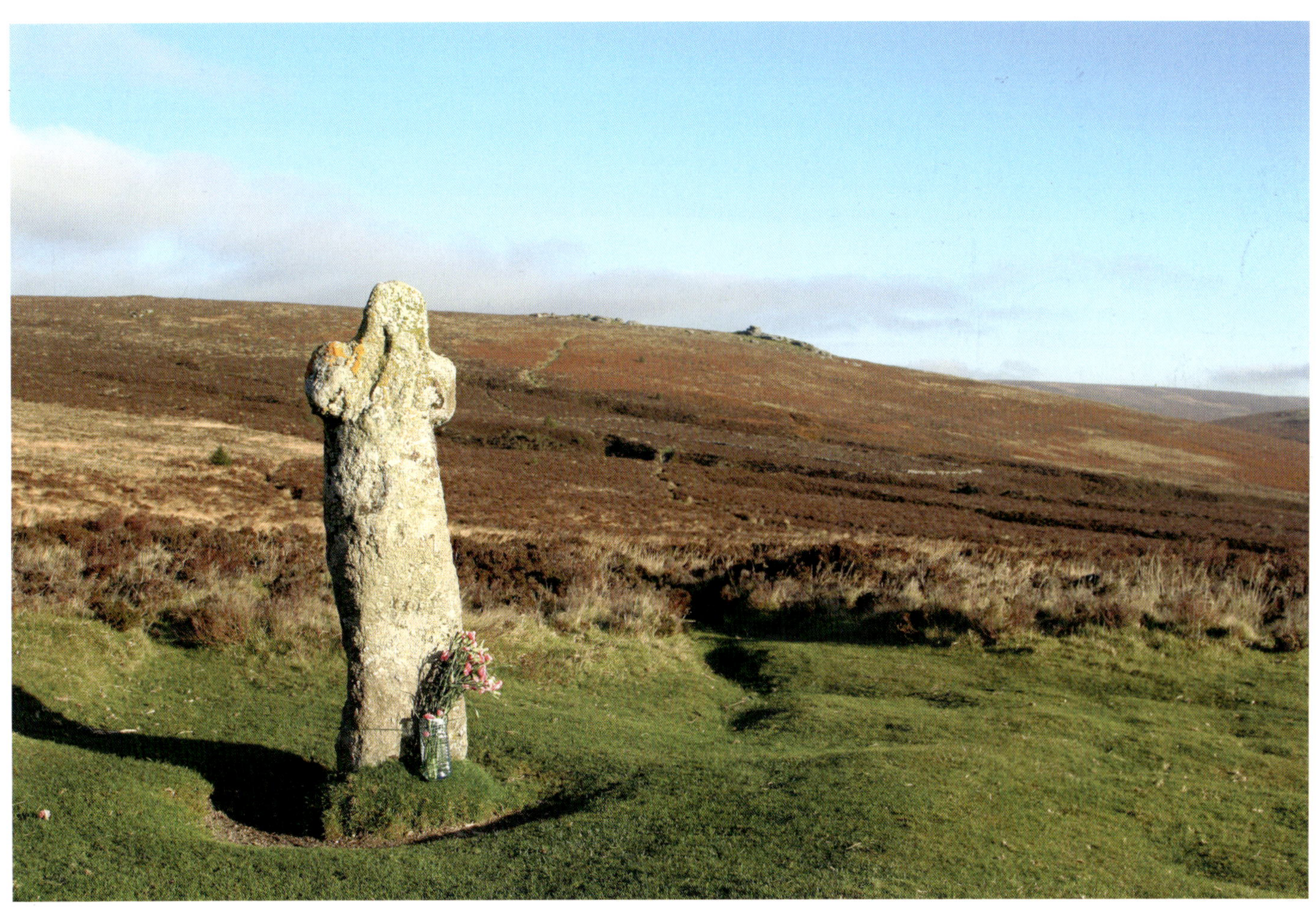

Bennett's Cross with flowers. In the distance is Birch Tor.

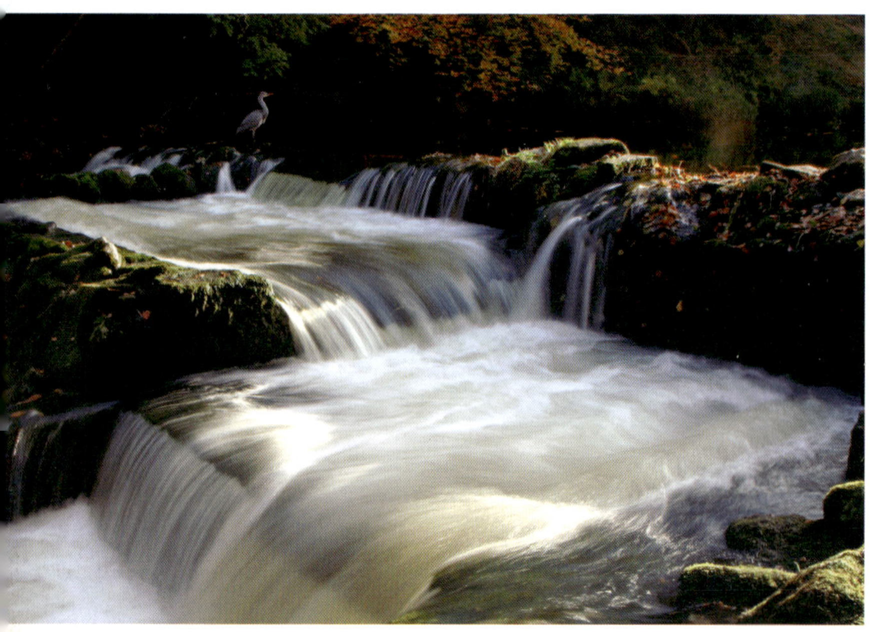

A heron sits patiently at the salmon leap along the Teign river from Fingle bridge.

Great Staple Tor with Brentor and its church in the distance.

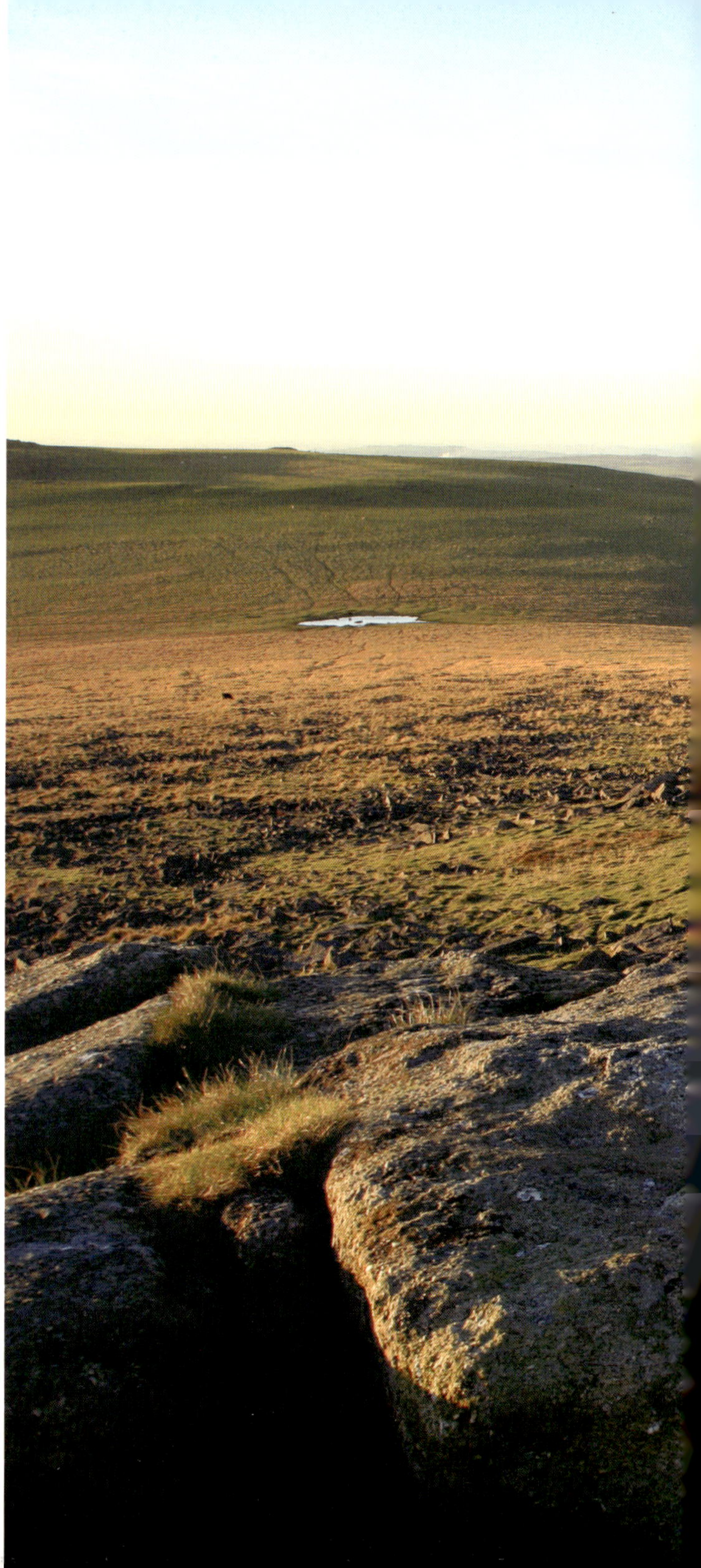

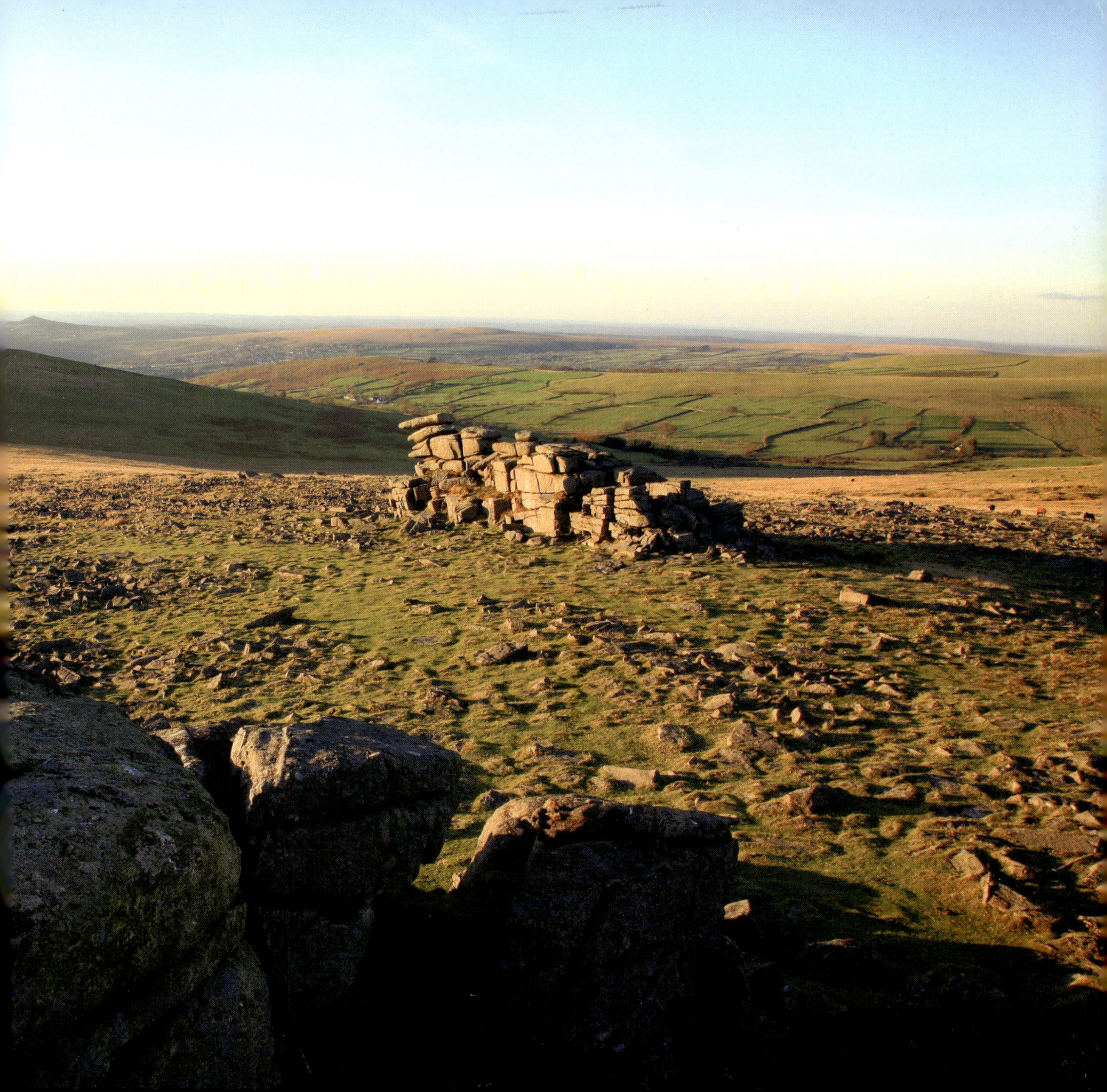

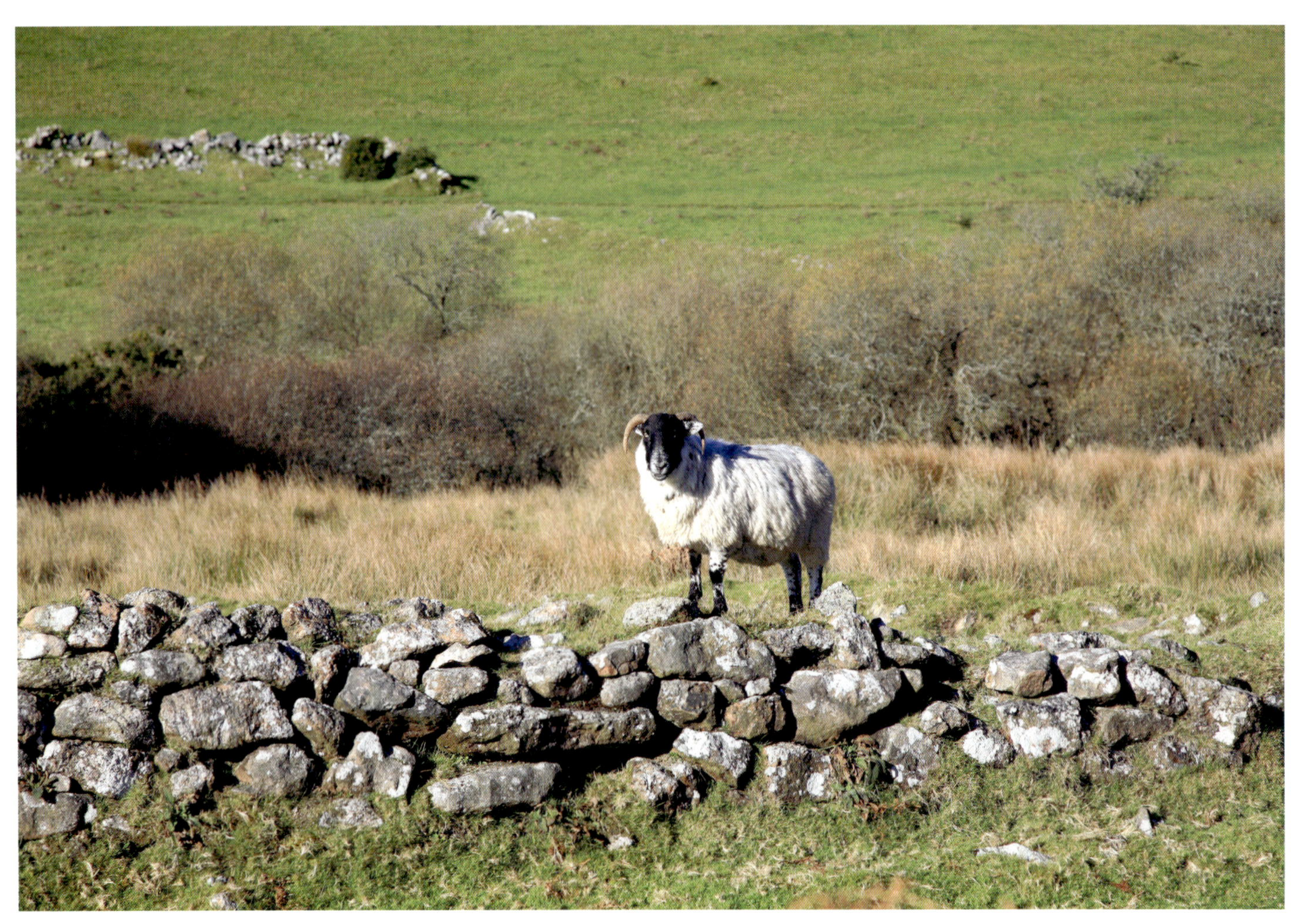

A lone ram stands on a wall near the medieval village remains at Challacombe.

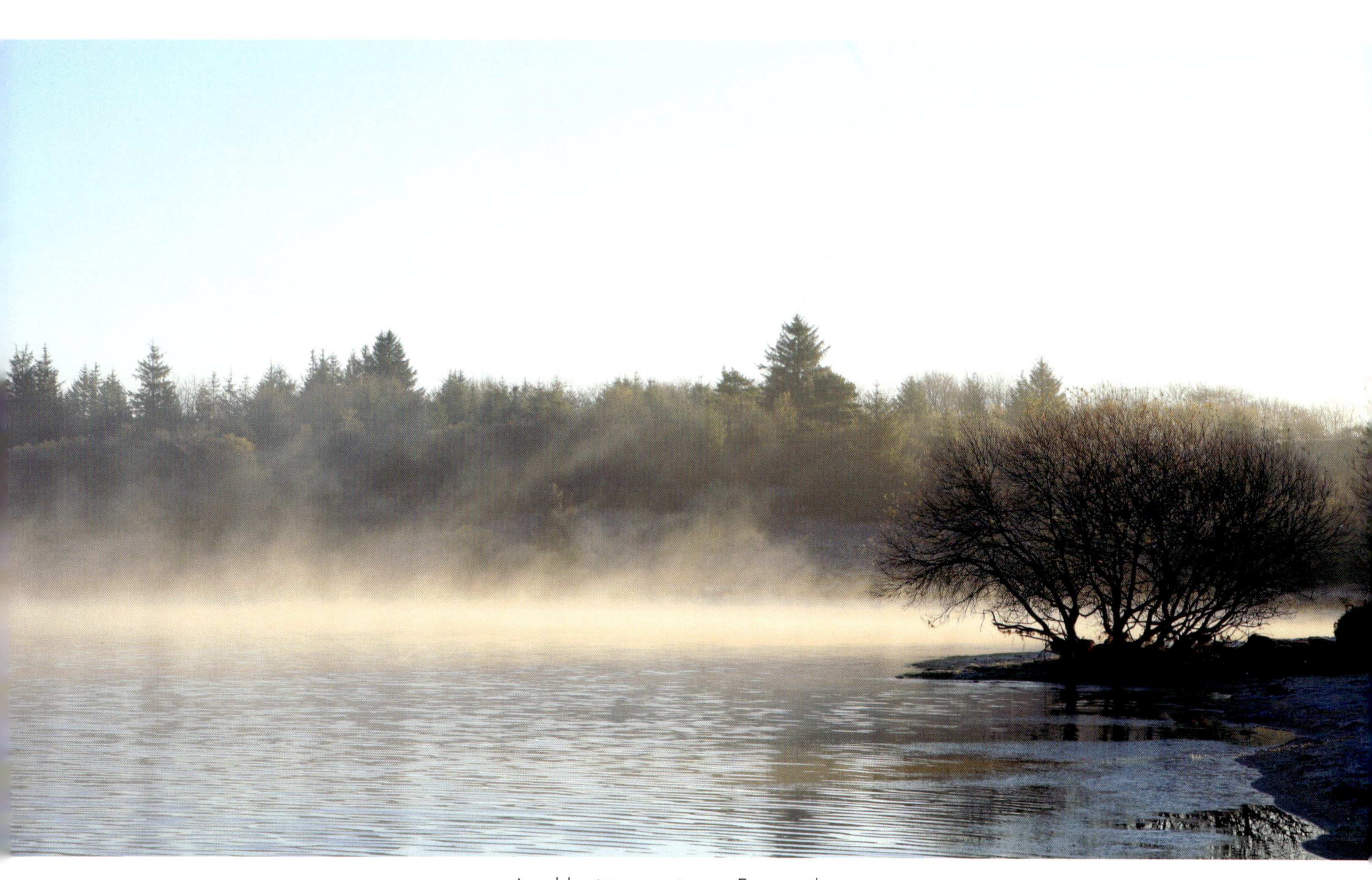

A cold misty morning at Fernworthy.

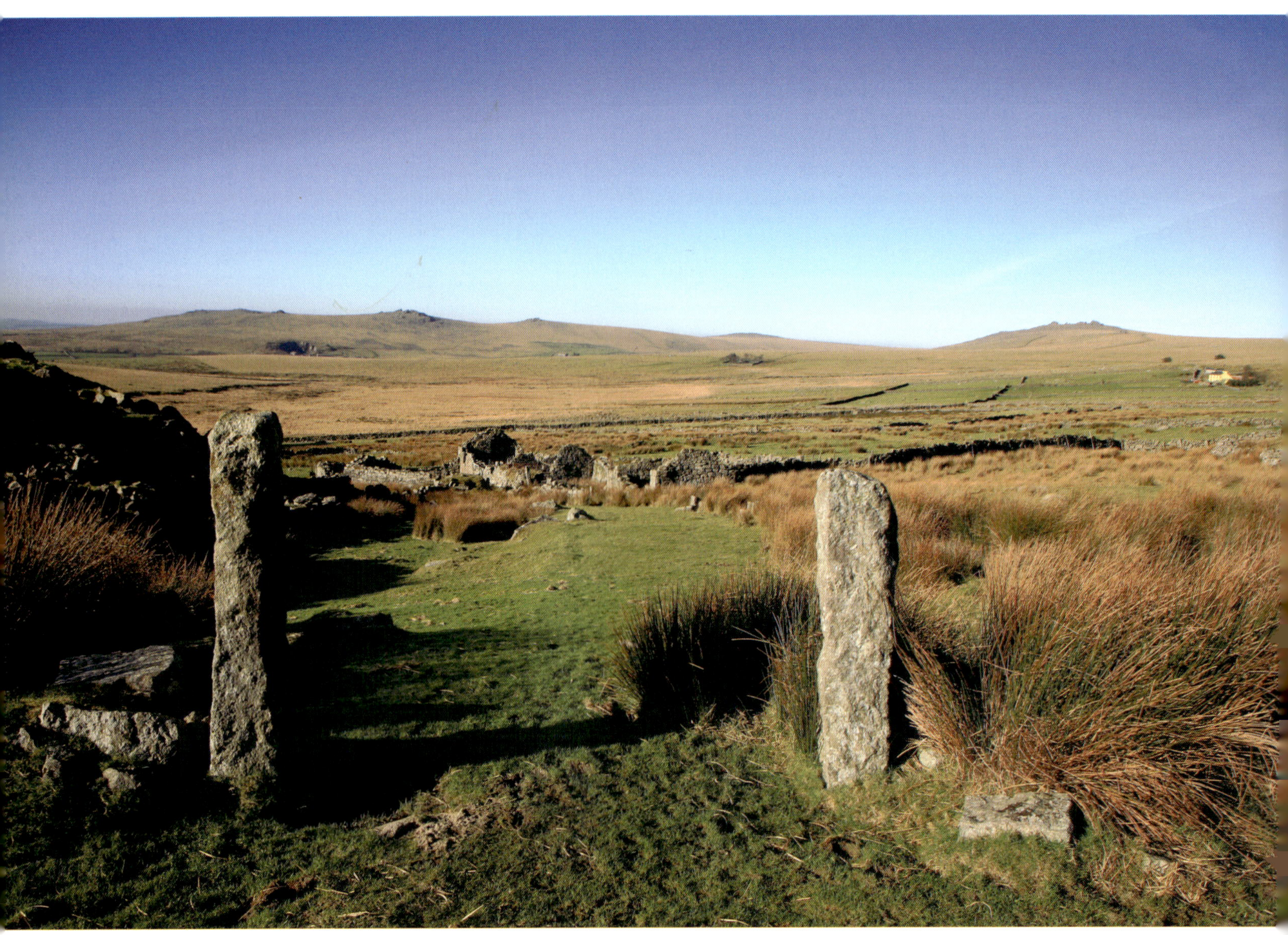

Looking through granite gate posts over ruins towards Great Staple and Great Mis Tors.

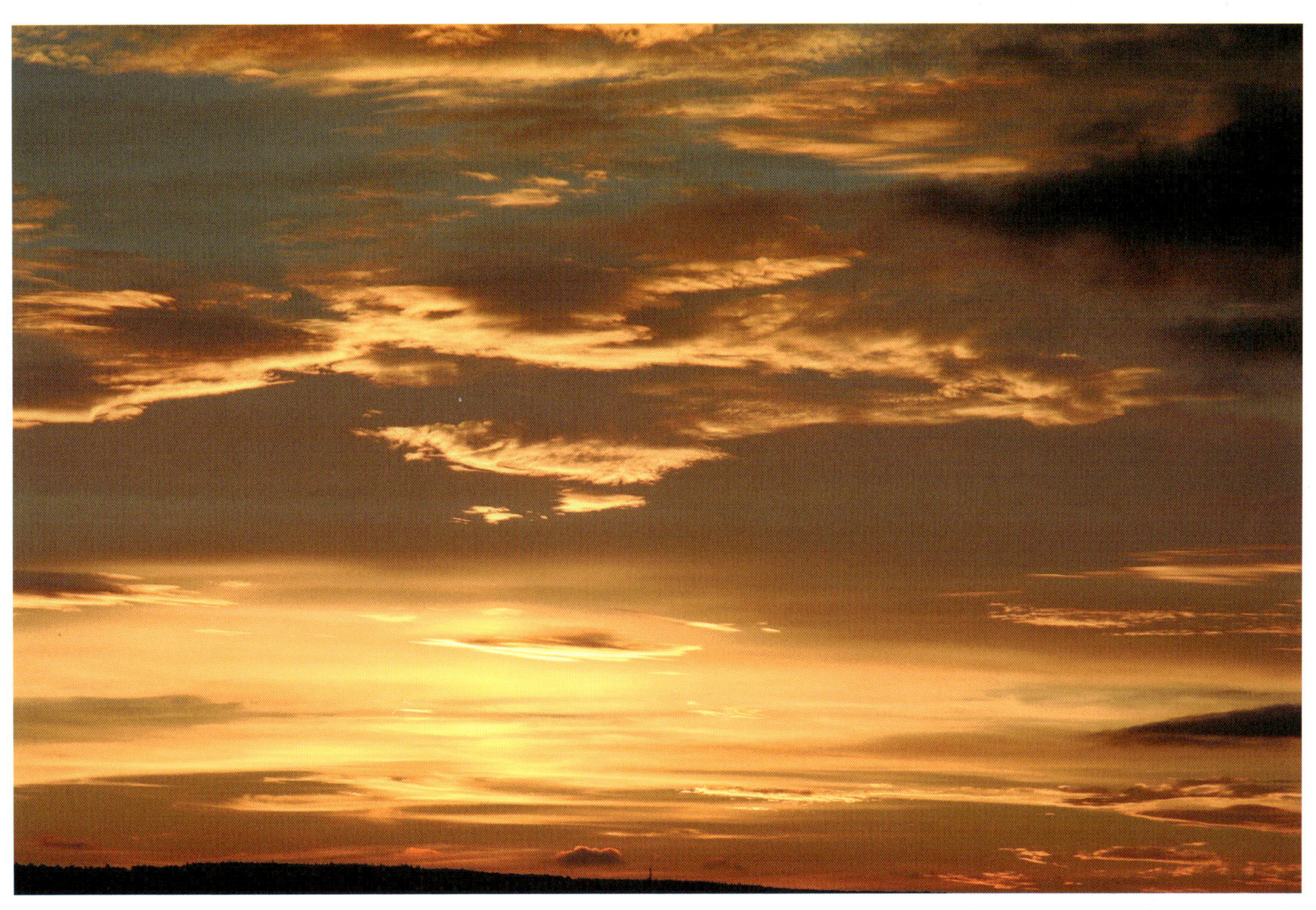

Rich autumn sunset over the moor.

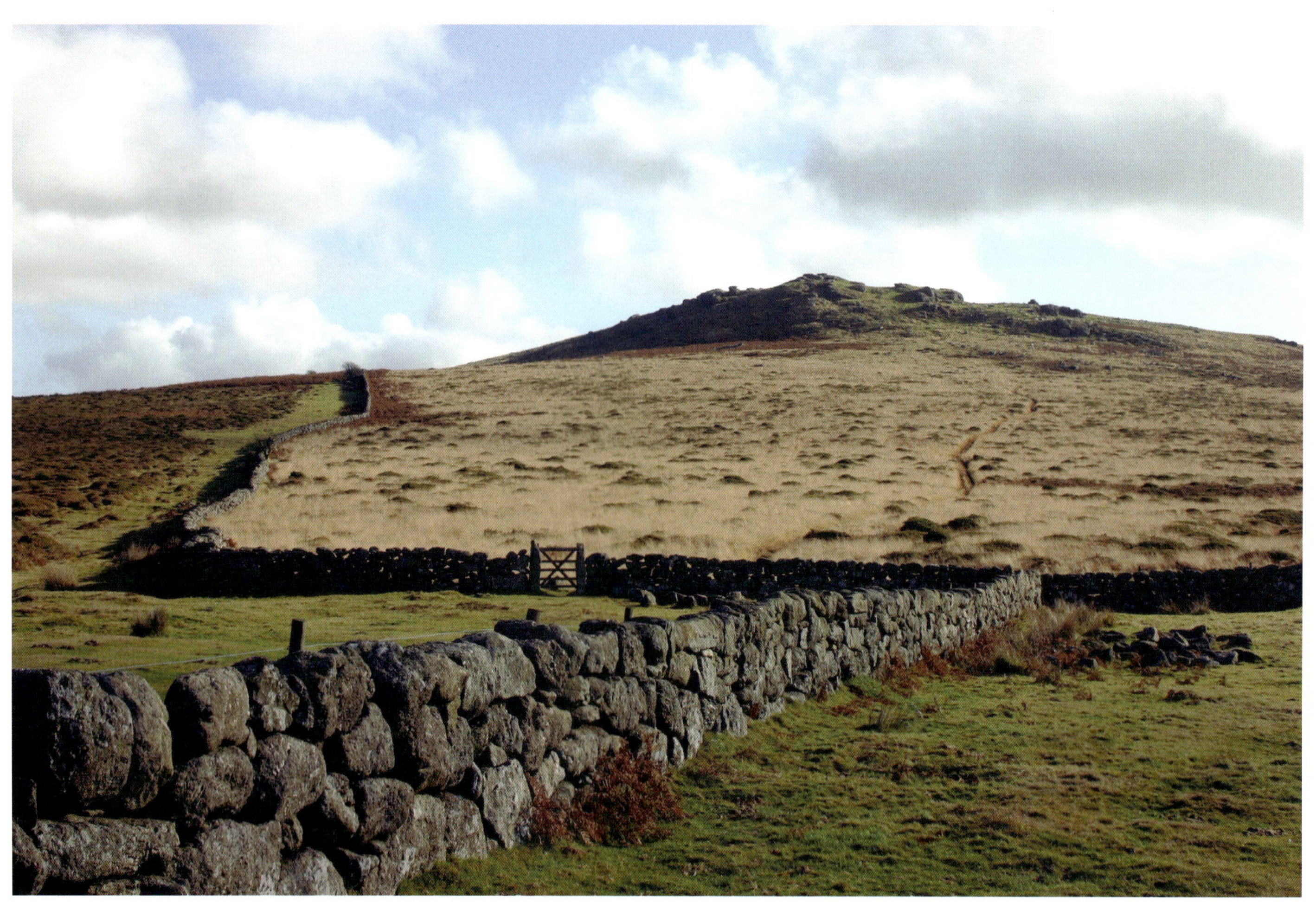

Granite walls wind their way around Rippon Tor.

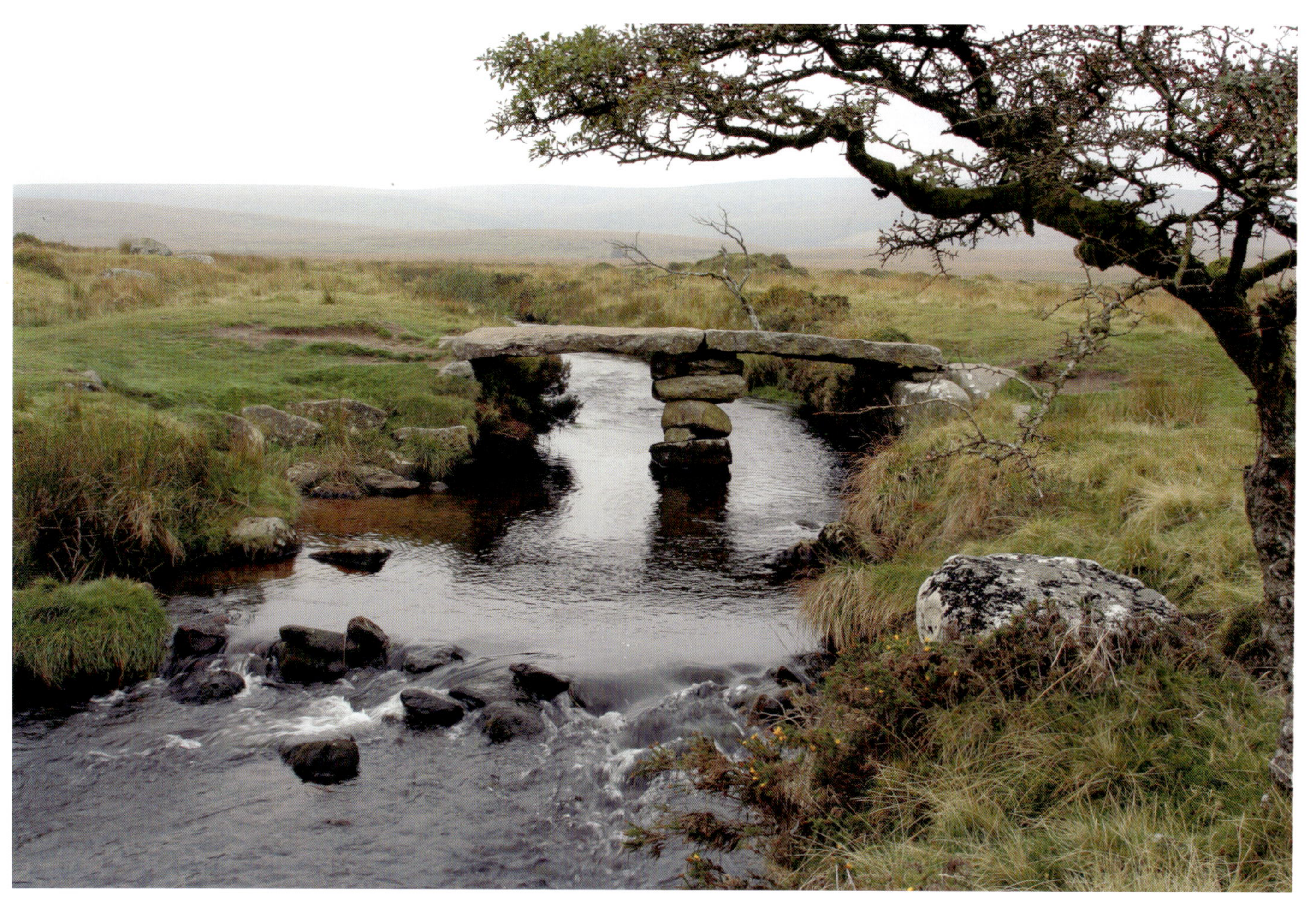

Clapper bridge near Batworthy on a stormy day.

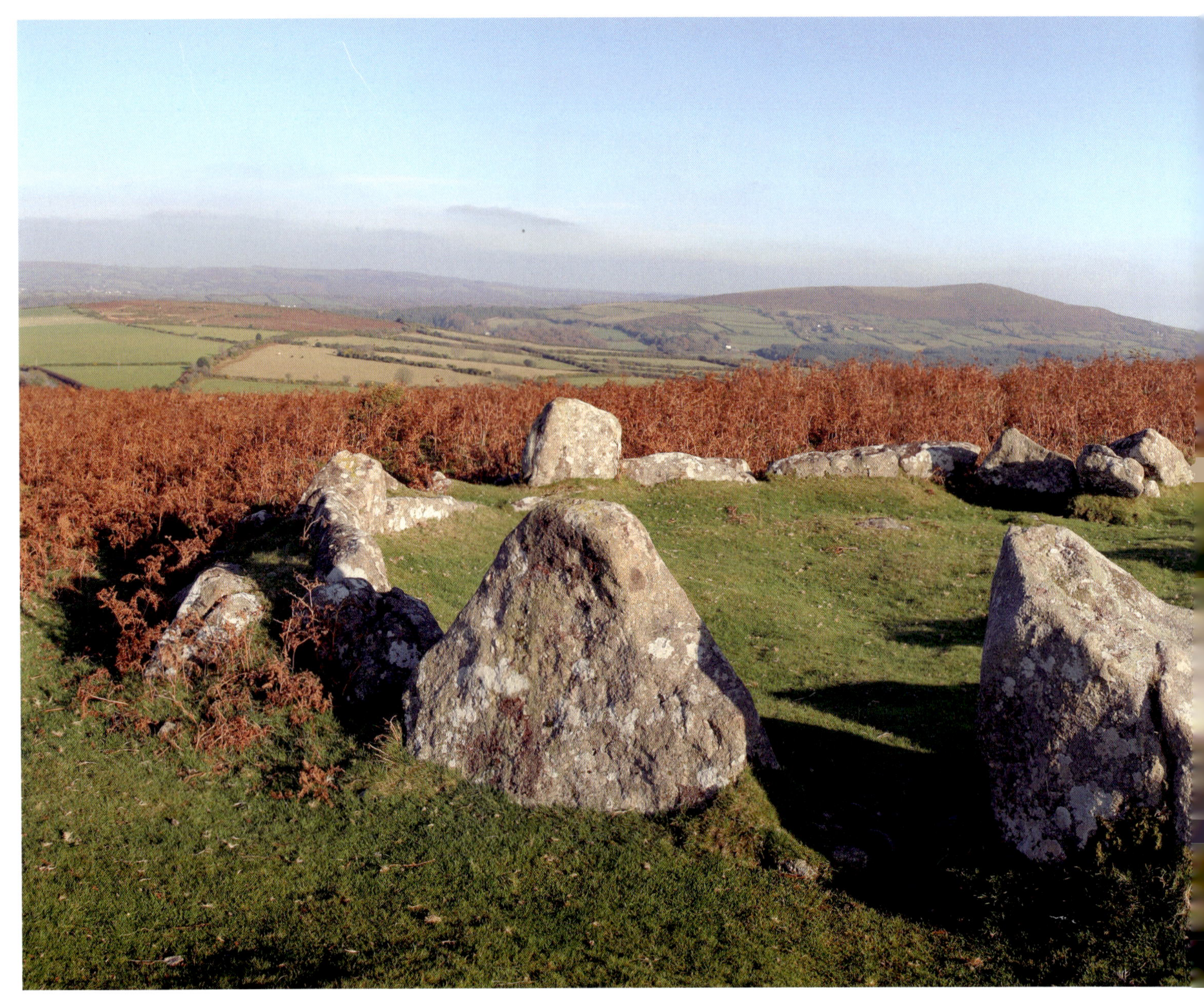

Prehistoric hut circle on Shapley Common.

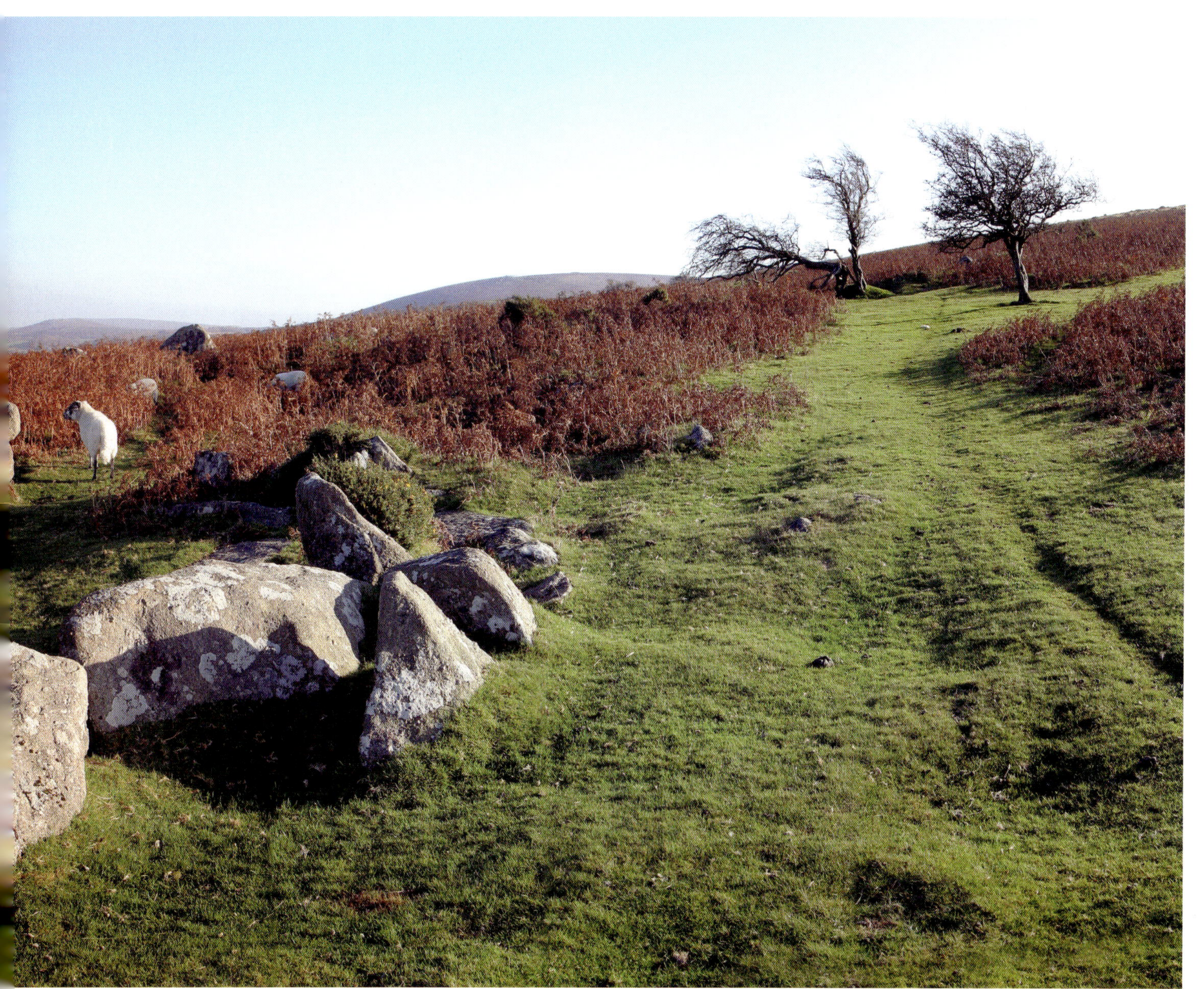

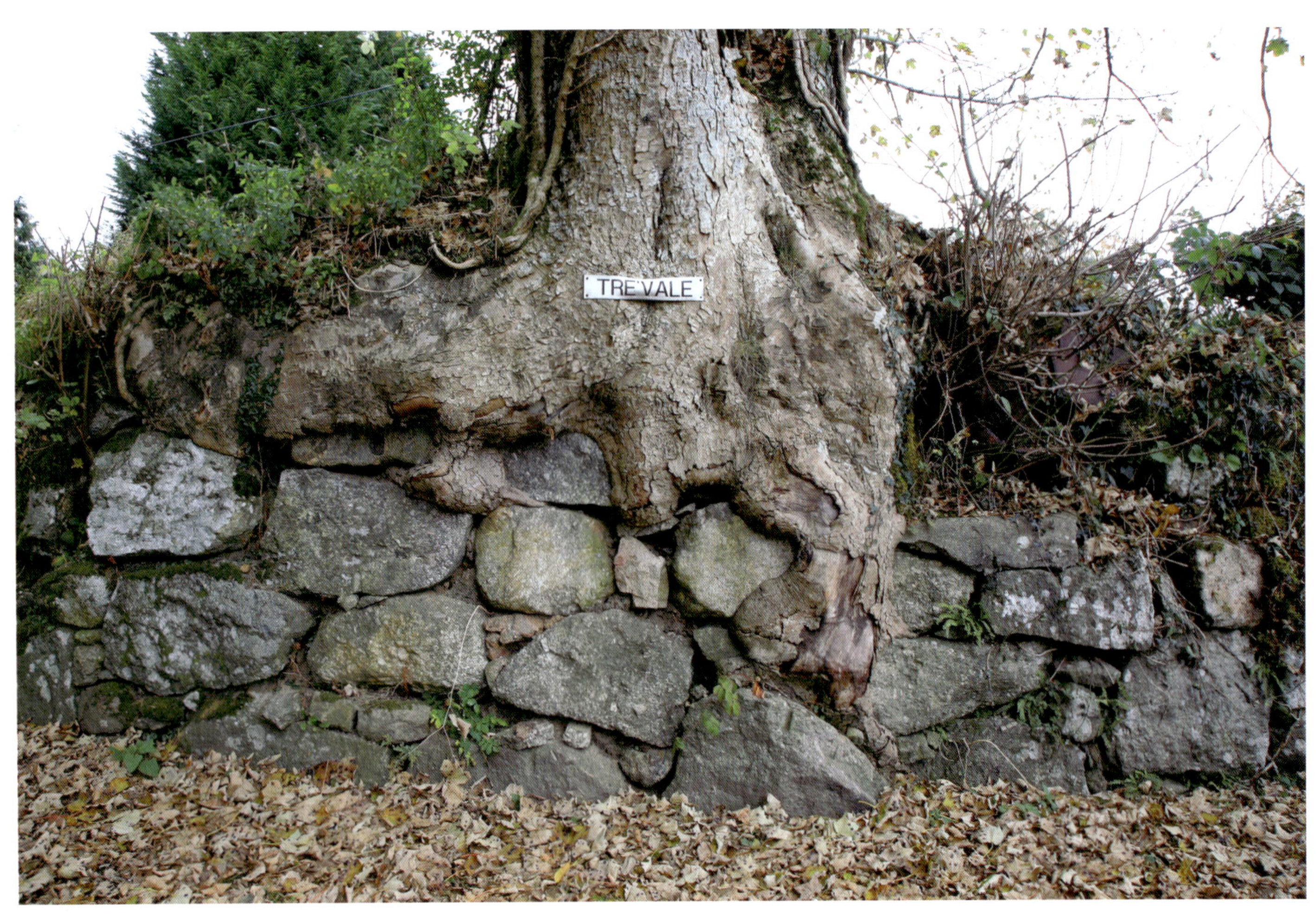

A very old tree grows out of an ancient wall near Widecombe-in-the-Moor.

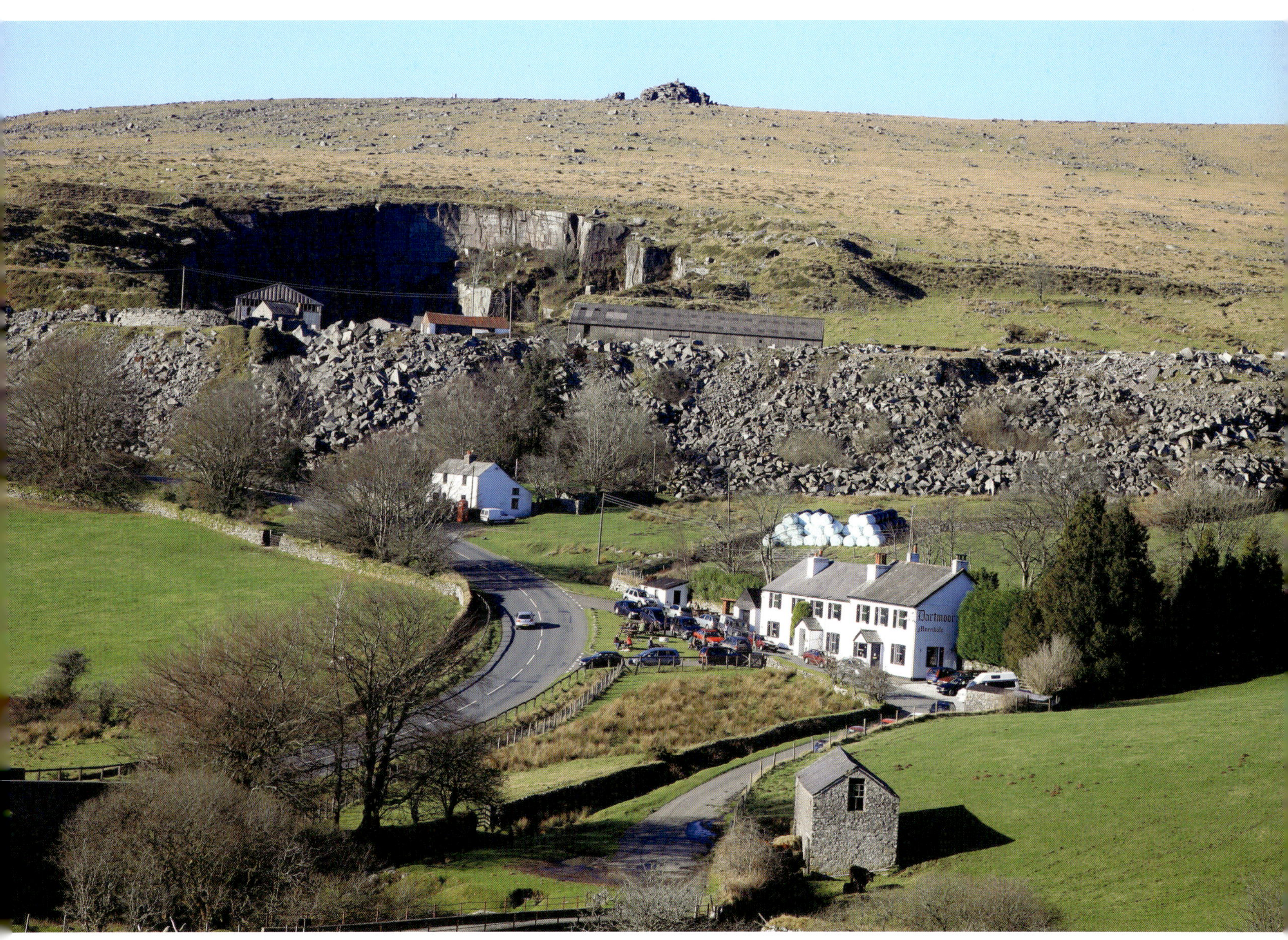

Enjoying the sun and refreshment at the inn at Merrivale.

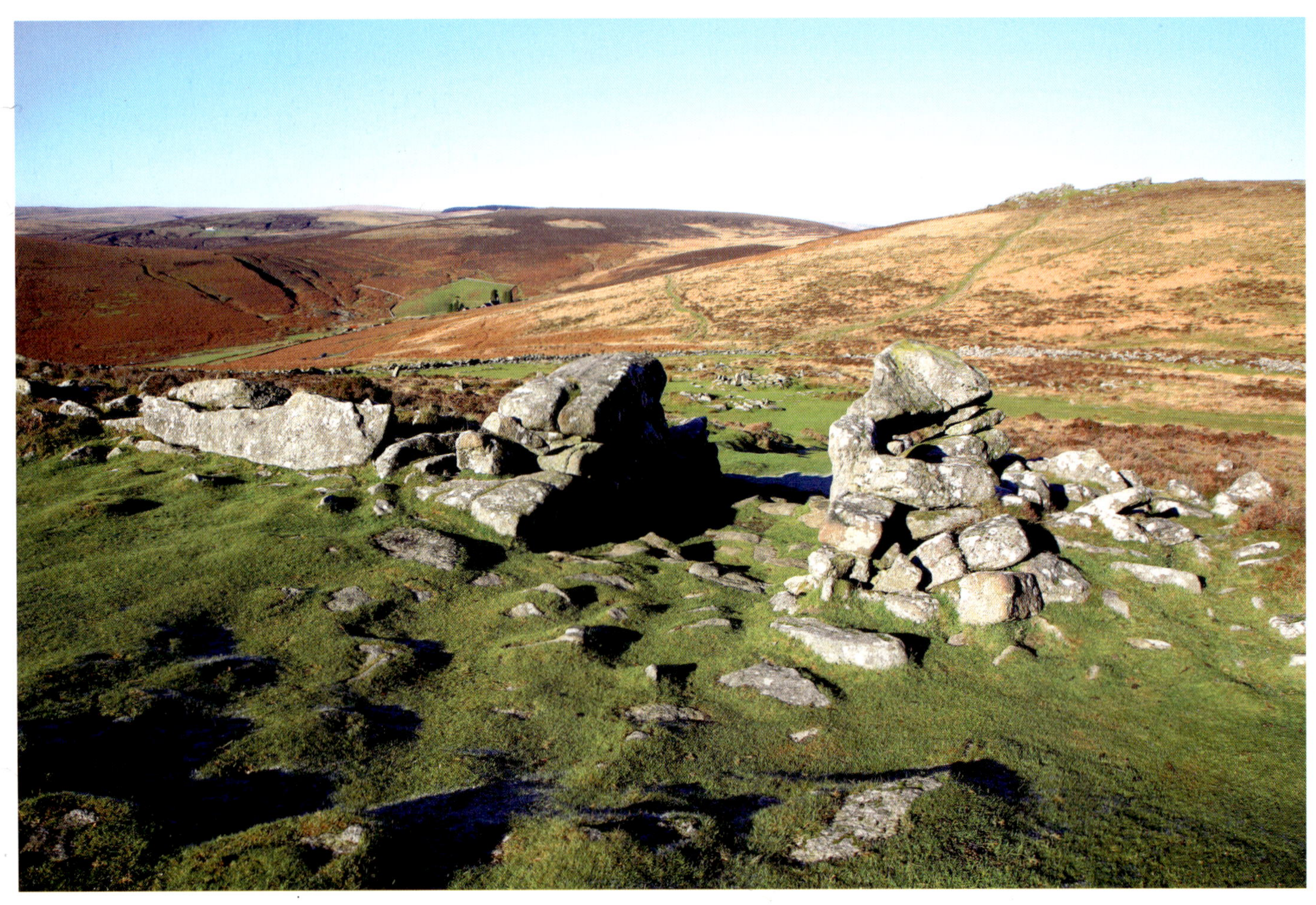

Entrance to Grimspound. The gateway to this Bronze Age settlement leads into a giant stone circle encompassing approximately 4 acres. Within are the remains of prehistoric stone dwellings known as hut circles.

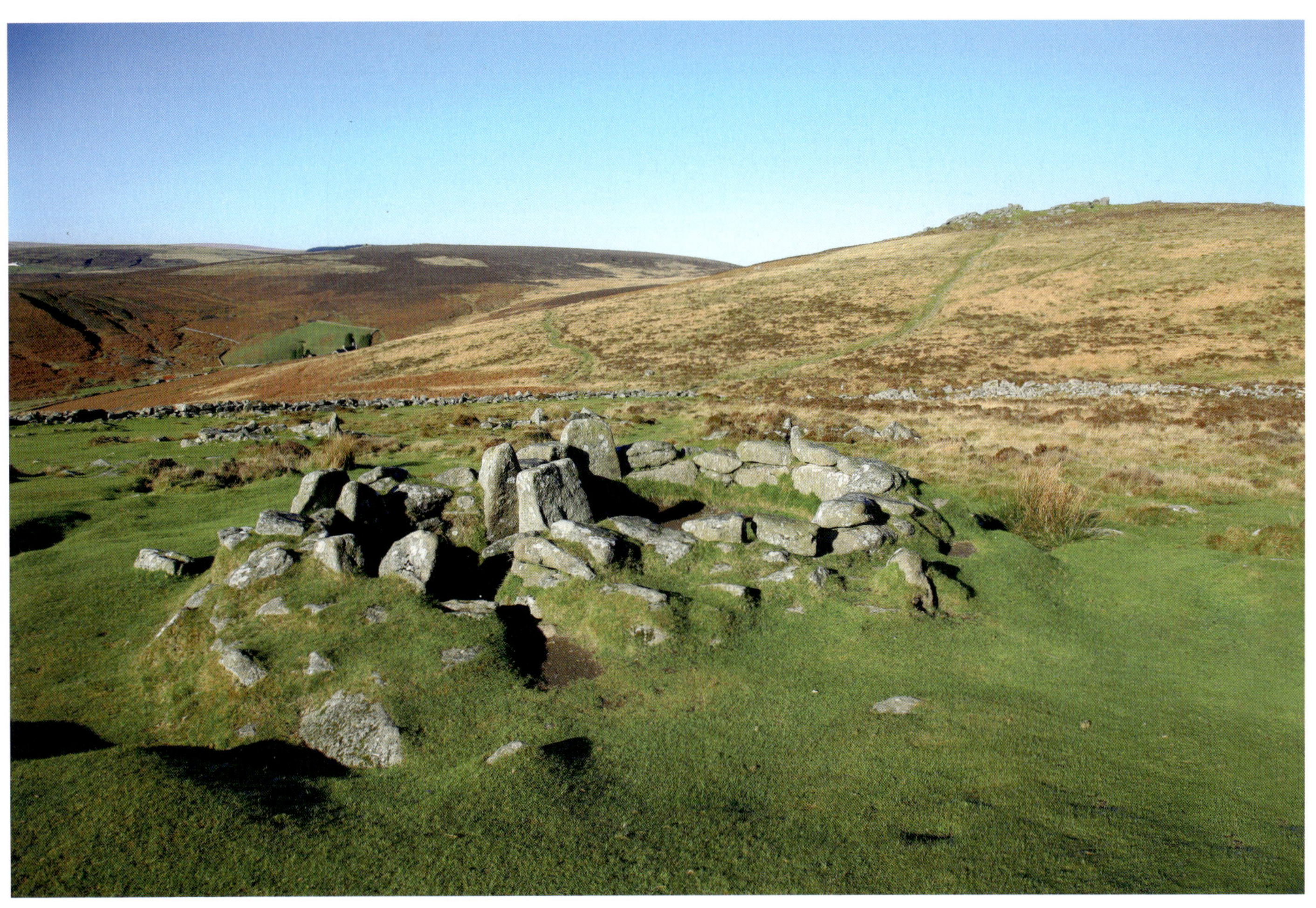

Hut remains at Grimspound, with Hookney Tor in the distance.

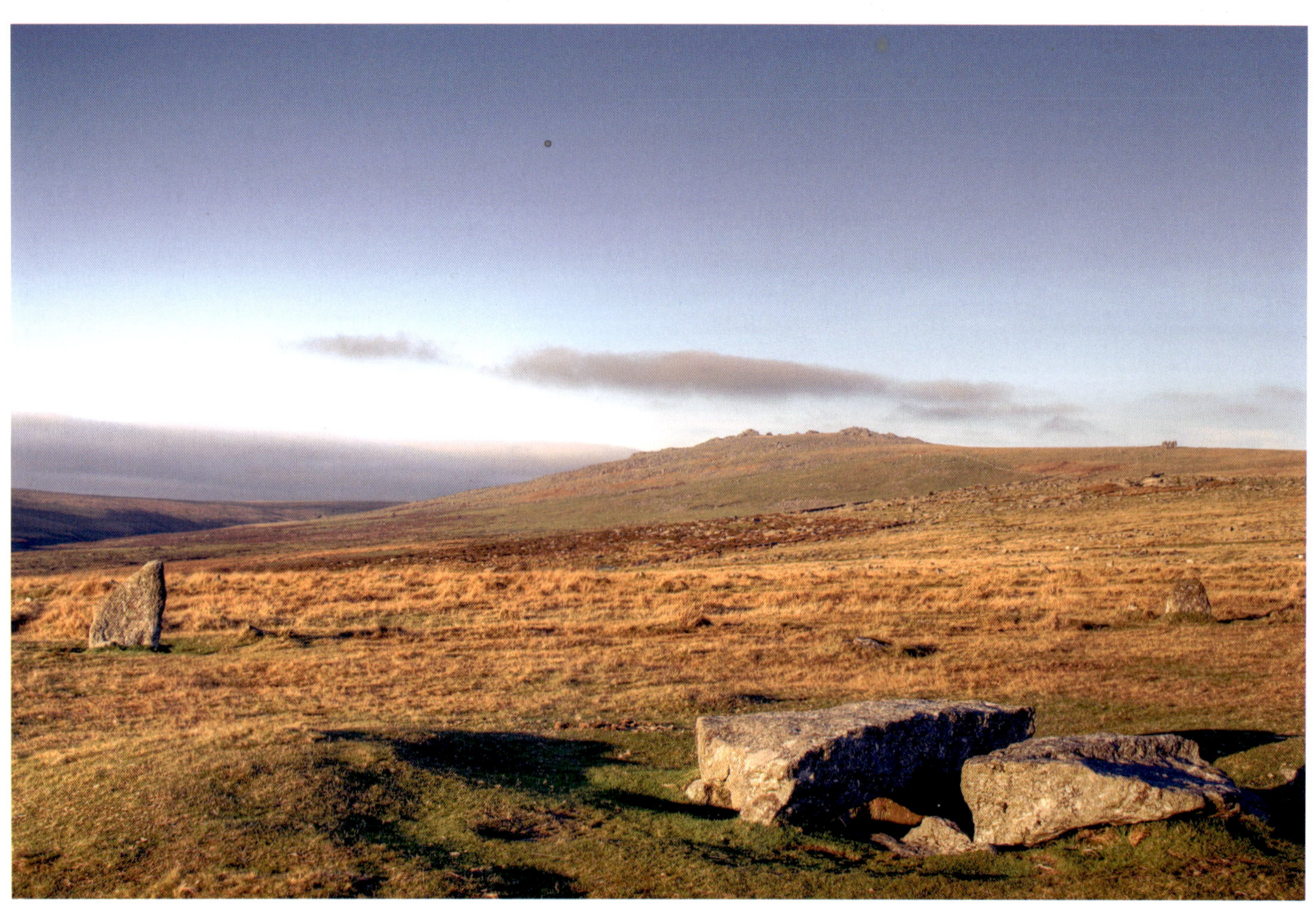

Sunset looking towards Great Mis Tor with a burial chamber in the foreground. This prehistoric grave, or cist, had its capstone split in two by stoneworkers over a century ago.

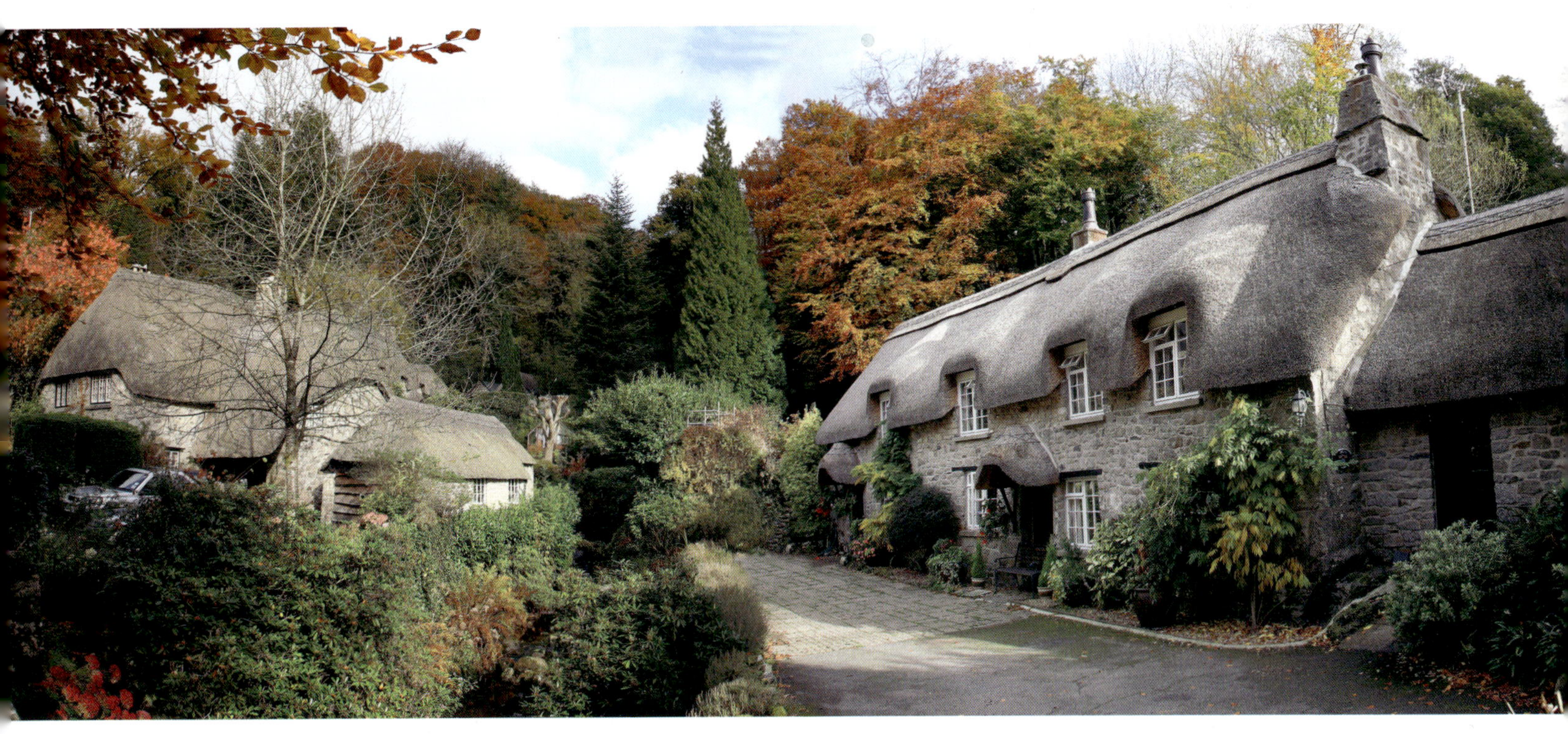

Some of the most attractive cottages on the Moor nestle in the small valley at Buckland.

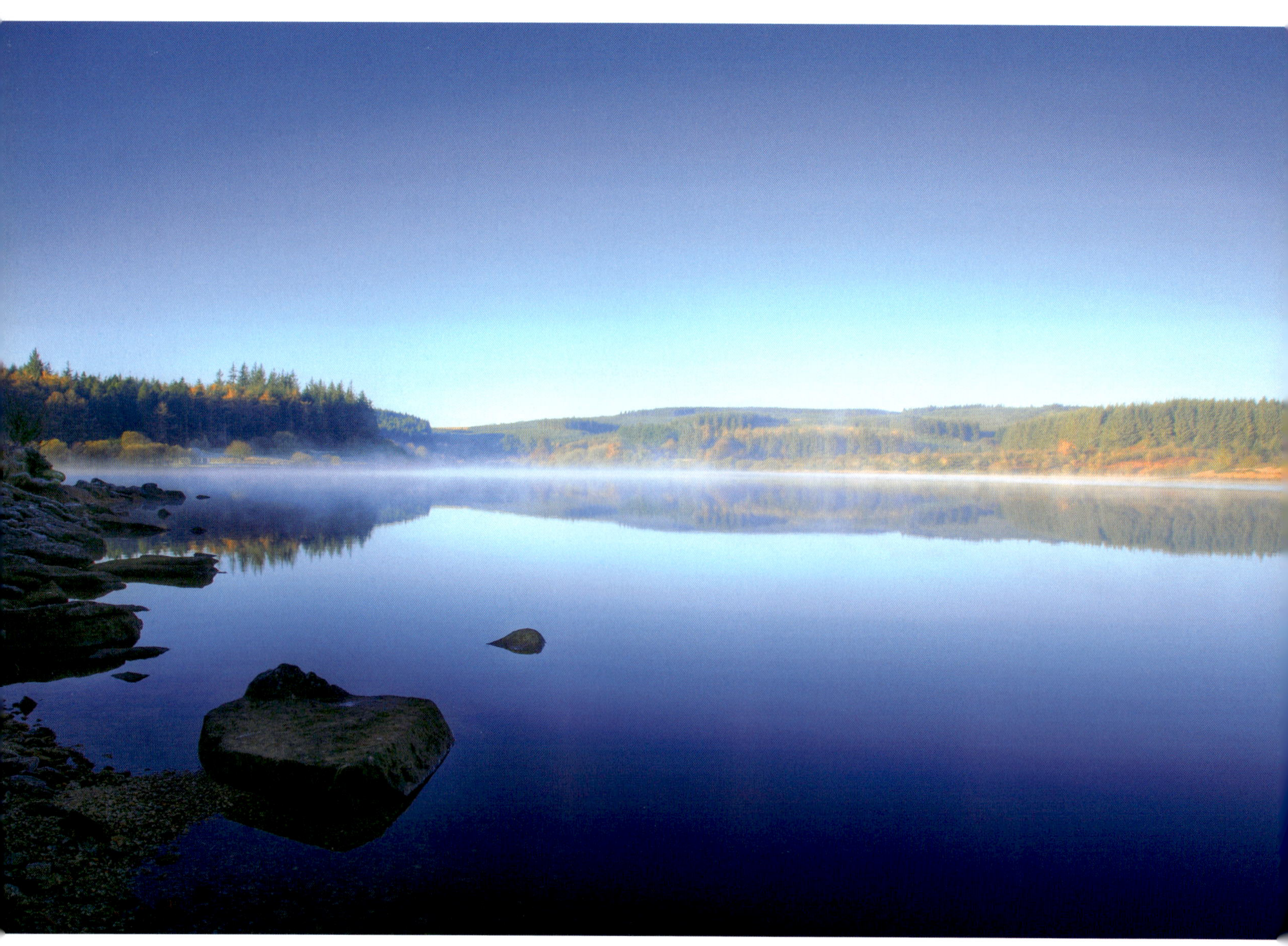

Beautiful autumn colours at sunrise over Fernworthy.

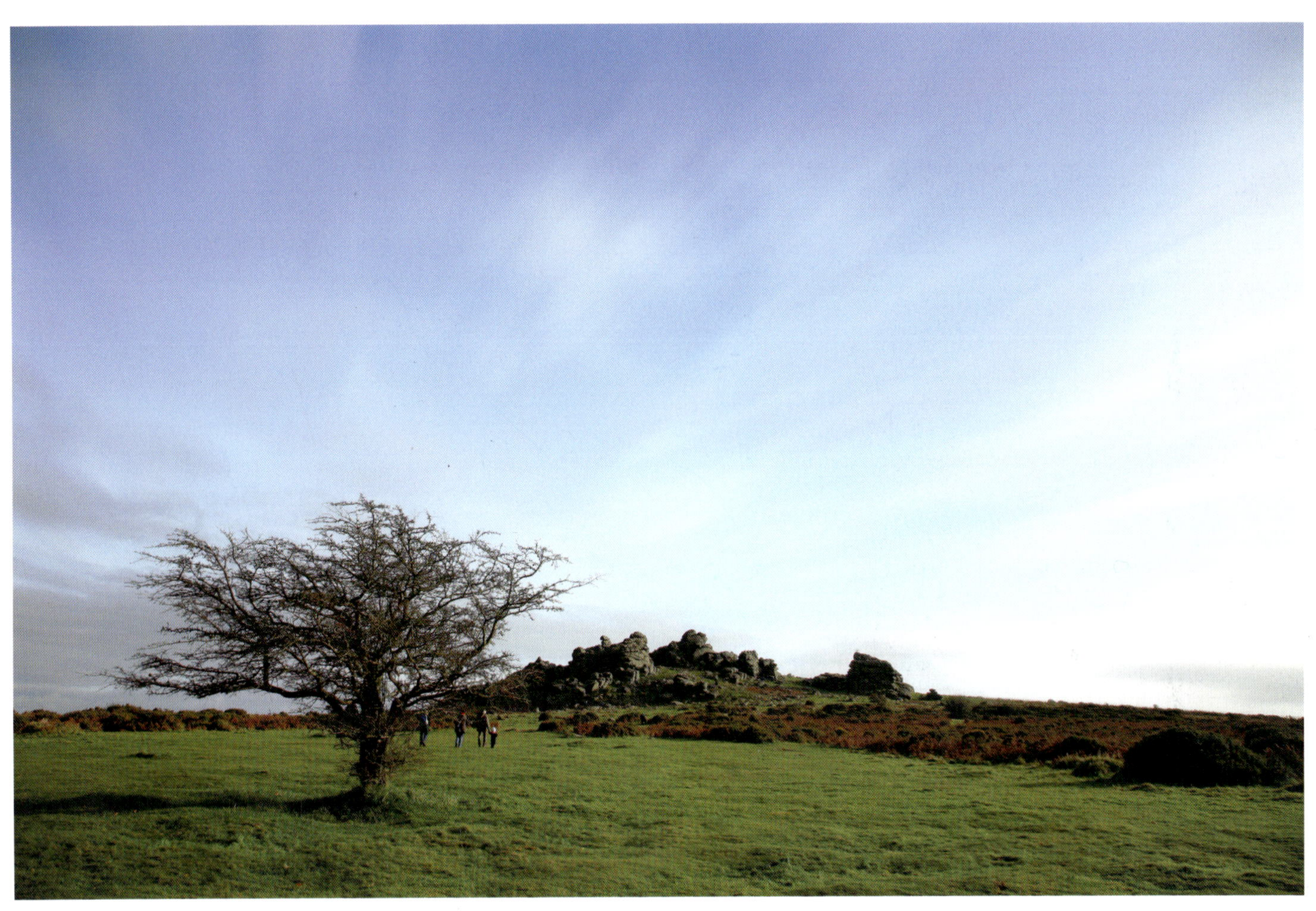

A family wander up to Hound Tor.

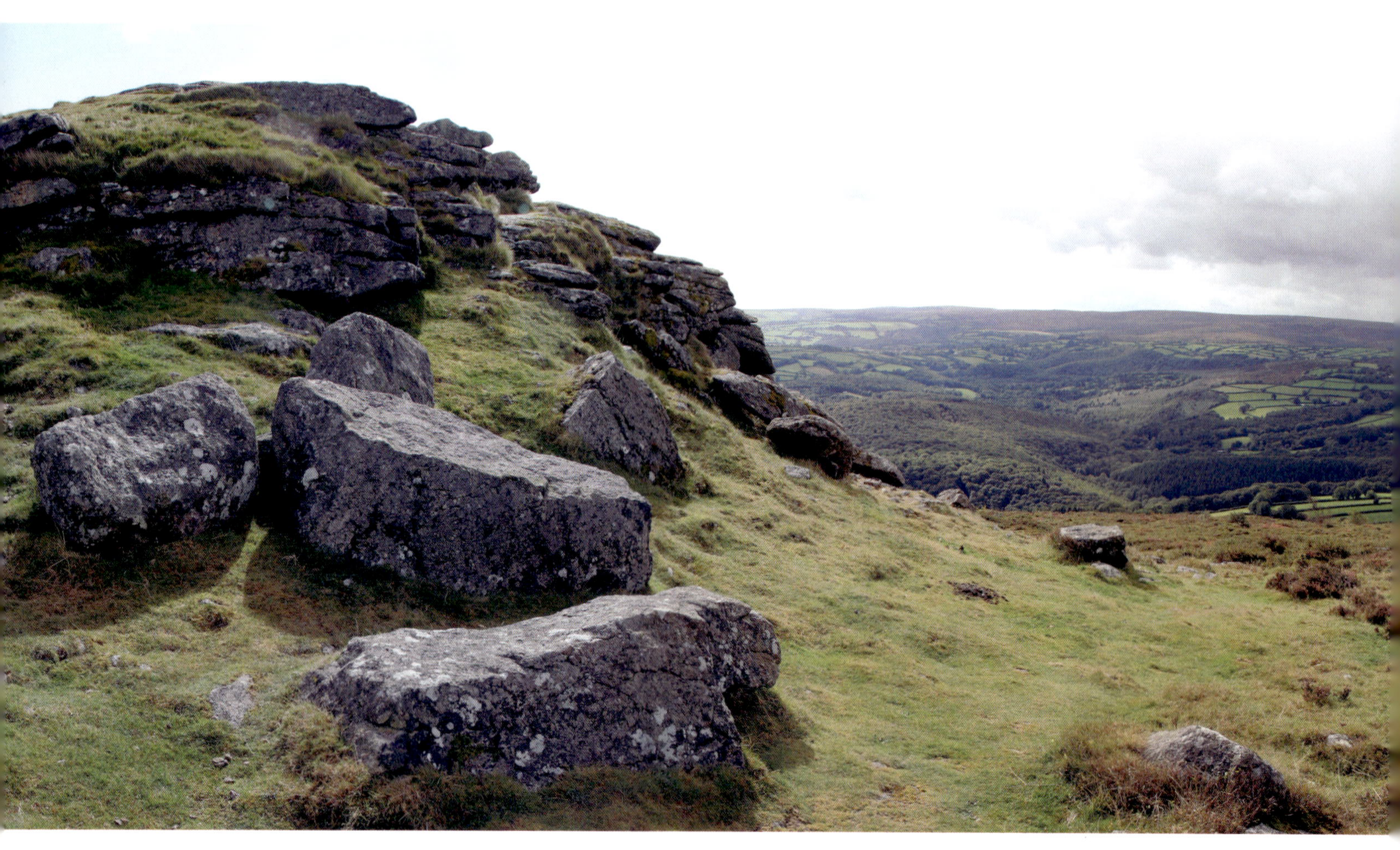

Panorama looking north from Buckland Beacon over the open moor, as the clouds thicken.

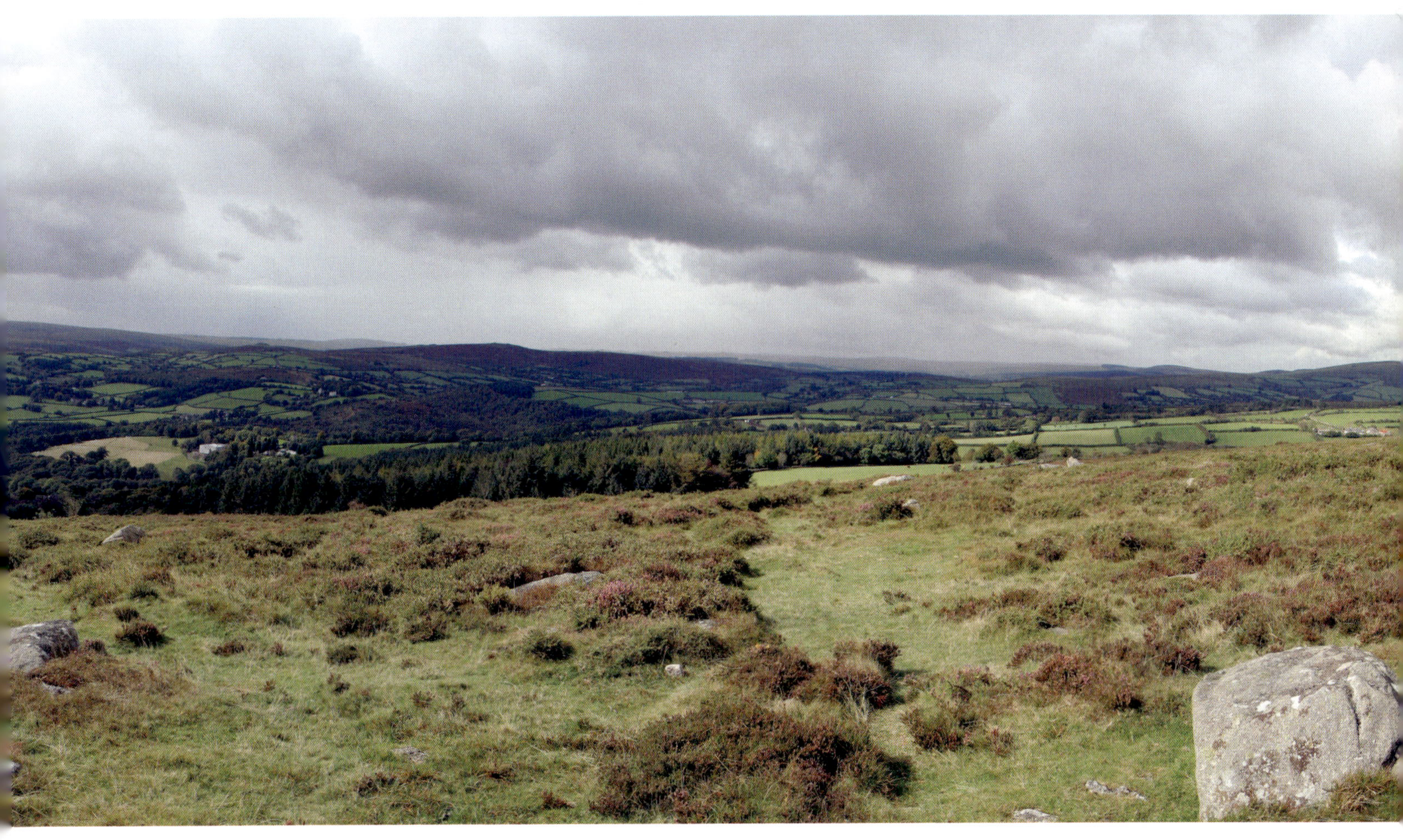

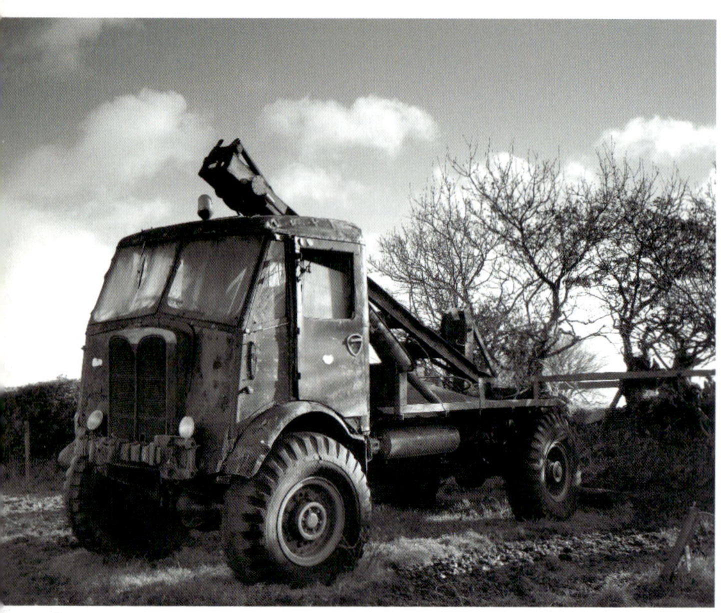

An old AEC Matador pre-war truck sits in the corner of a farmers field. Formerly used for removing unexploded bombs, this vehicle is still in use on the farm today.

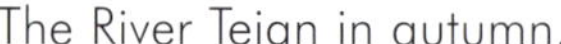

The River Teign in autumn.

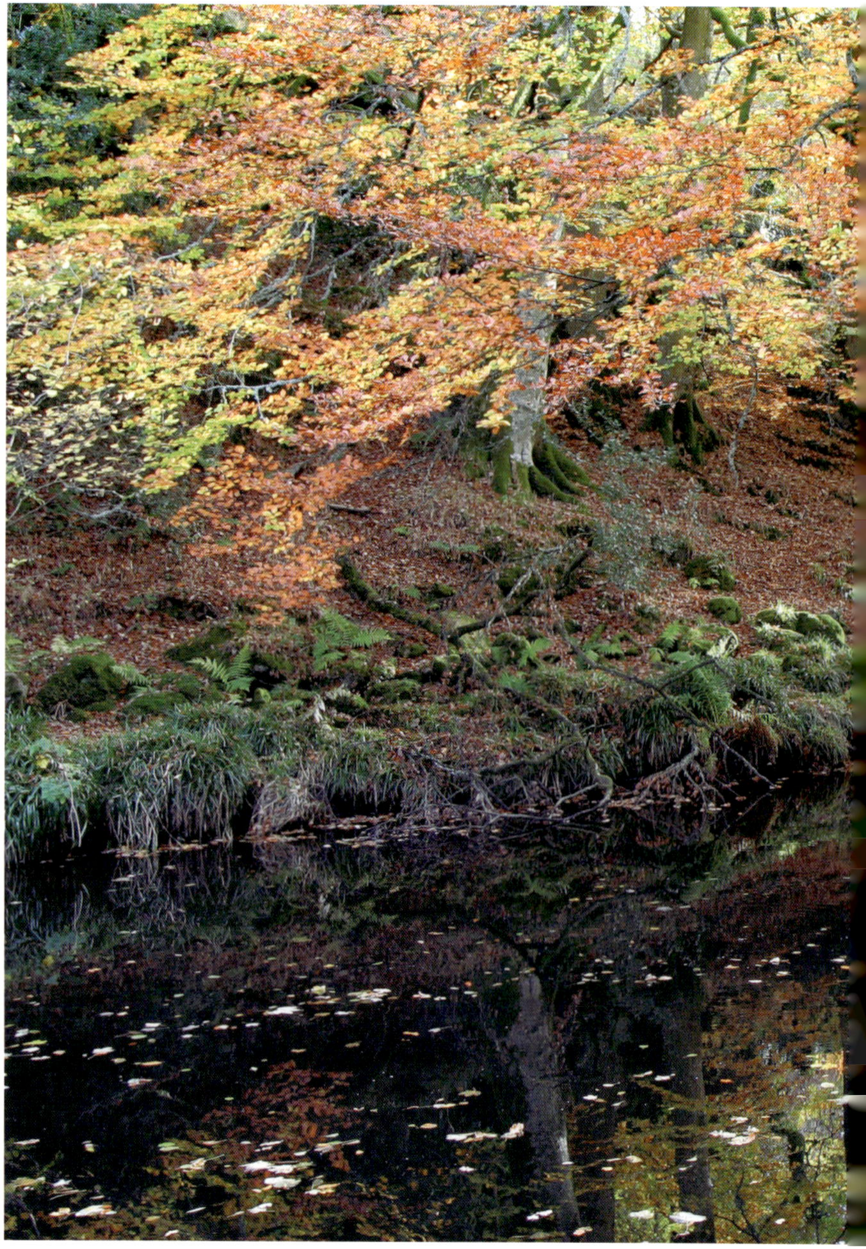

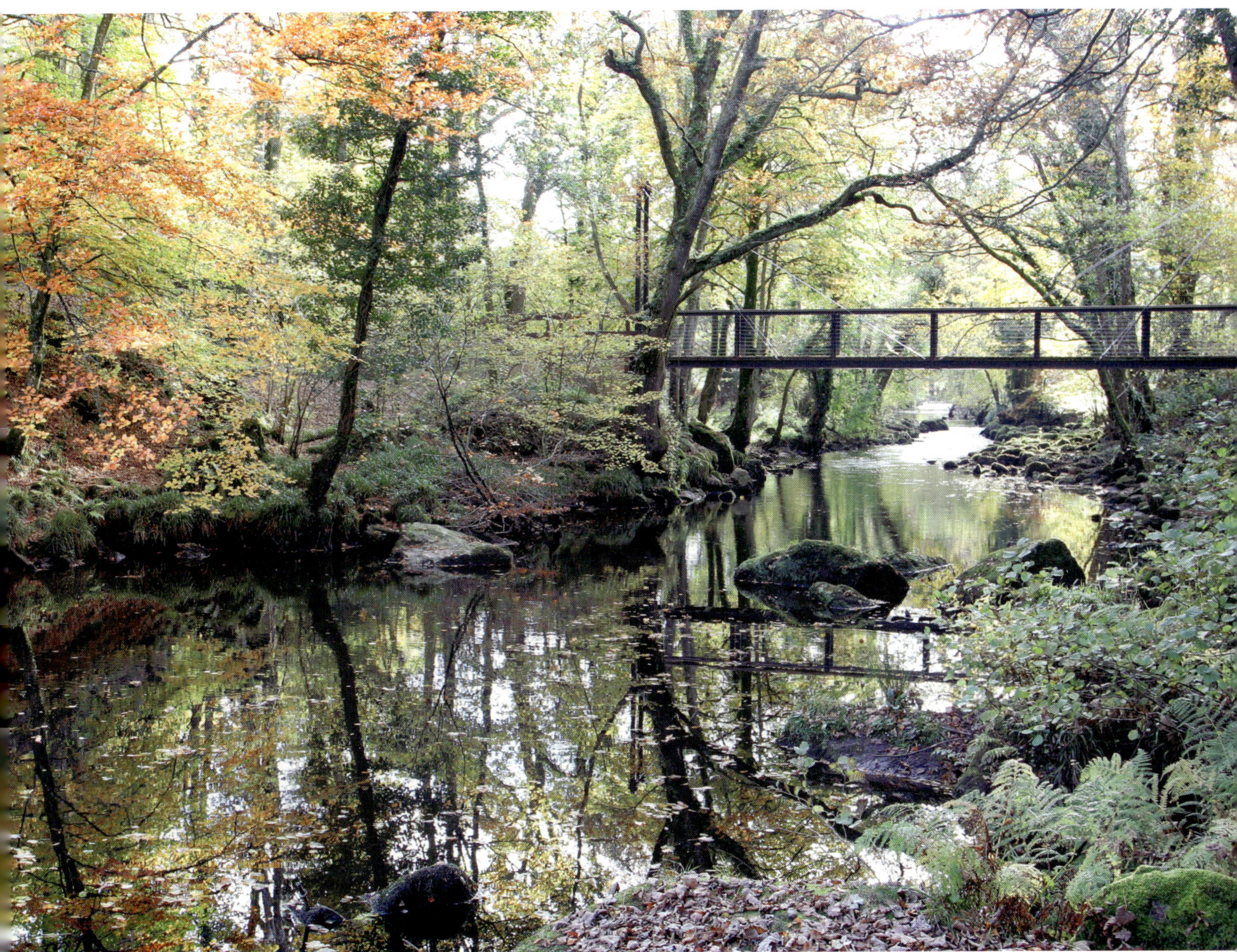

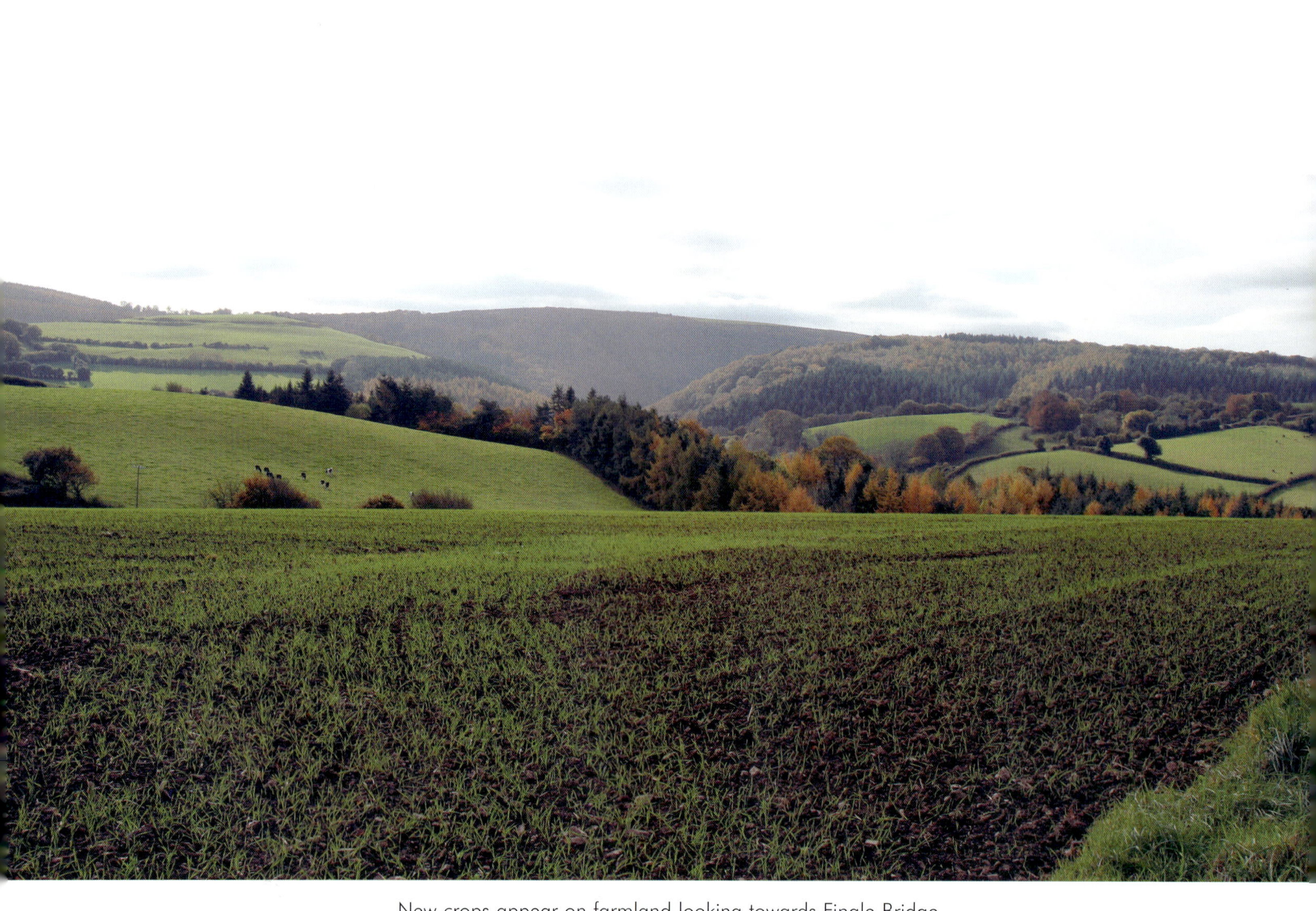

New crops appear on farmland looking towards Fingle Bridge.

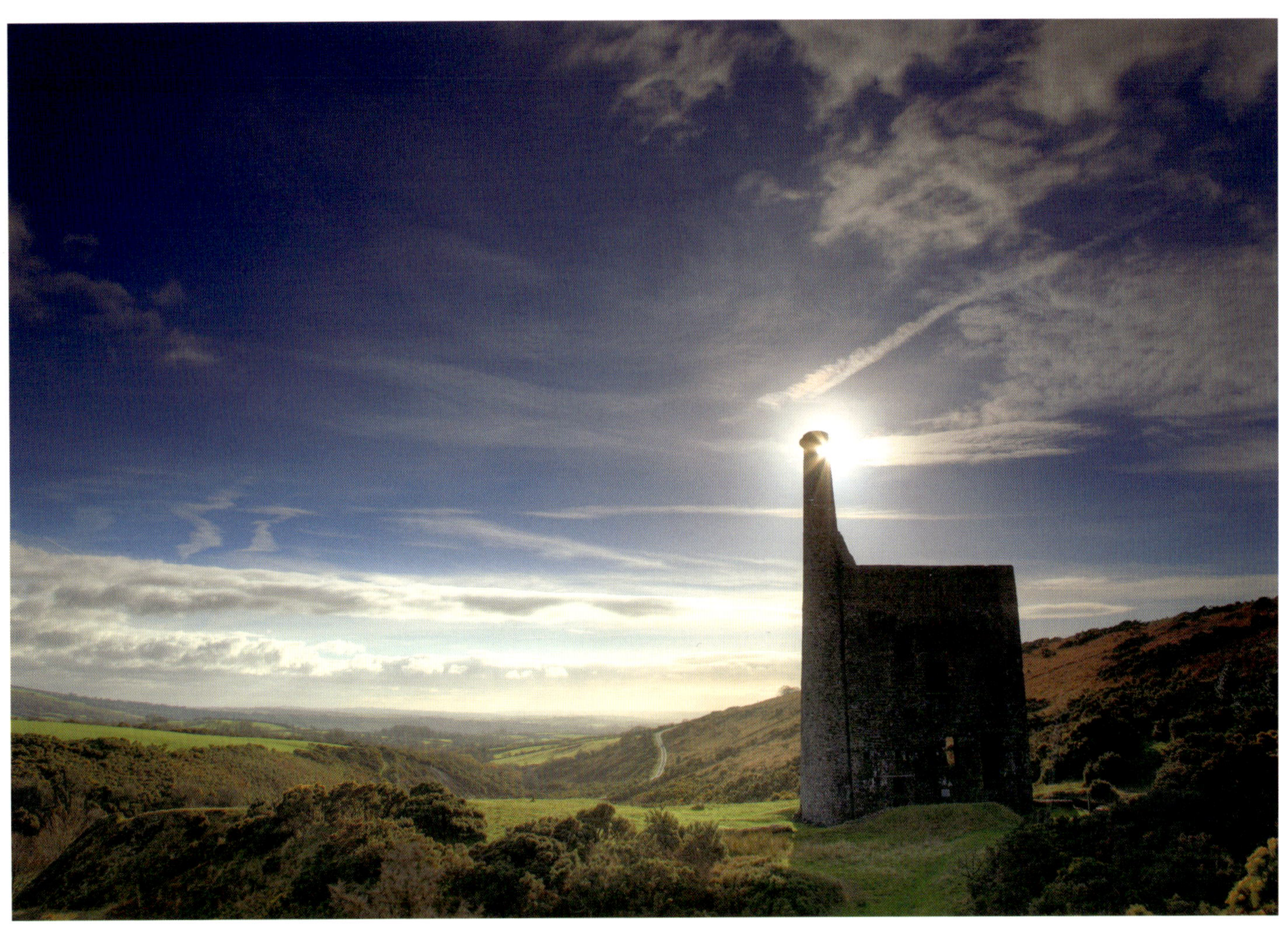

Wheal Betsy at sunset.

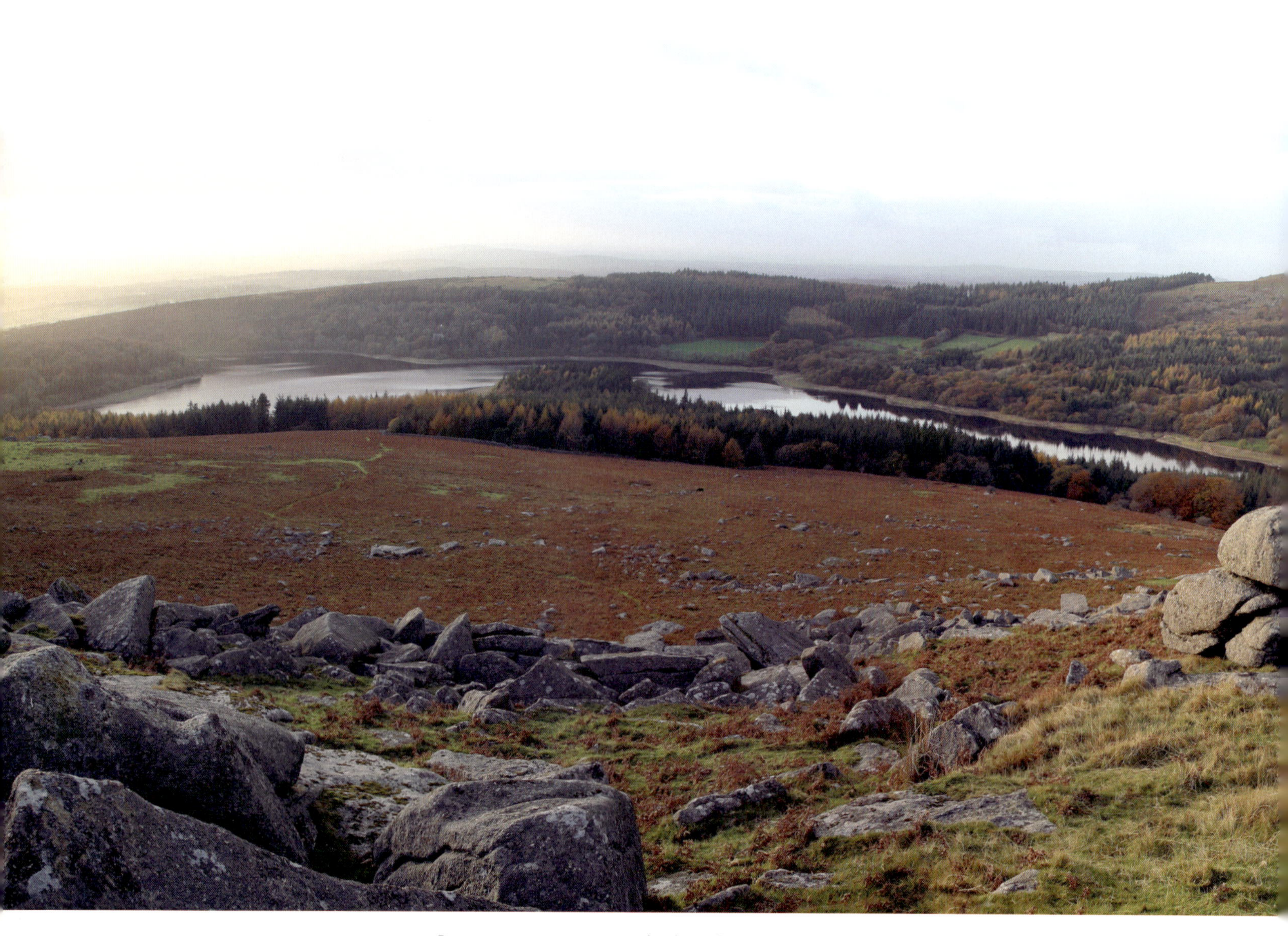

Panorama at sunset overlooking Burrator reservoir.

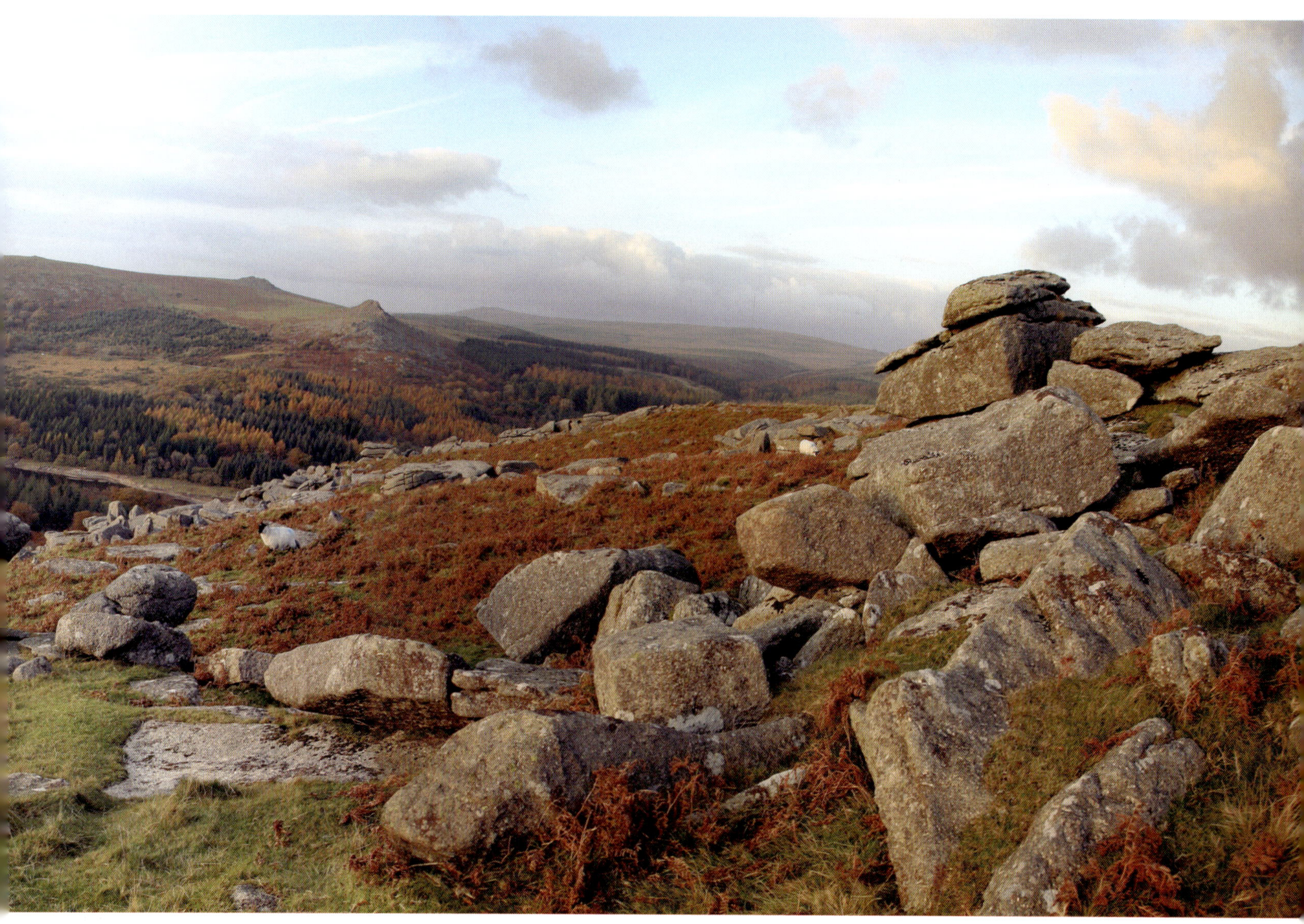

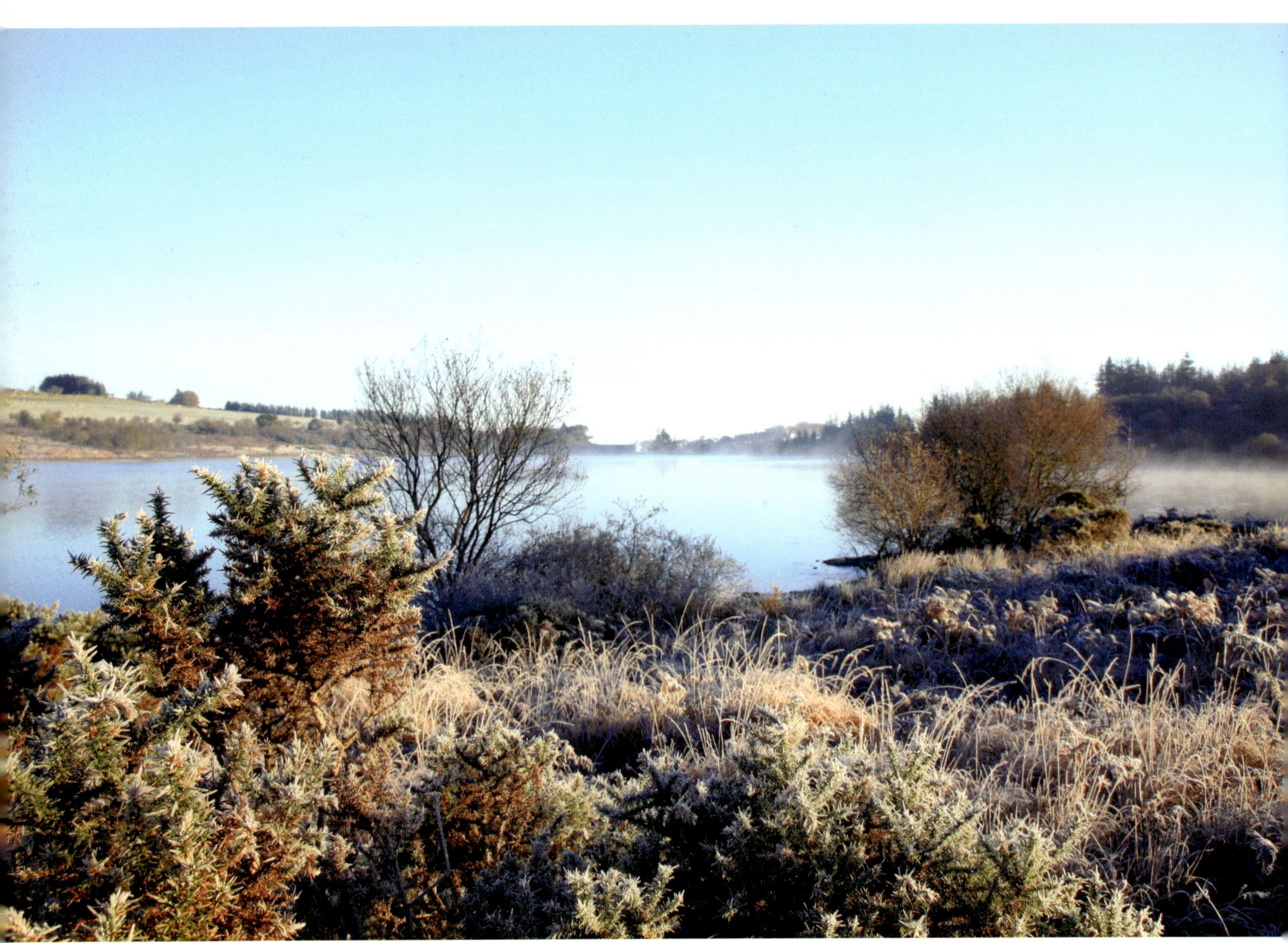

Thick frost on the gorse and heather remains long after the sunrise.

Sheep wander in the road near Burrator.

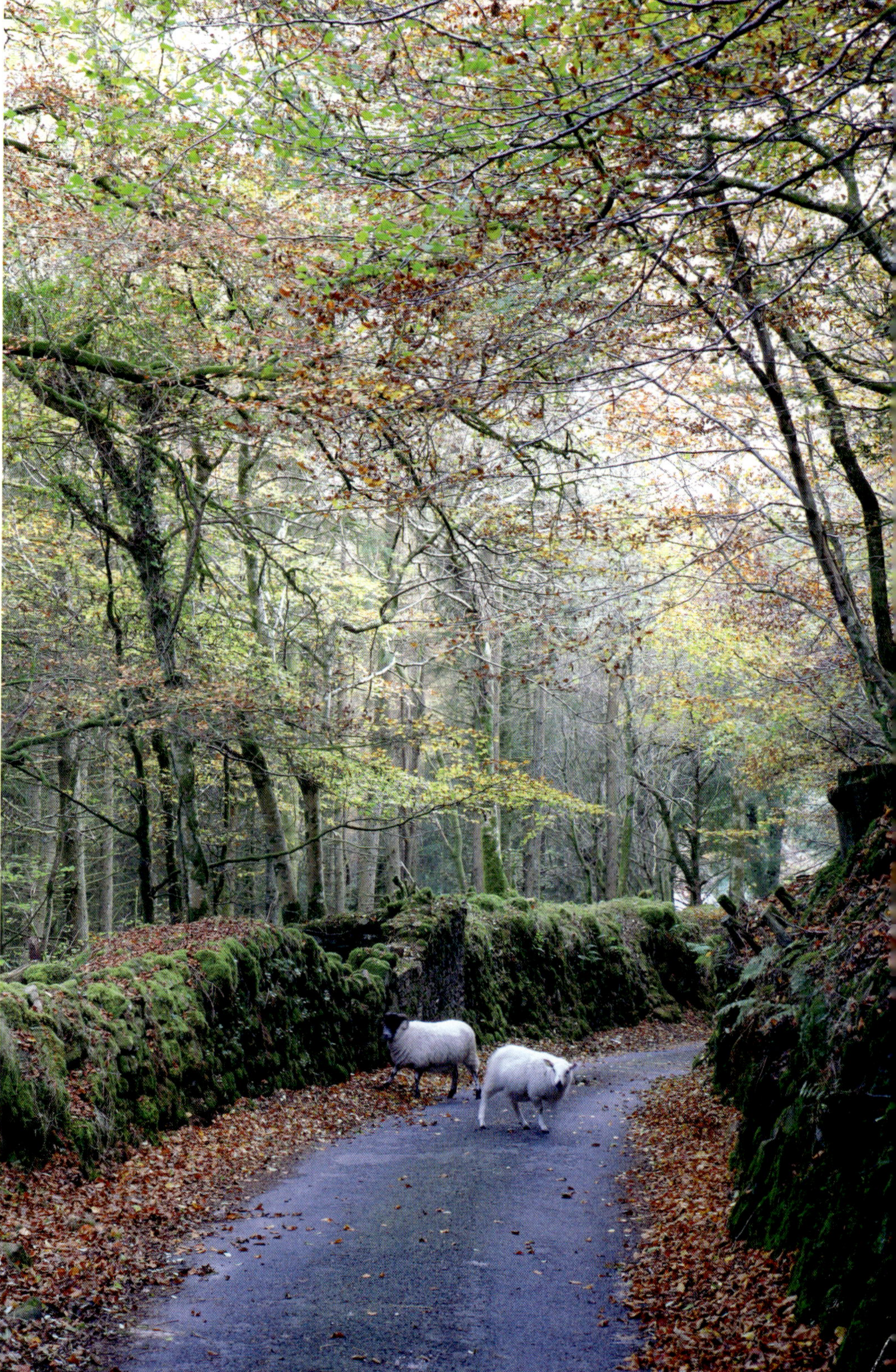

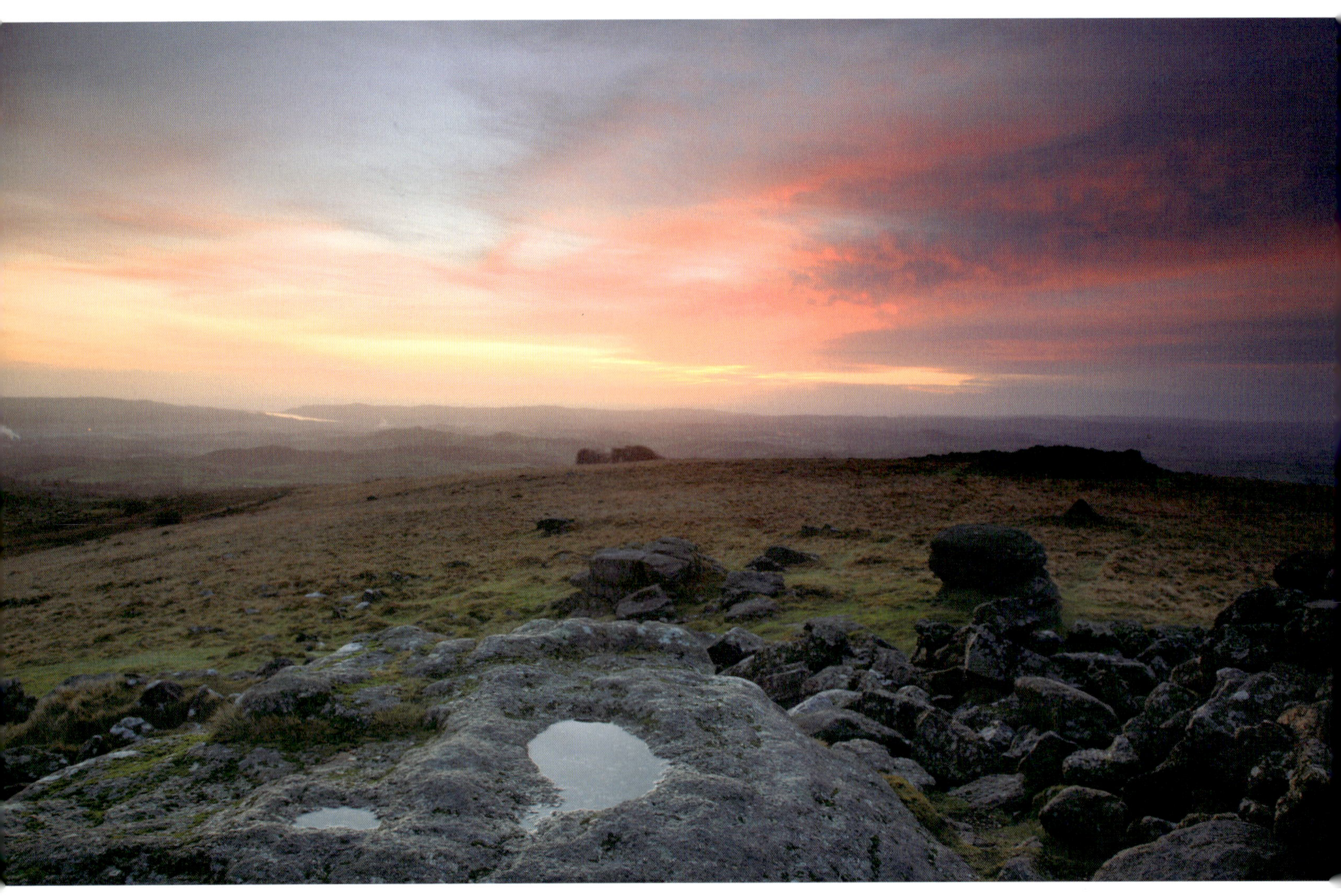

Pink sunrise over the moor looking from the top of Rippon Tor, with the Teign Estuary in the distance.

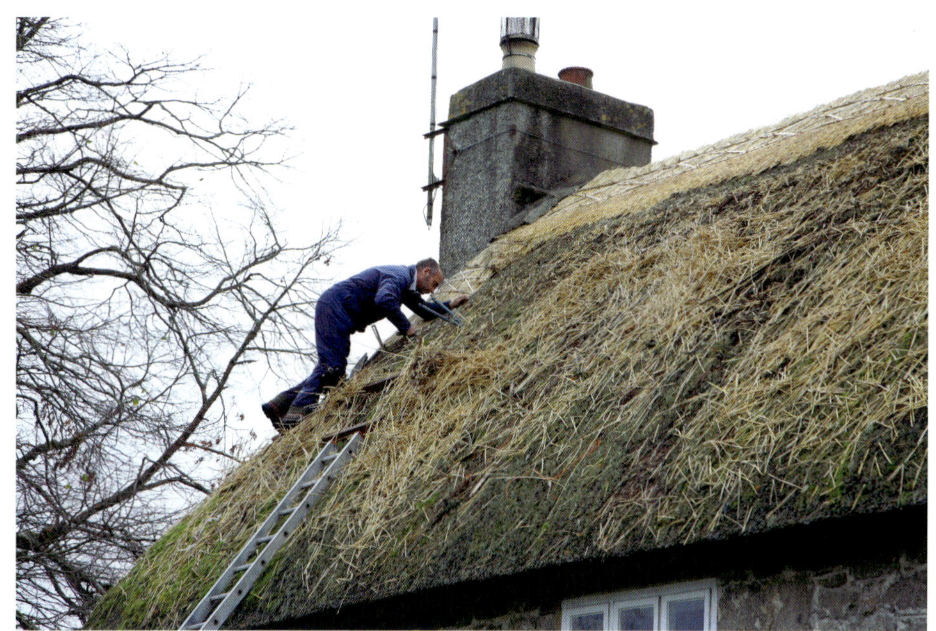

A thatcher works on a roof at Manaton.

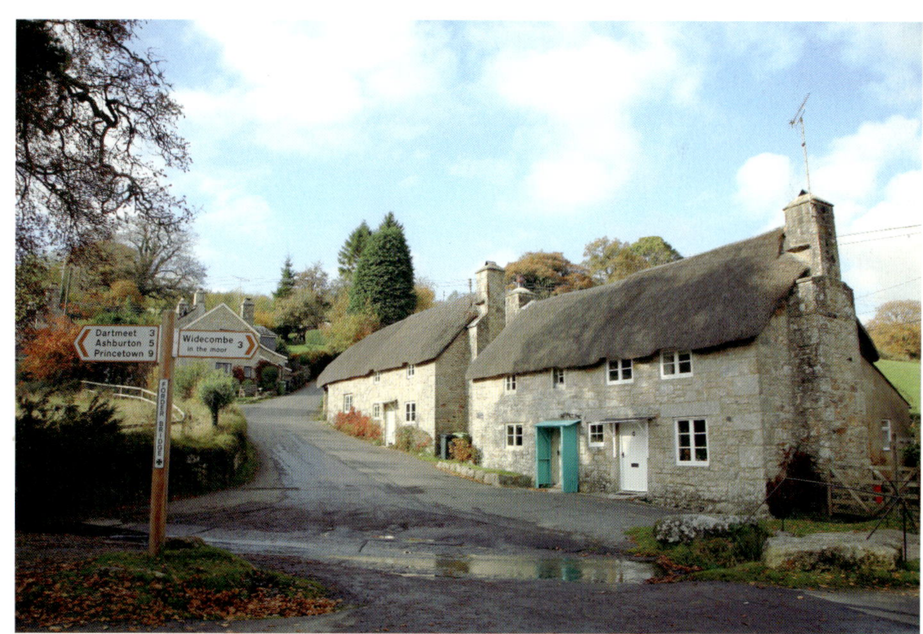

Cottages at the ford in Ponsworthy.

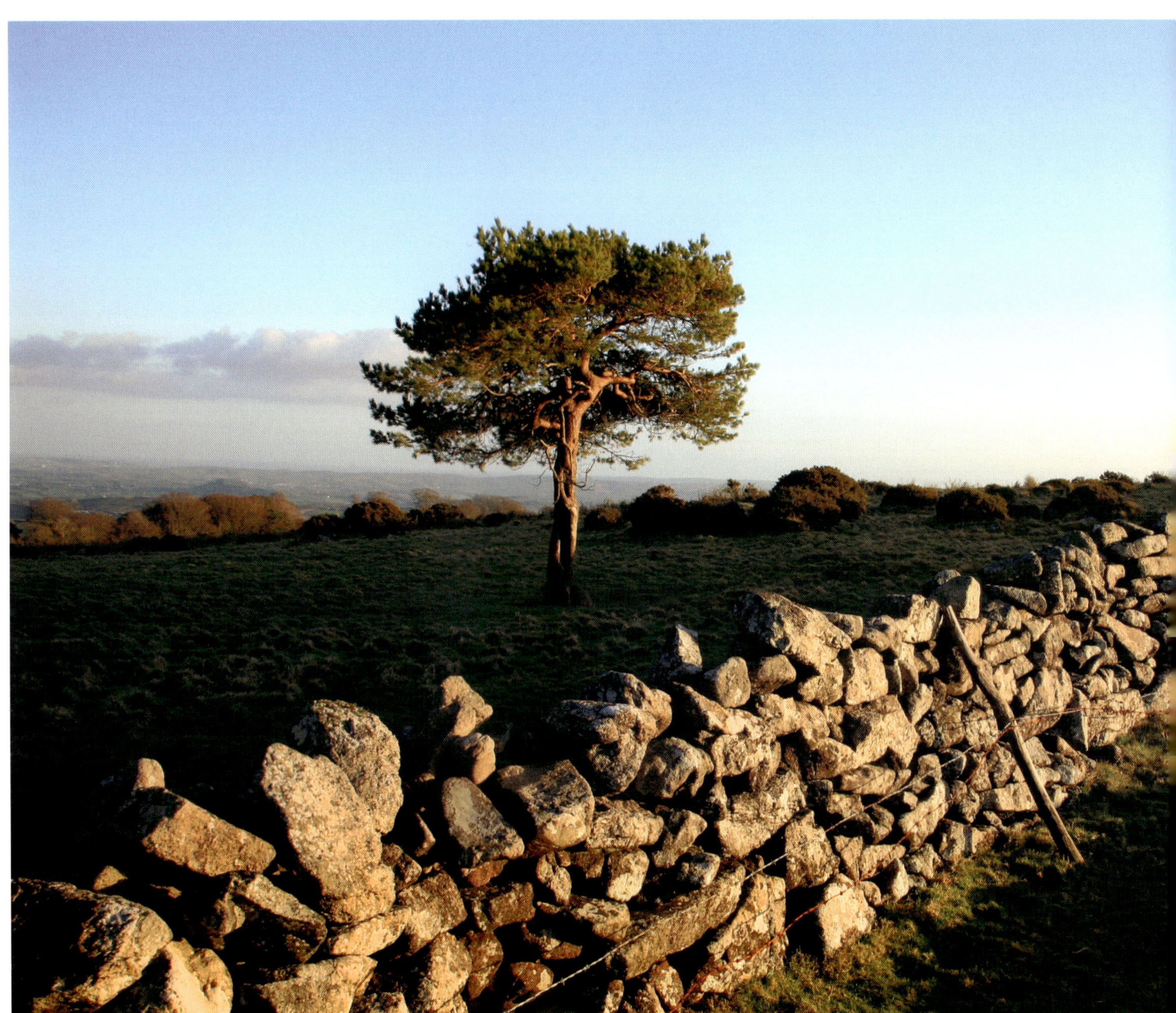

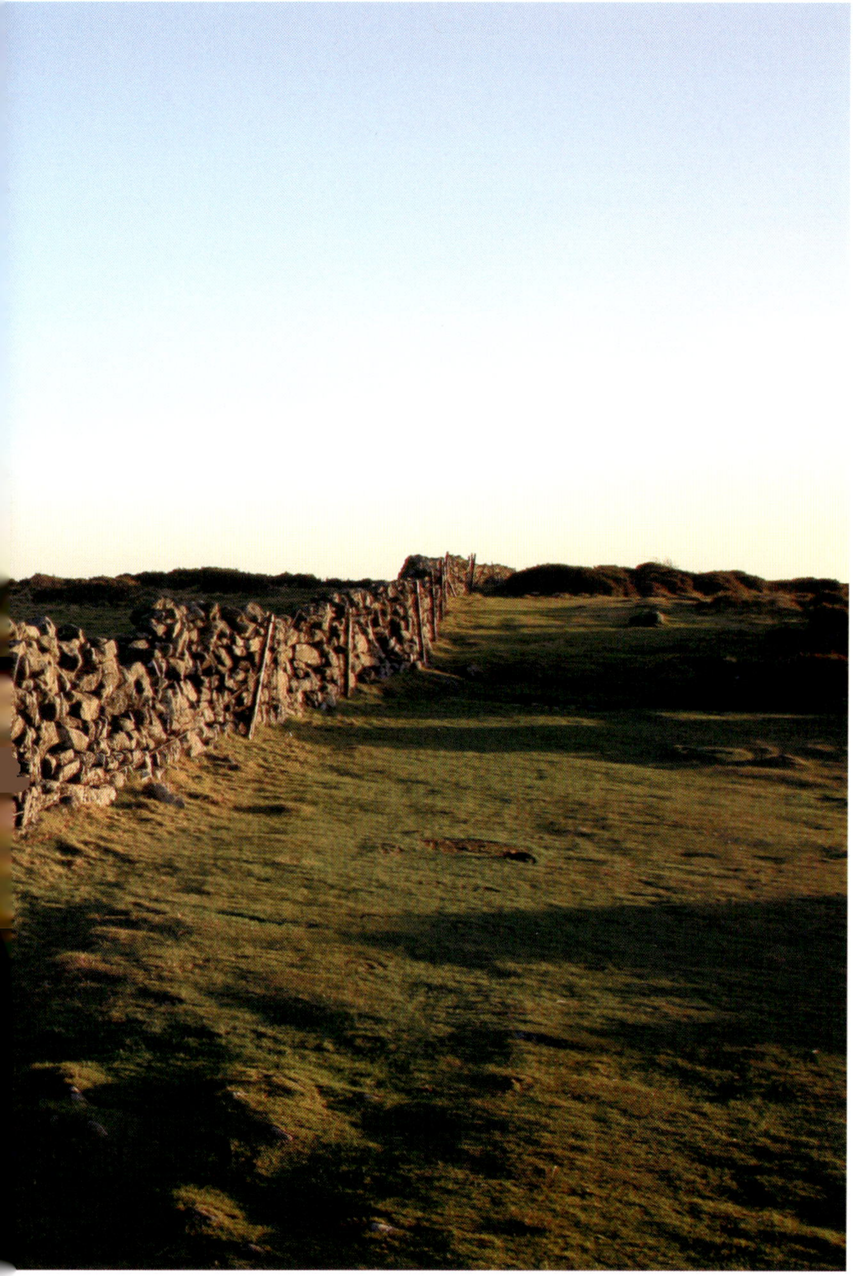

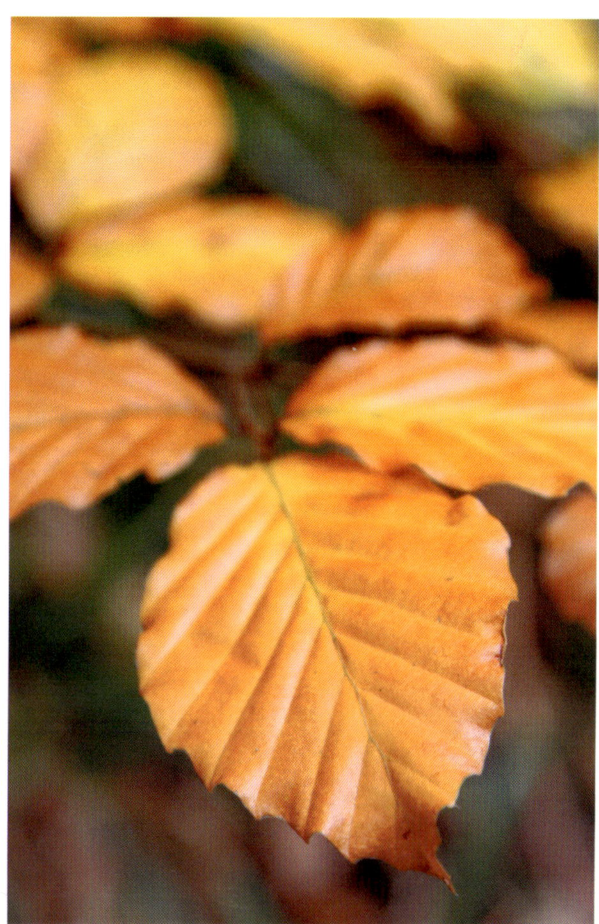

Dartmoor autumn gold.

Soft winter light illuminates a lone tree on the top of the moor.

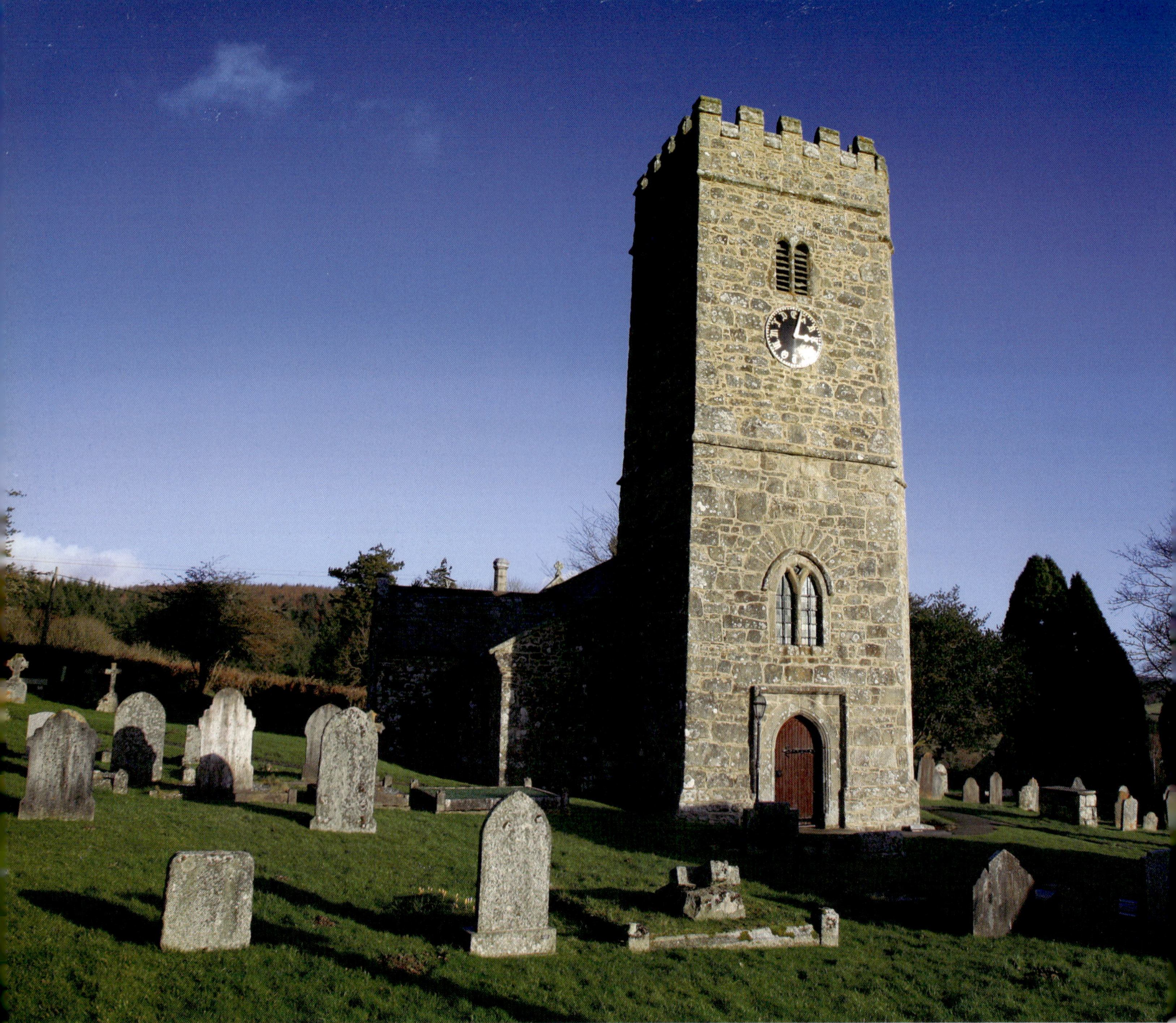

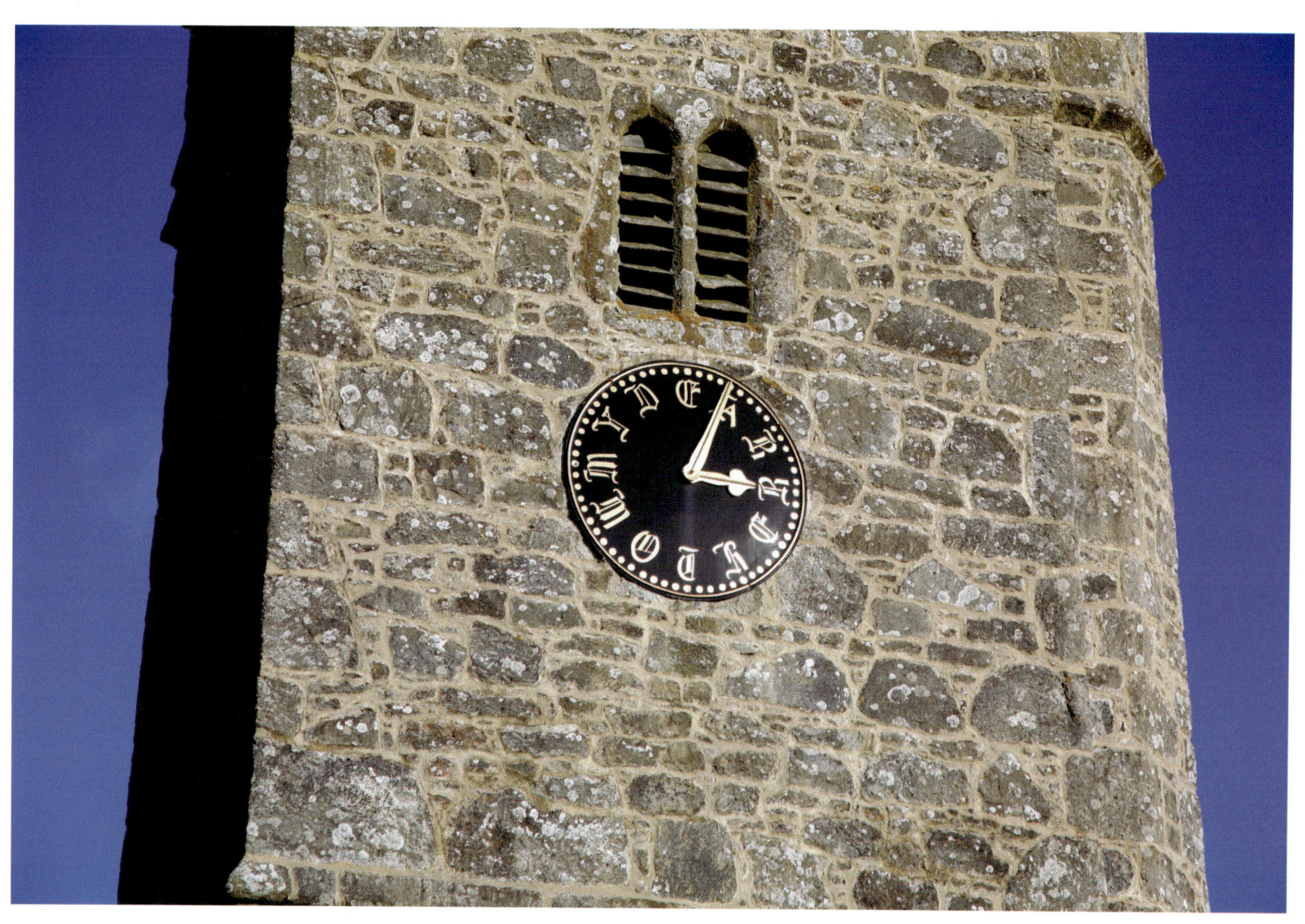

There has probably been a church at Buckland since Saxon times. The tower has an interesting clock that has no numerals. Instead it has the words 'My dear mother' around the face.

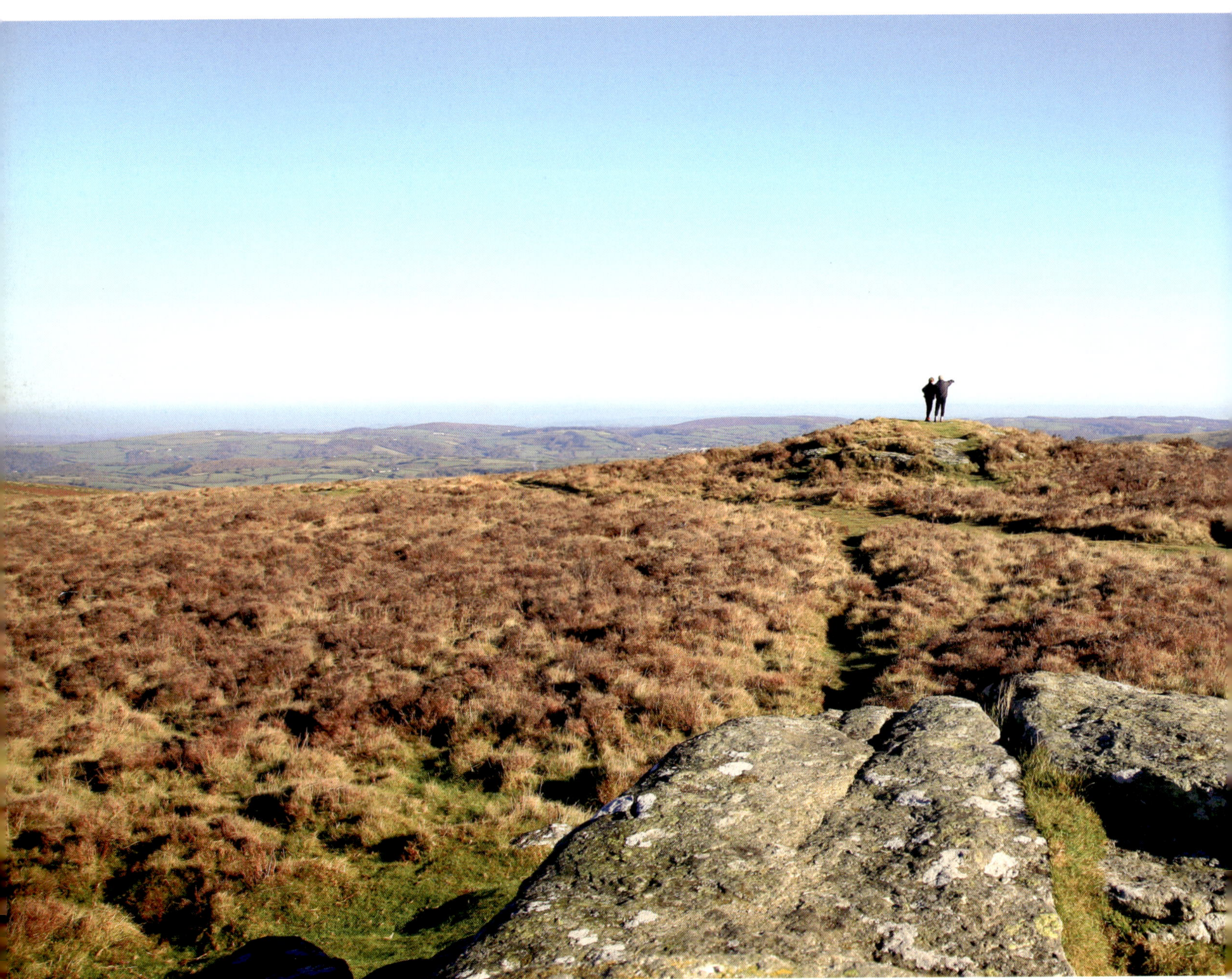

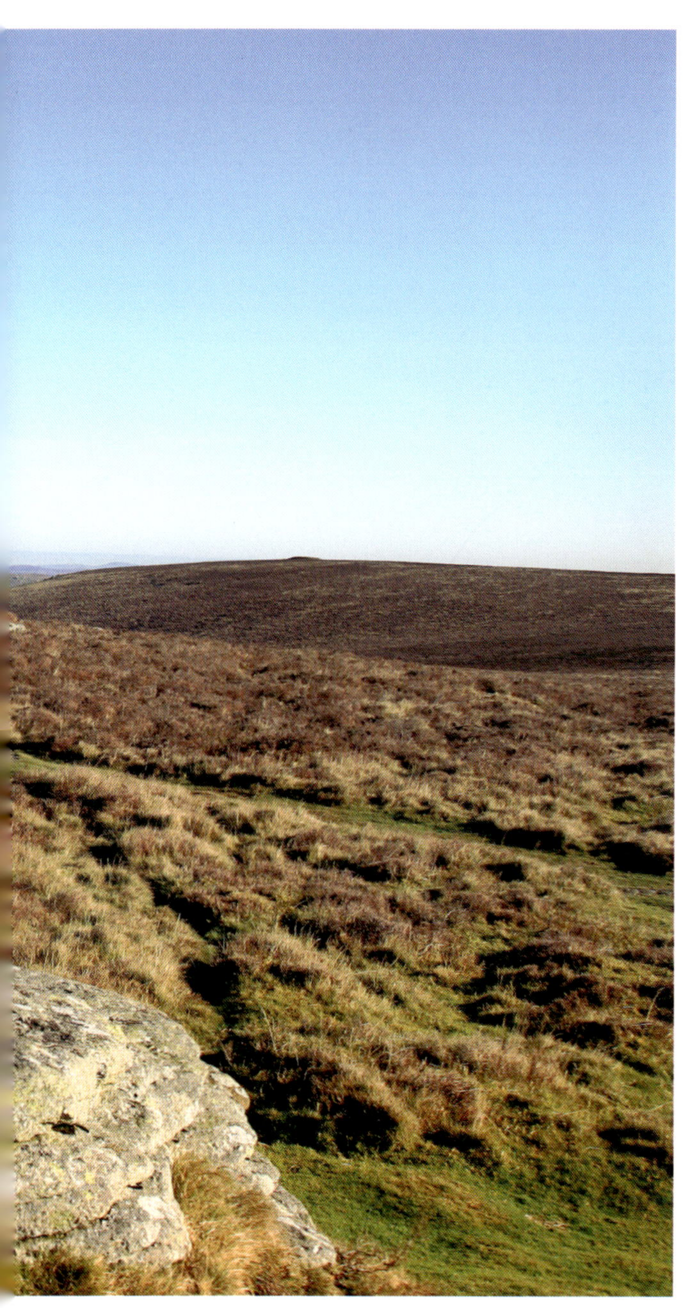

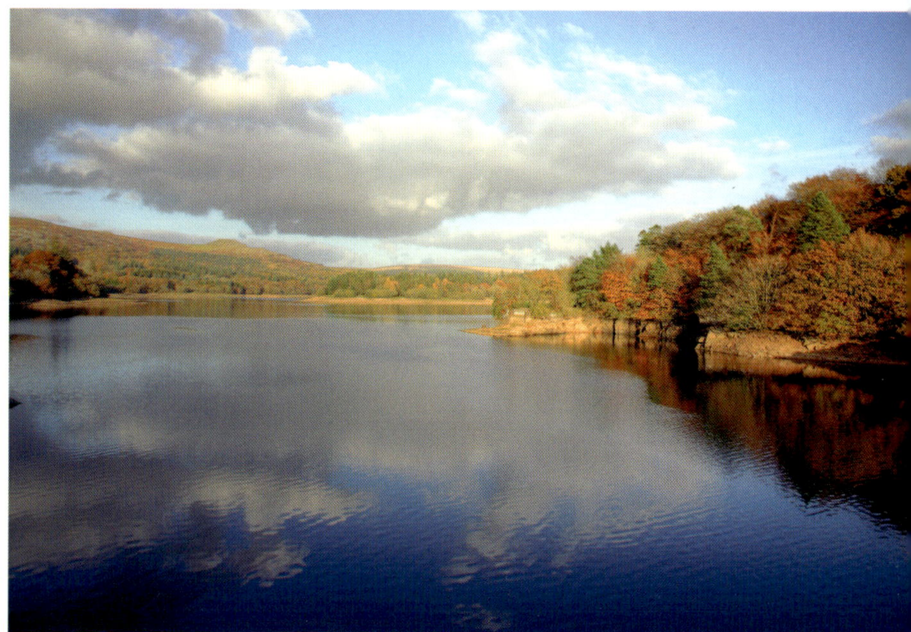

Autumn colours over Burrator.

Walkers look out across the open moor
on a beautiful autumn day.

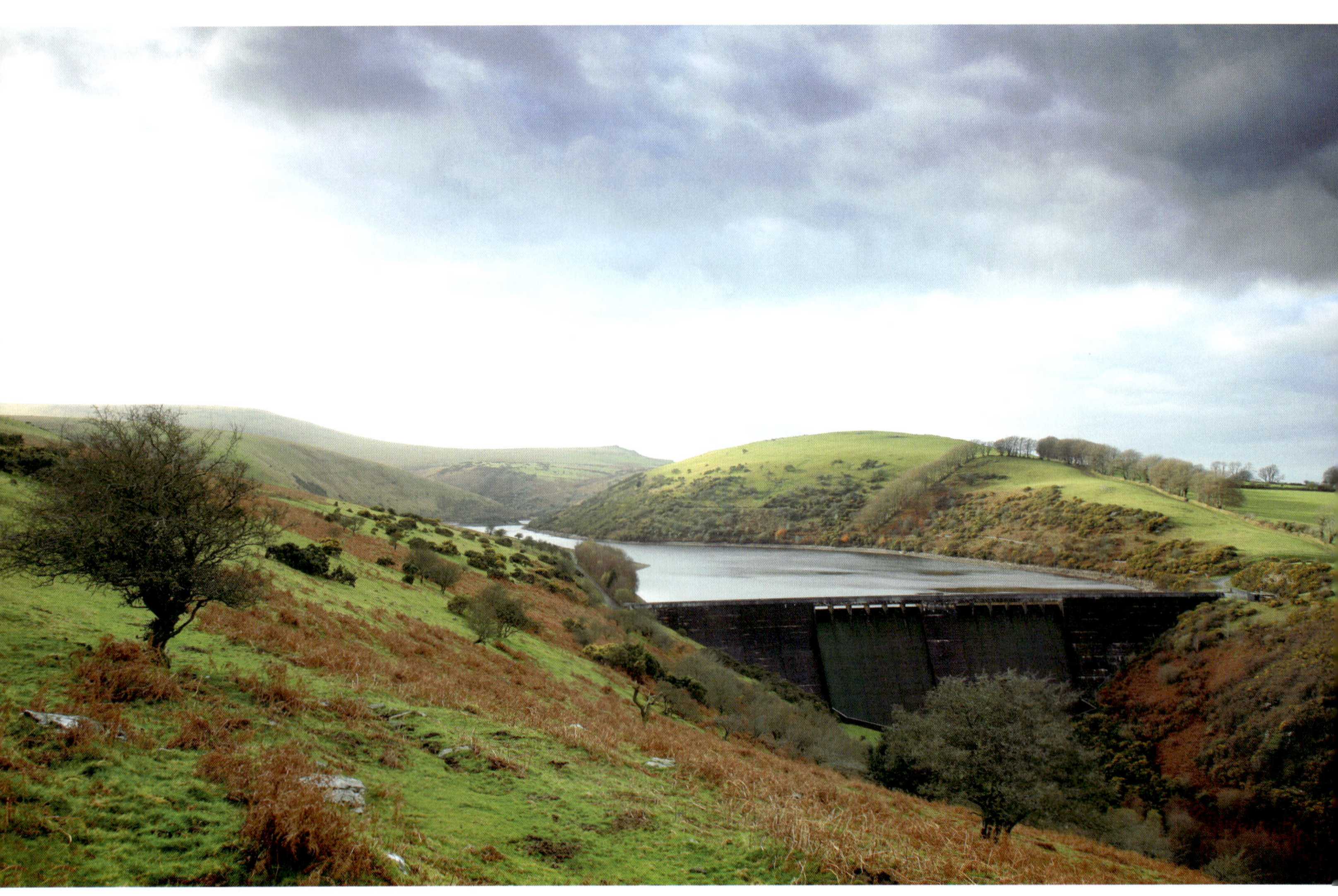

Meldon Dam was built in 1972 and was the last dam to be built on Dartmoor.
It blocks the West Okement valley to produce the reservoir.

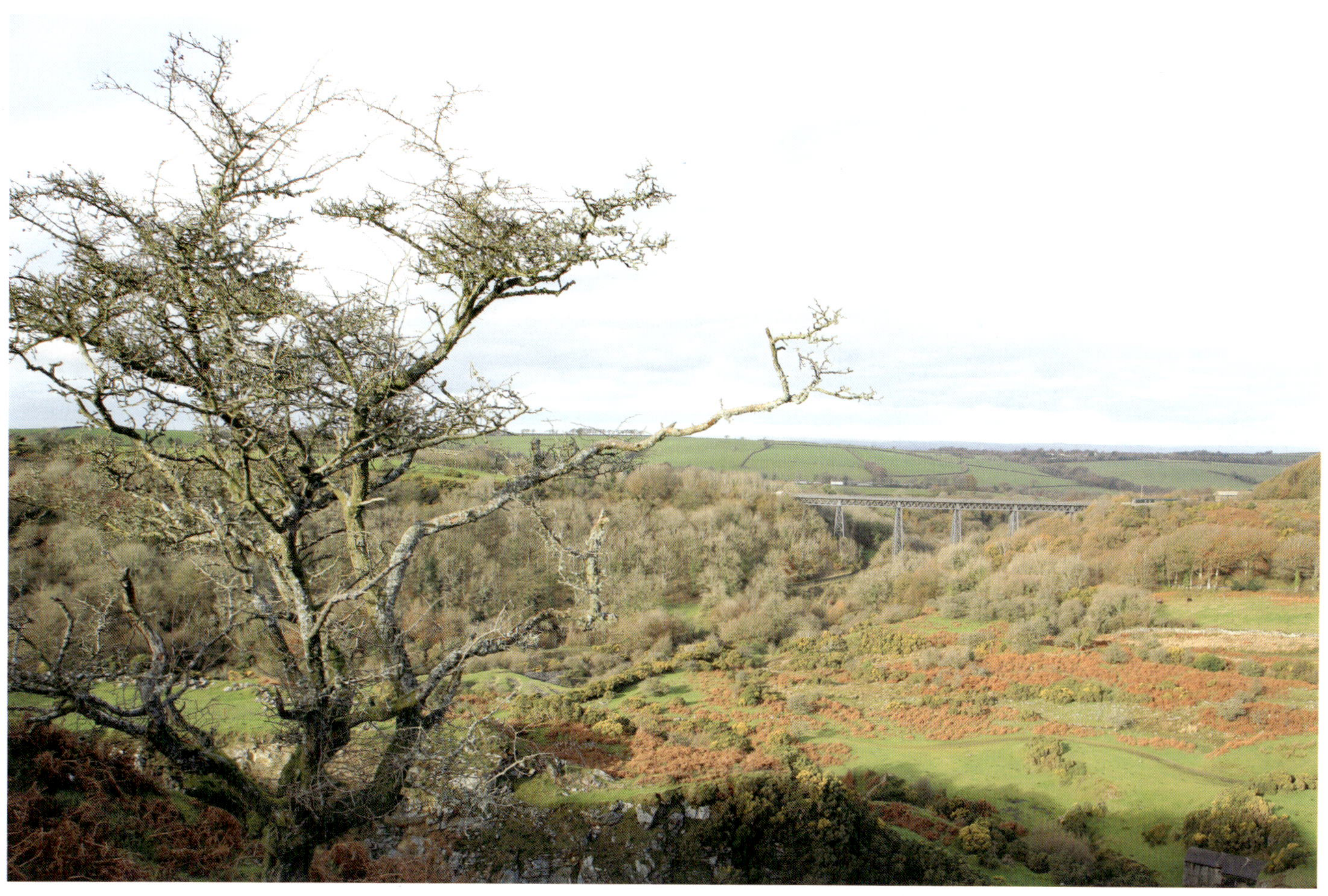

Meldon Viaduct looking from the disused quarry. The viaduct was built in 1874 for the London & South Western railway main line between Waterloo and Plymouth. It was closed to trains in the late1960s, was refurbished from 1996, and is now used by walkers and cyclists.

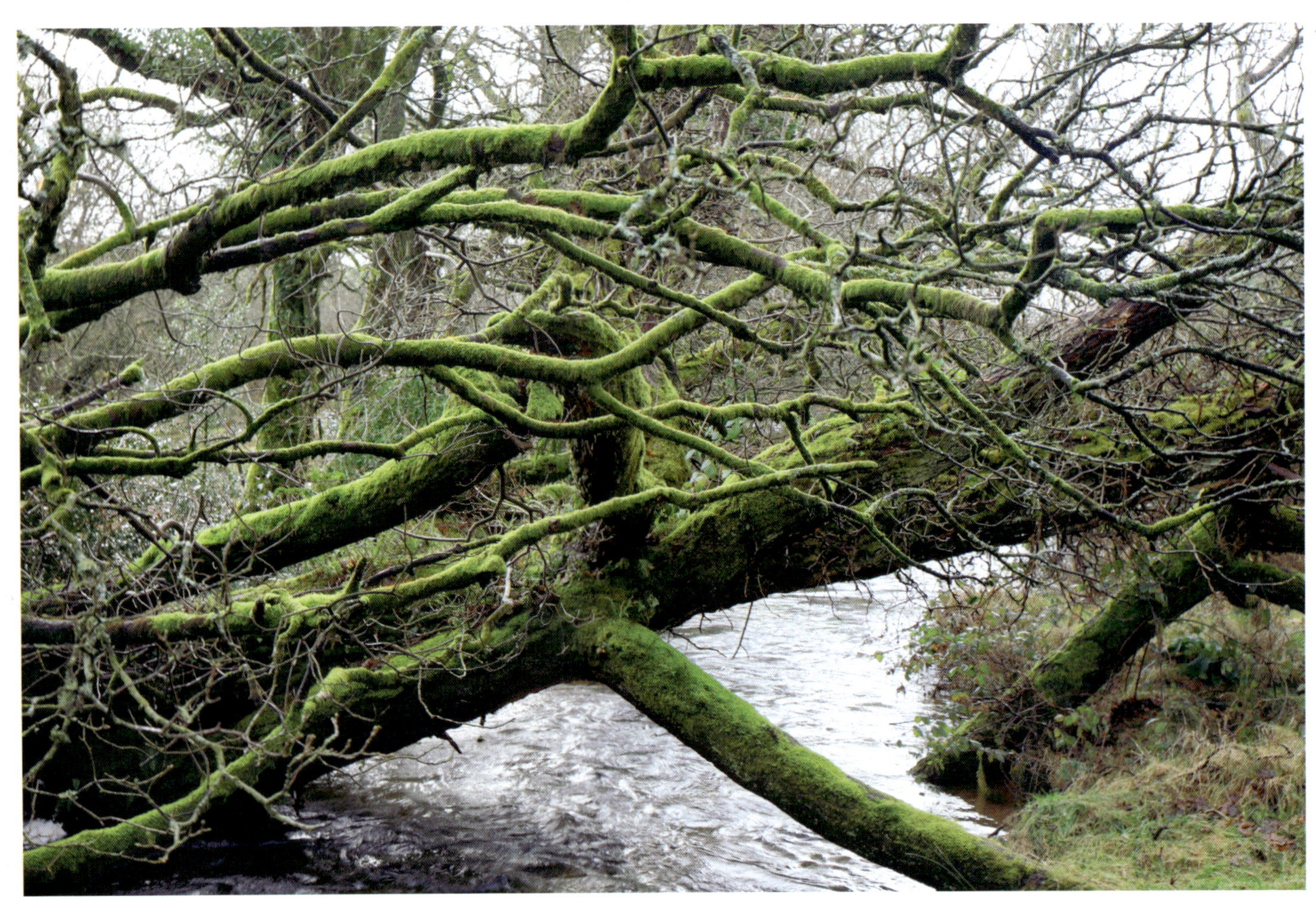

In winter, rocks and trees seems to attract a wonderful rich and thick carpet of moss, often inches thick.

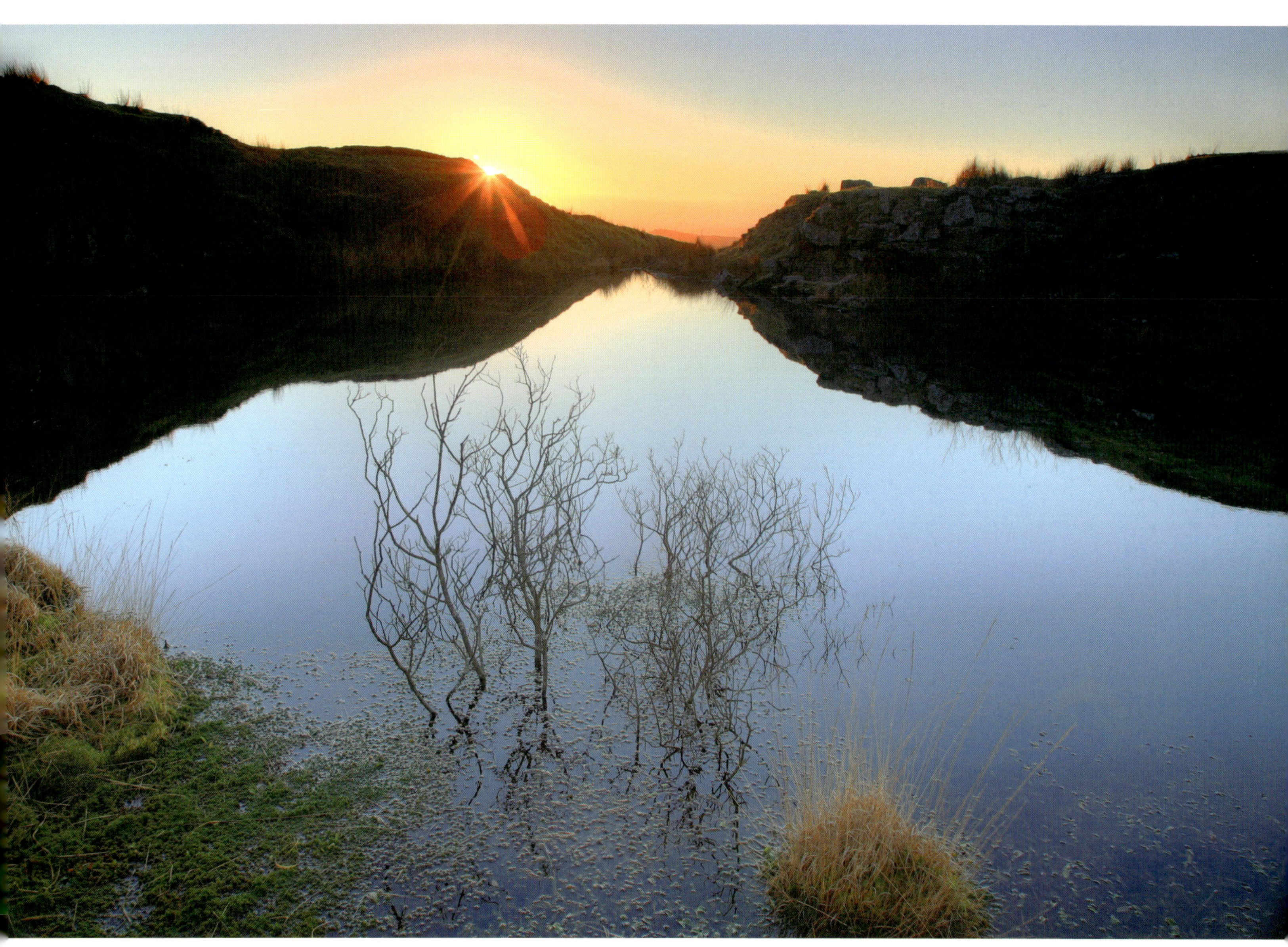

One evening, wandering the open moor, I came across this small granite quarry. Other than from its immediate edge it was virtually invisible. I took this magical image from the base of the quarry, looking through what was once the entrance, as the sun set. The bush growing out of the water was perfectly healthy.

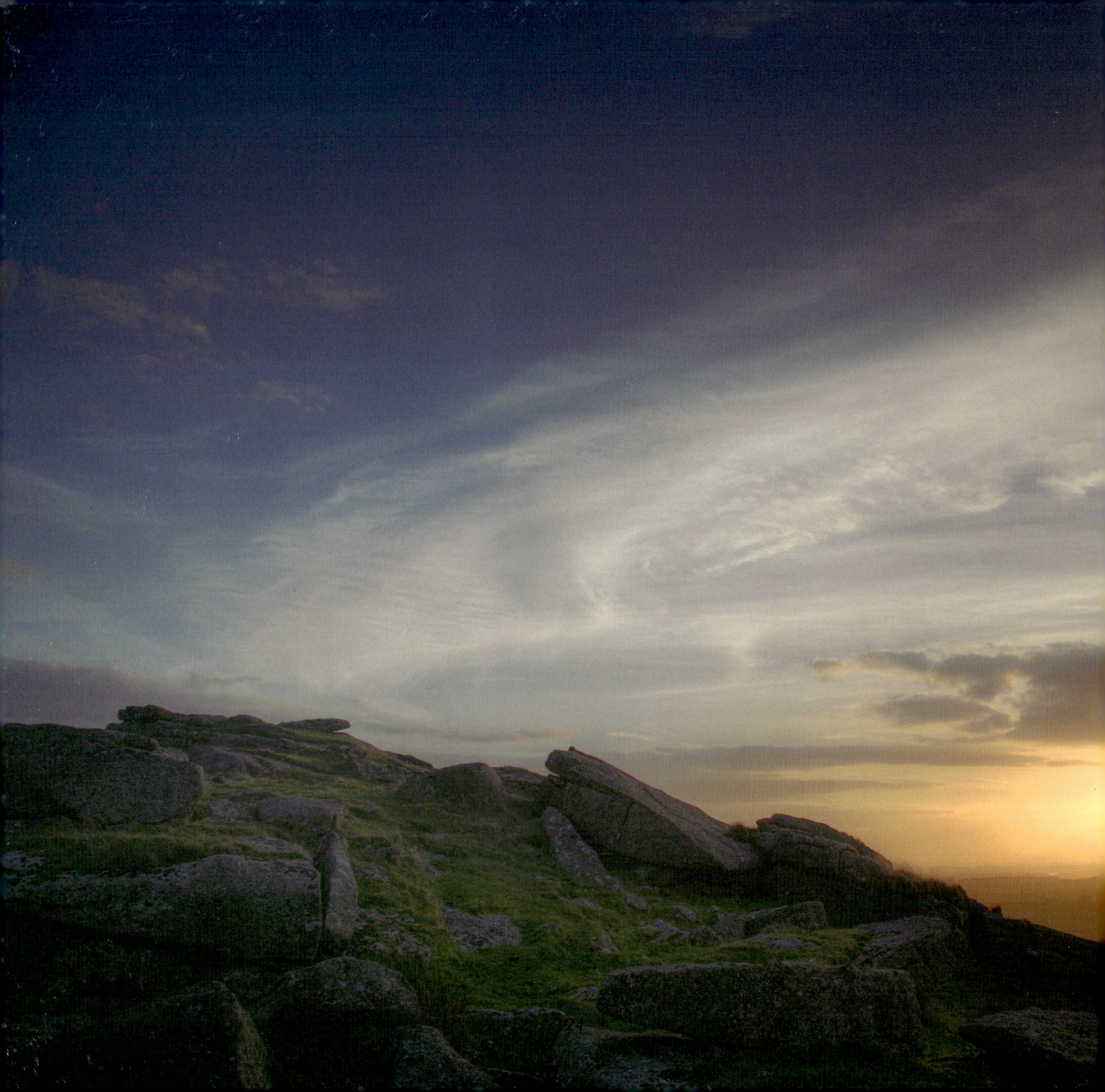

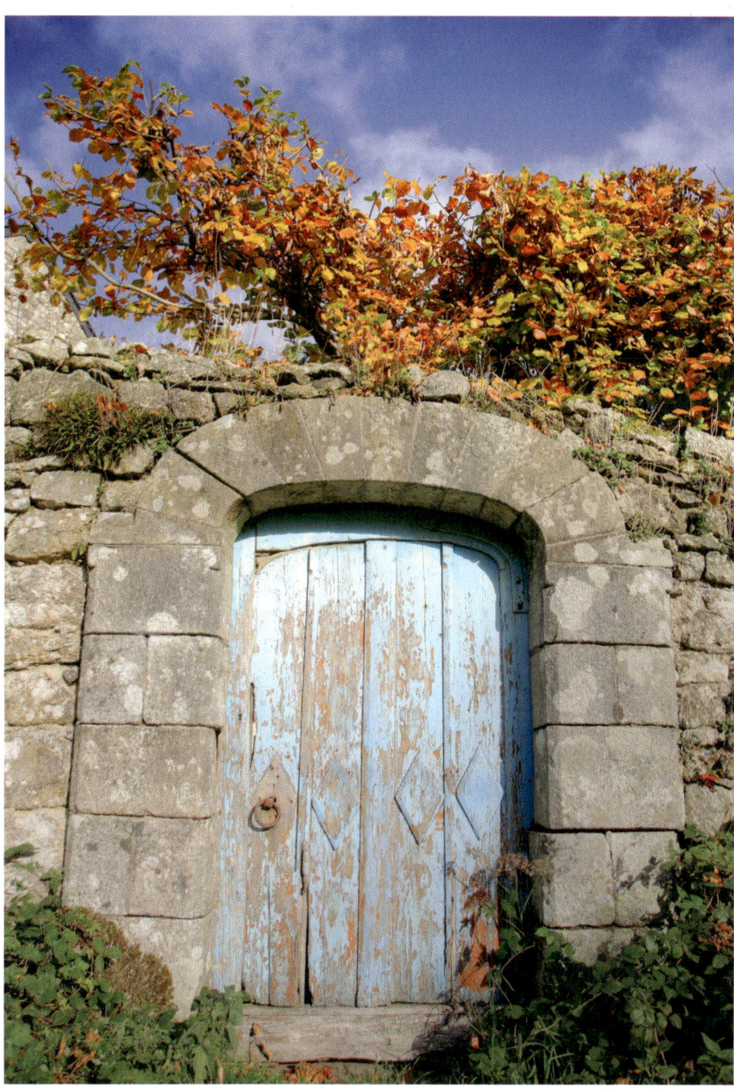

An old blue door and a Dartmoor granite arch near Buckland.

Sunset from Sheepstor.

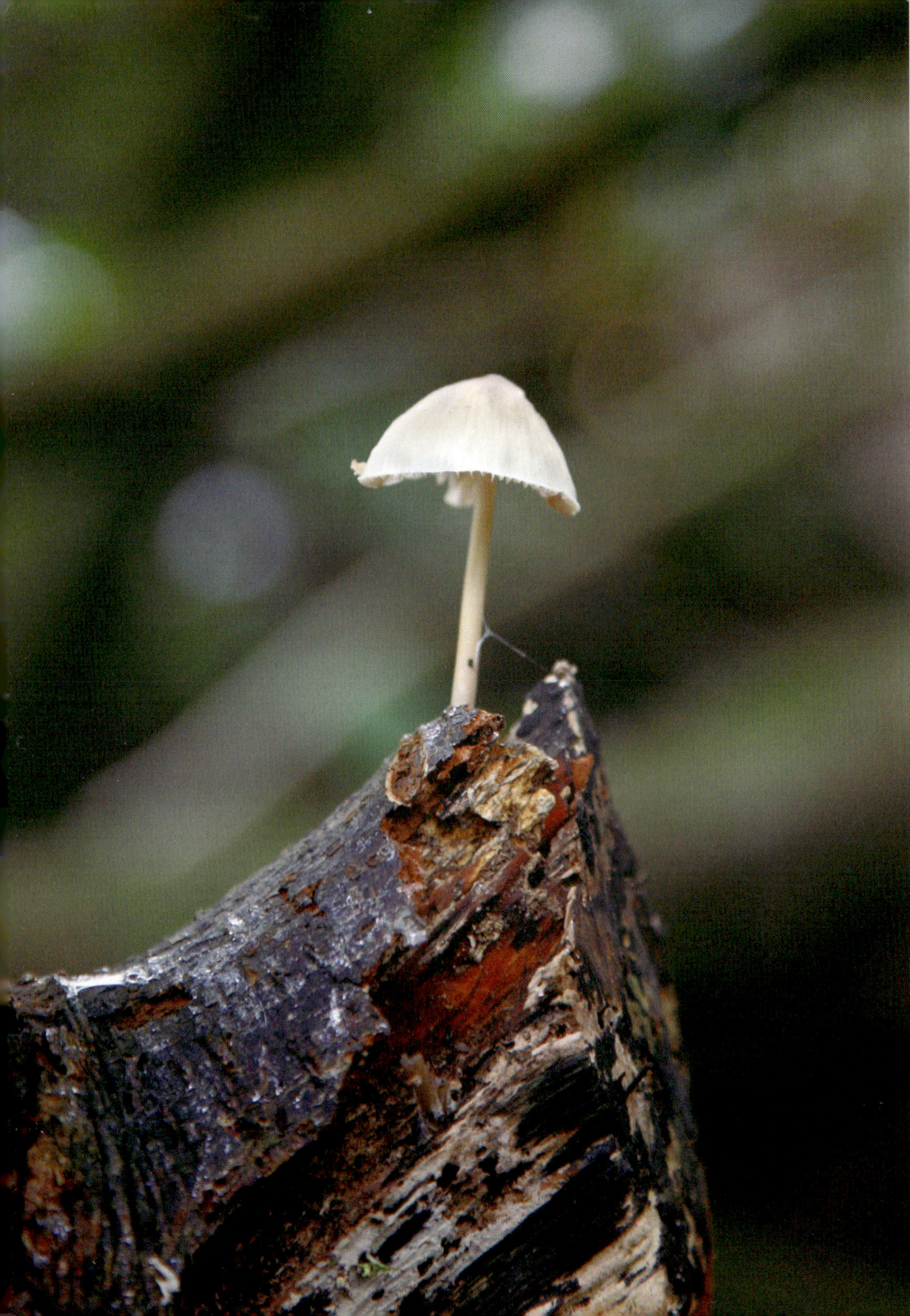

A fungus sits happily on
a rotten tree stump.

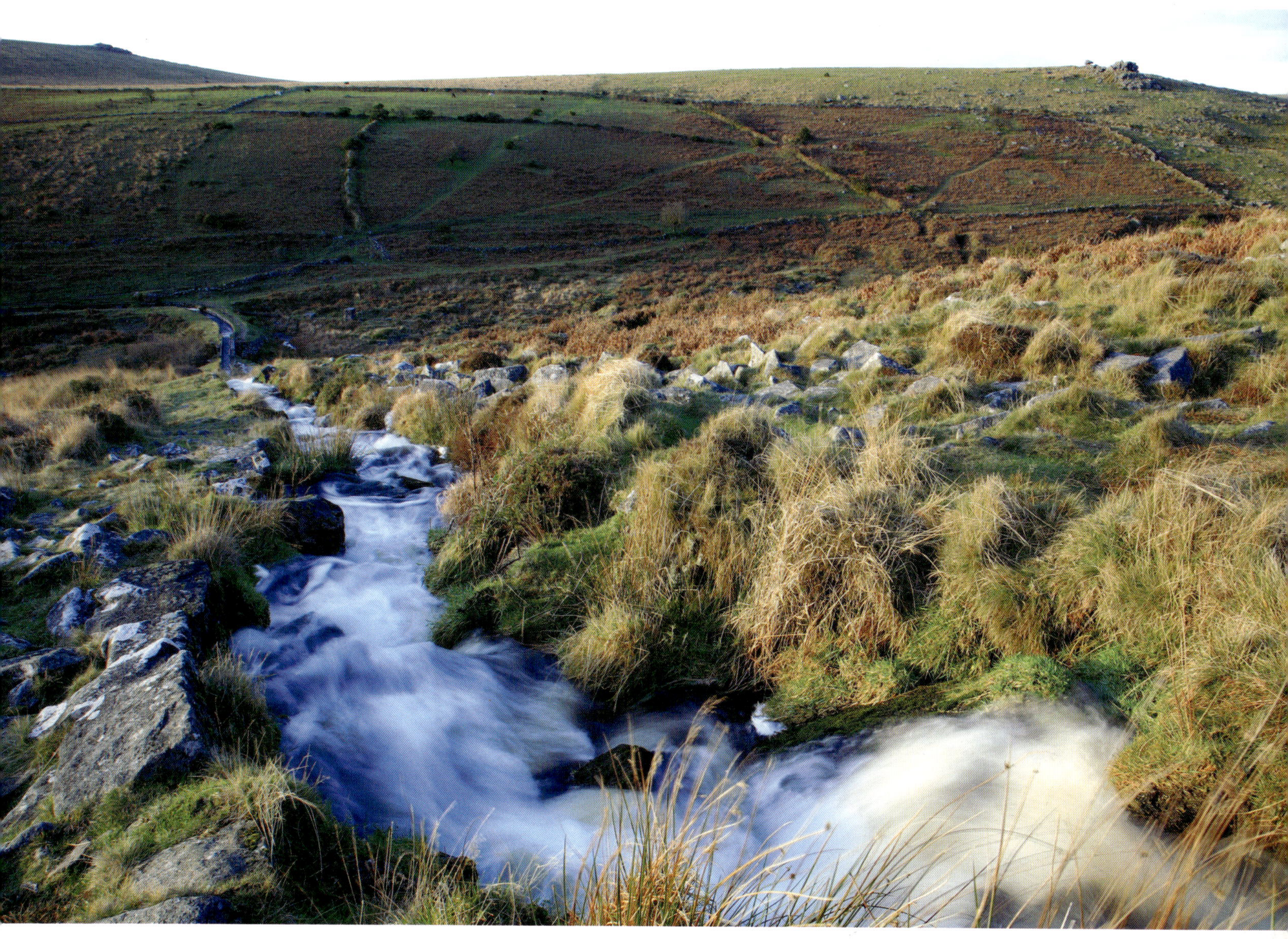

The Devonport Leat runs down the entire side of Raddick Hill and over an aqueduct: Black Tor in the distance.

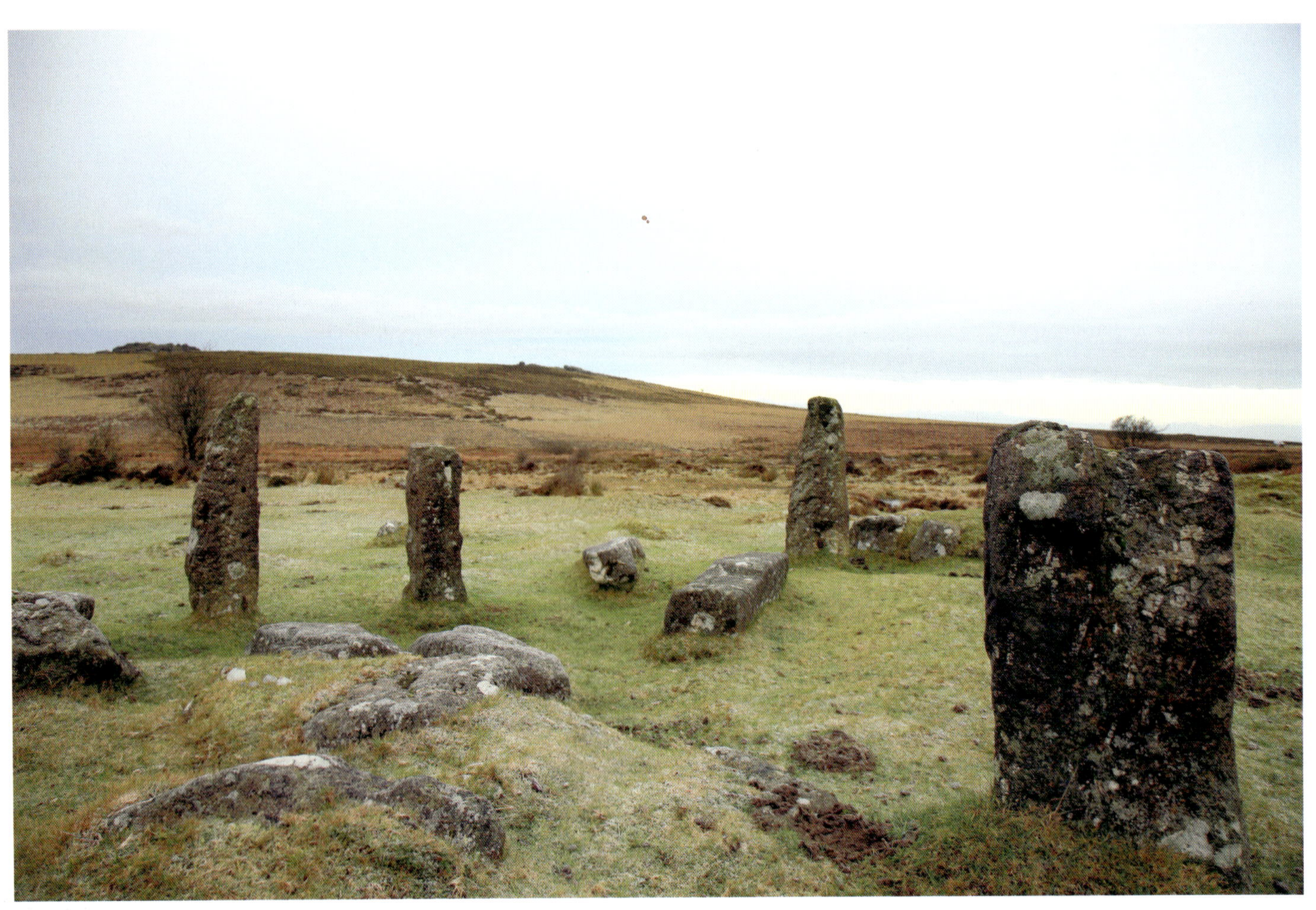

Near Hemsworthy Gate, the remains of the Newhouse Inn that burned down around 1850.

A large stone engraved with A and 1793 sits beside the road near the site of the Newhouse Inn. This is a boundary stone for Ashburton.

Many such markers can be found over the moor. Usually inscribed with letters or numbers.

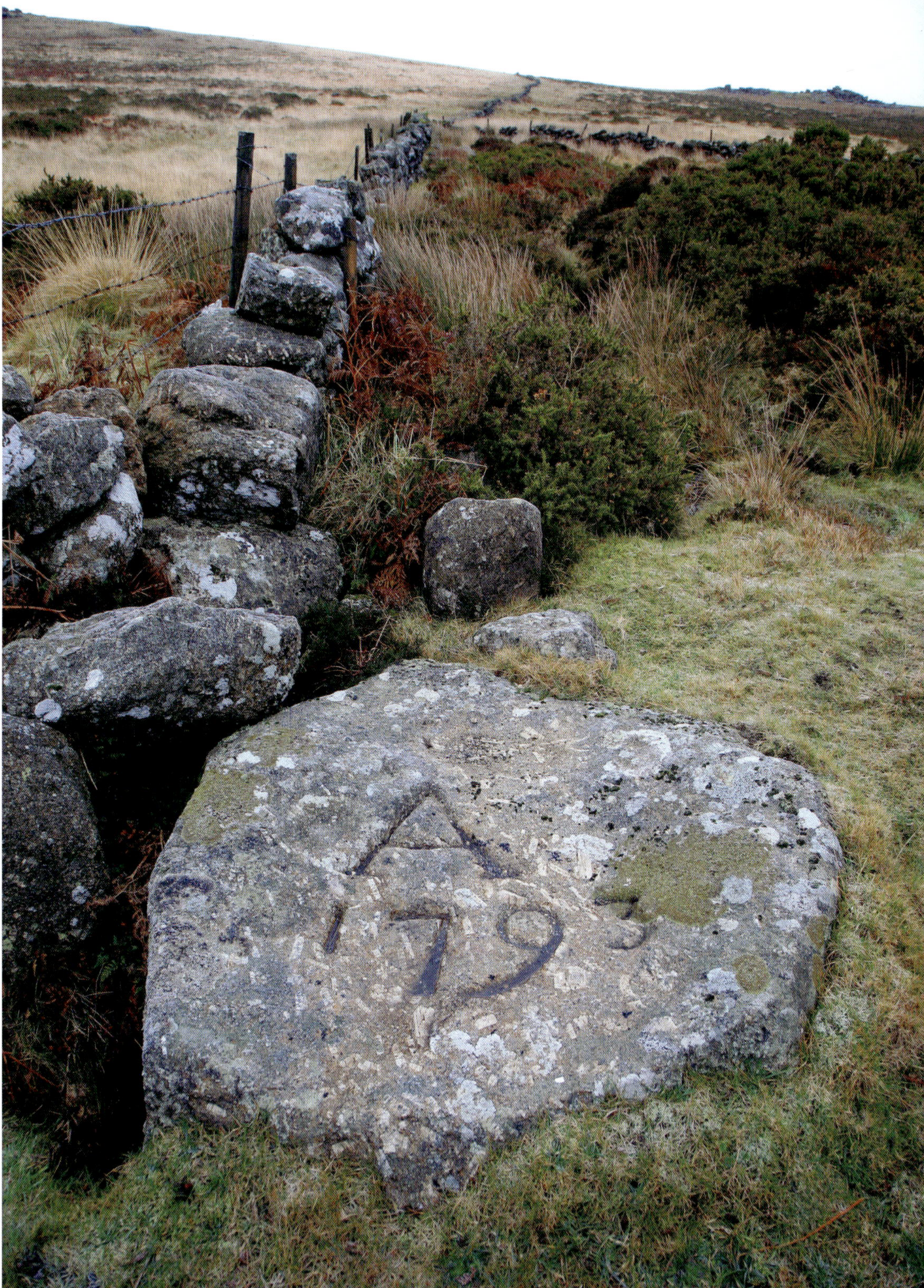

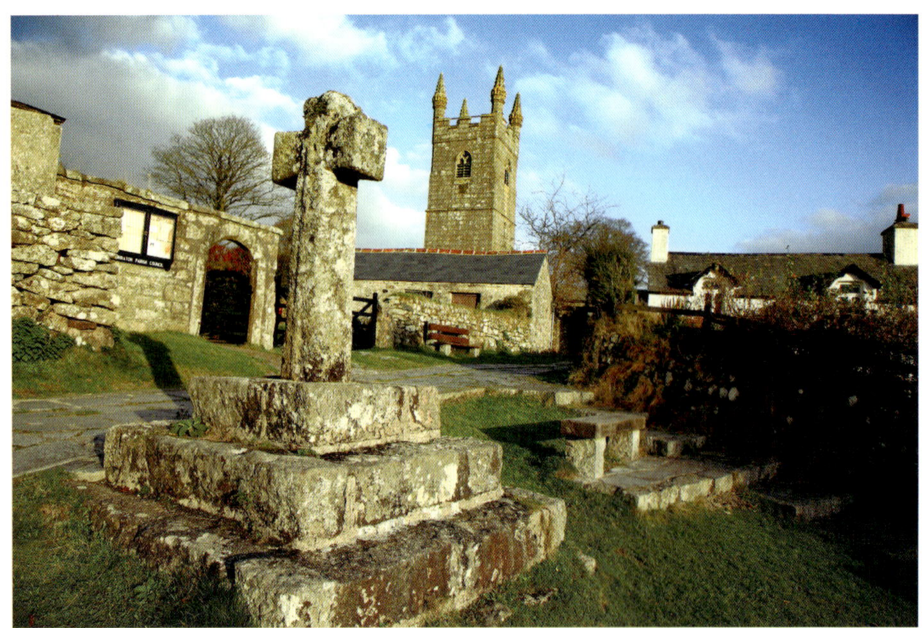

Sheepstor Village church with one of many Dartmoor granite crosses.

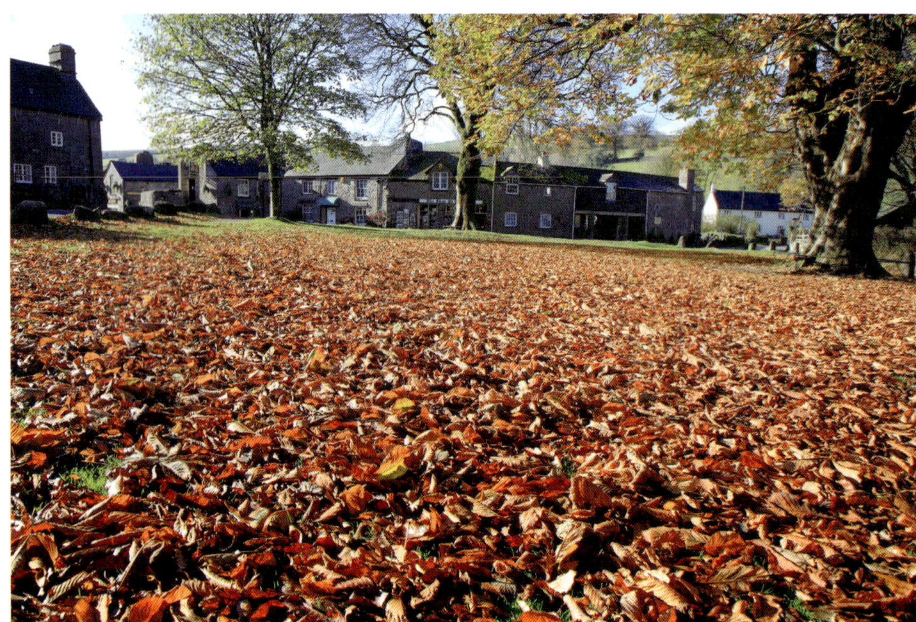

A blanket of autumn leaves on the village green, Widecombe-in-the-Moor.

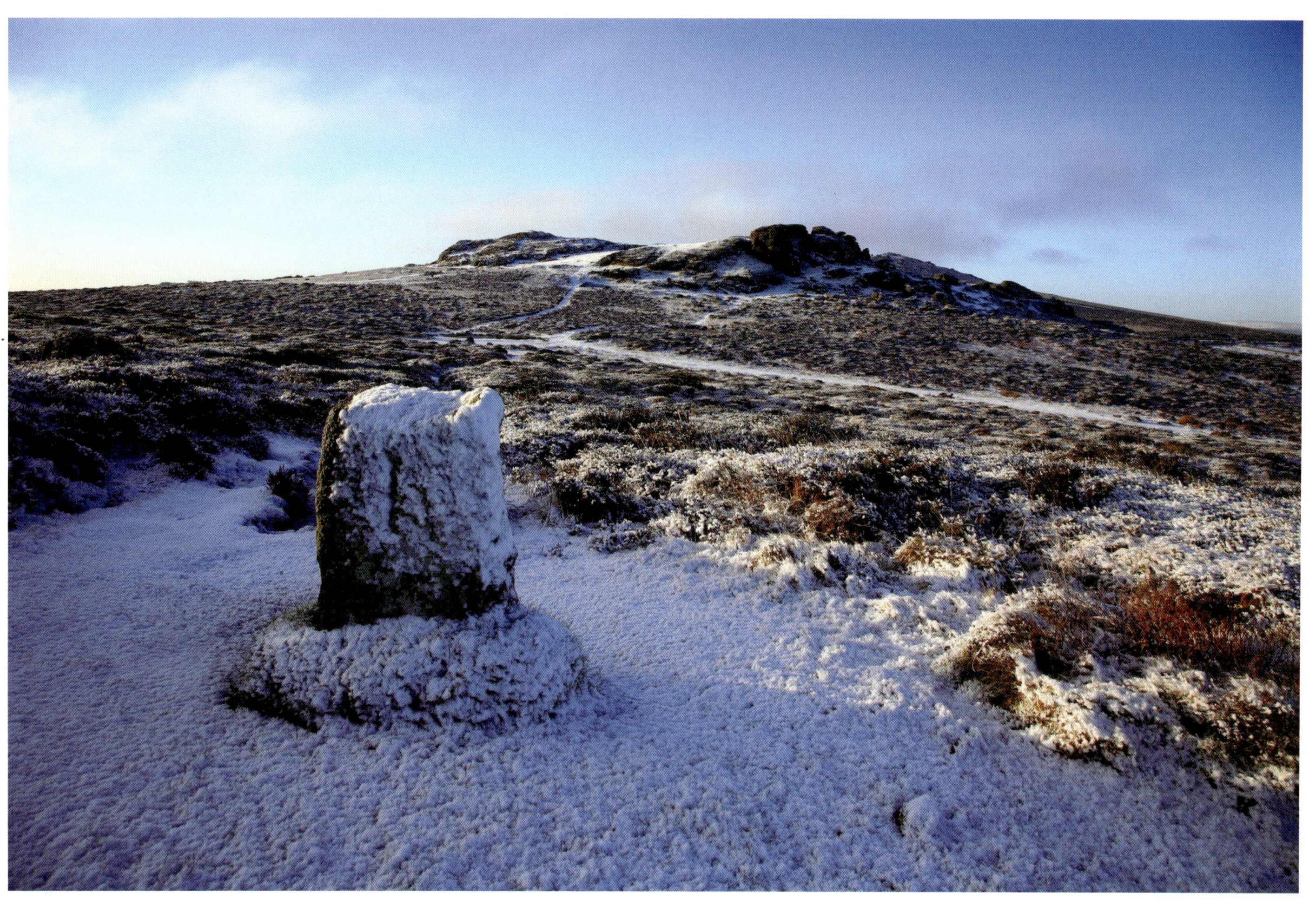

Saddle Tor.

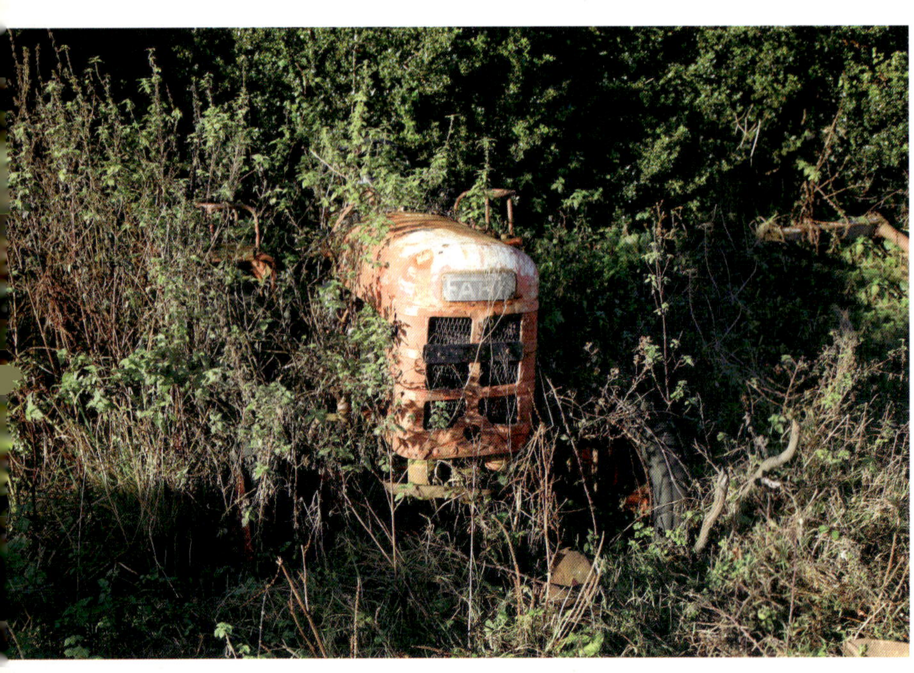

A tractor of uncertain age covered in overgrowth.

Late autumn sunset at Staple Tor.

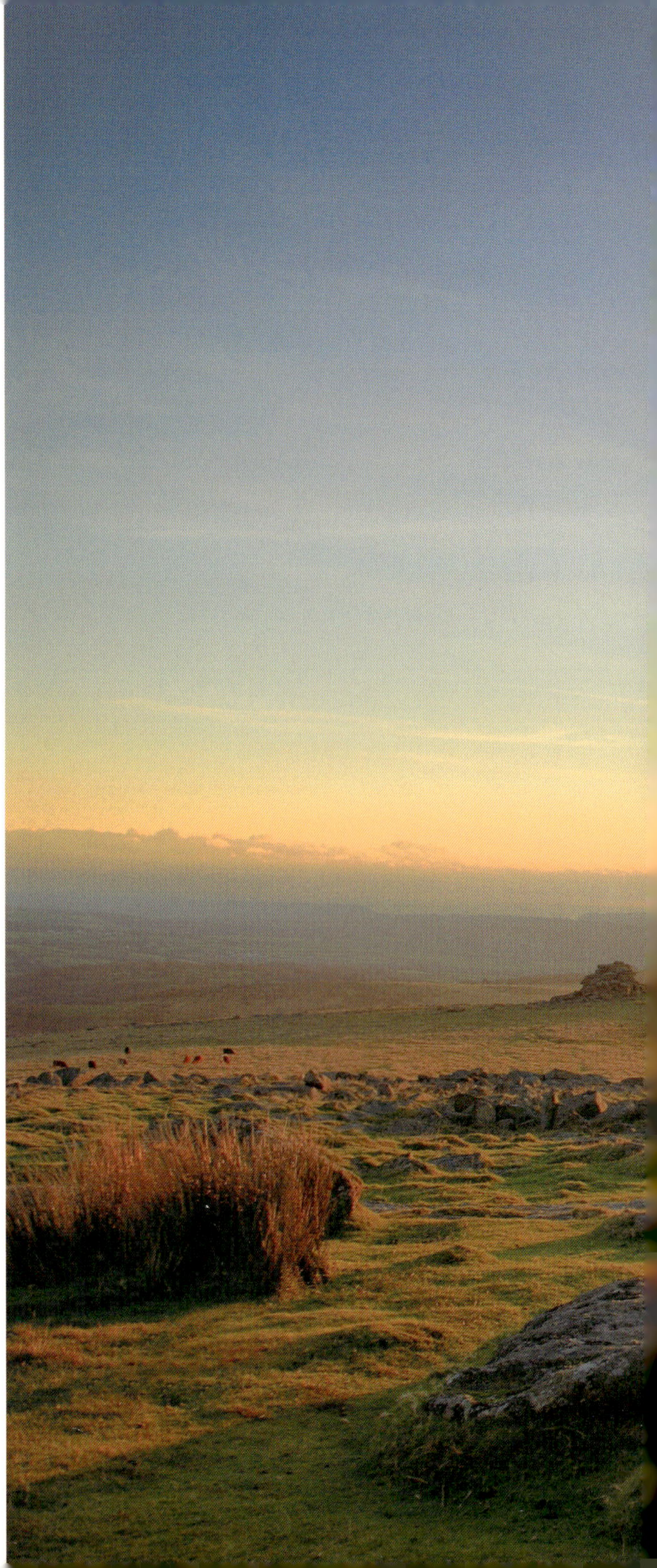

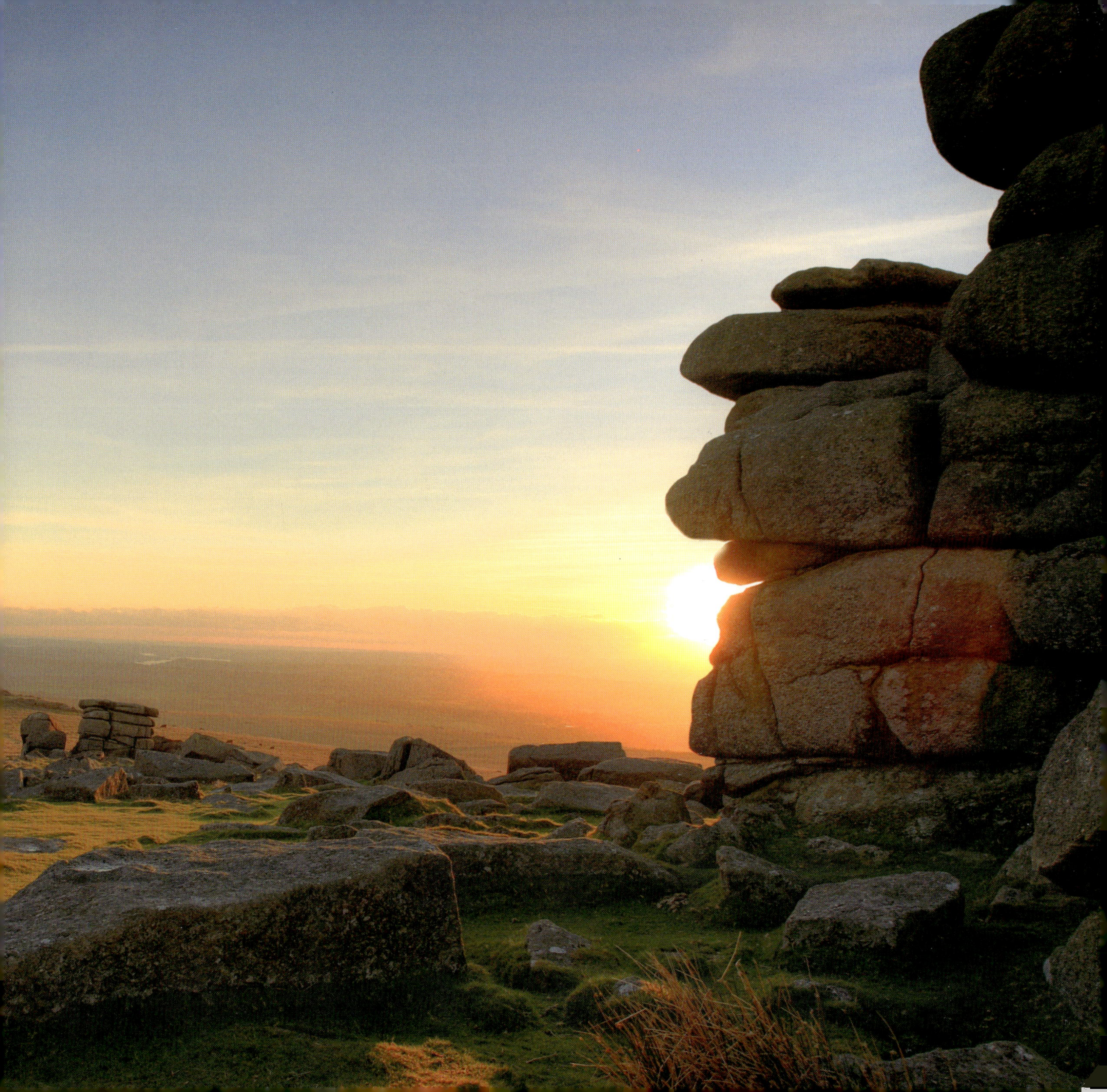

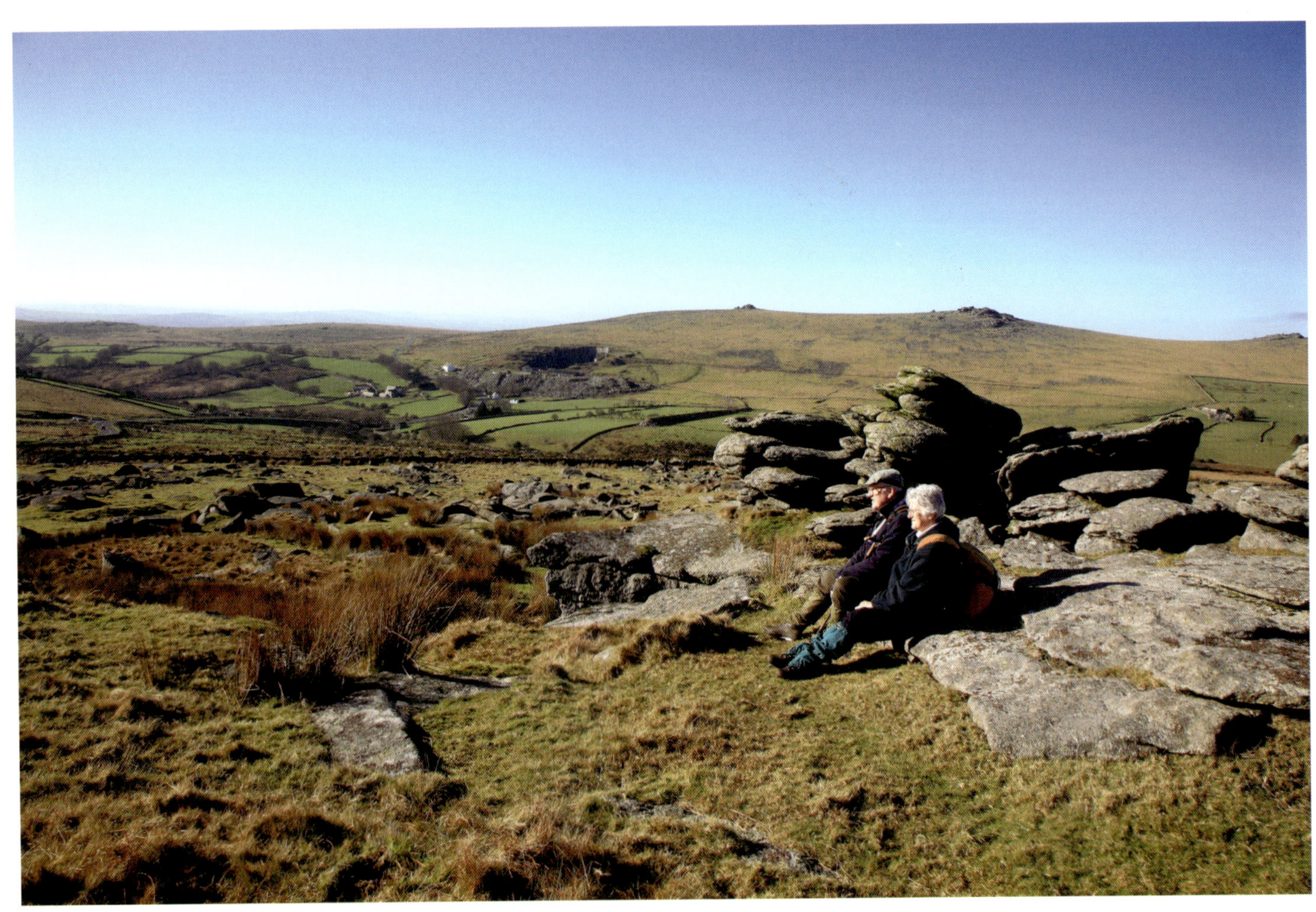

Walkers enjoy a well-earned rest in the winter sun.

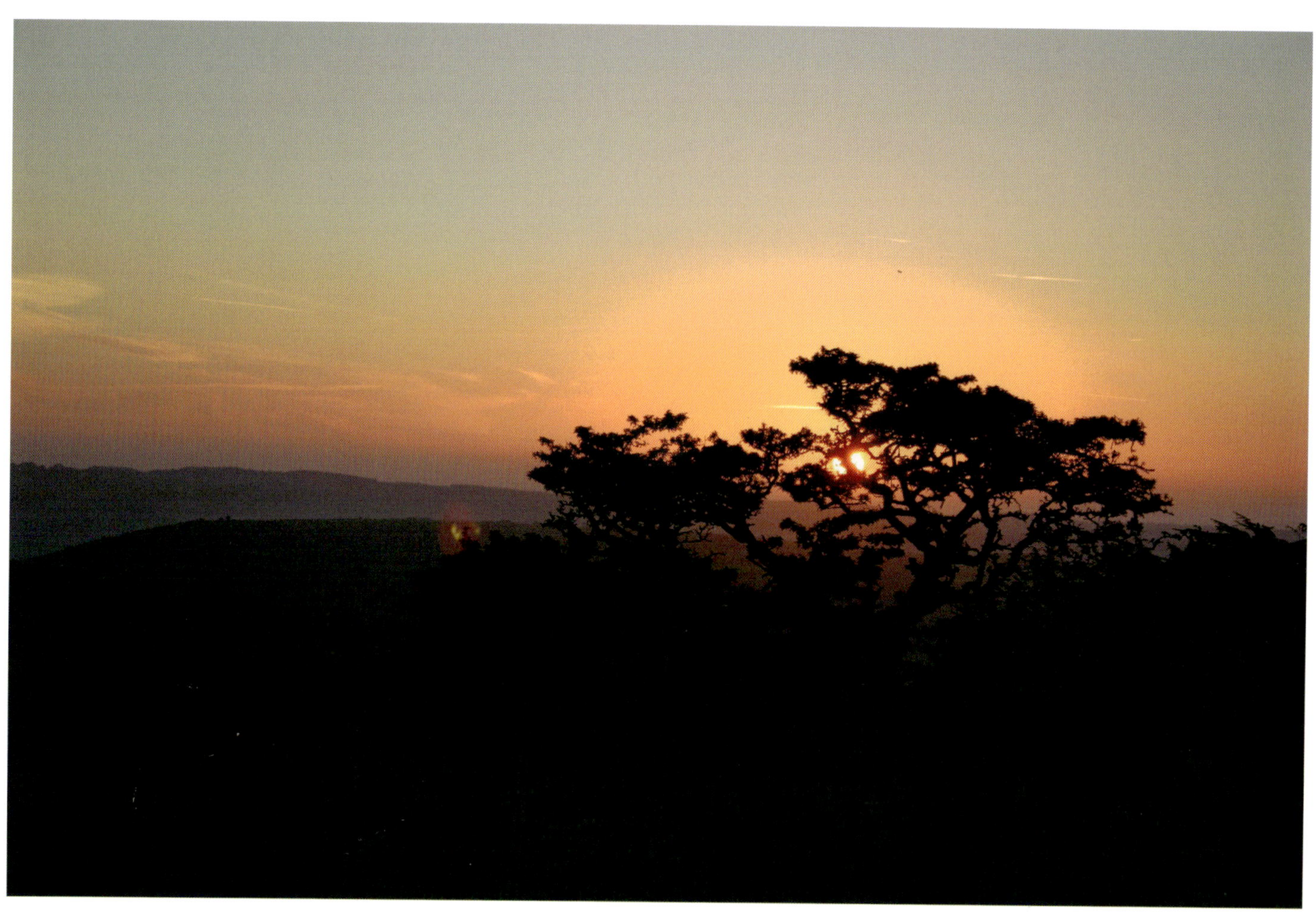

The sunrises and sunsets will always draw me to the moor. I sat and waited patiently for the sun to appear near Bowermans Nose and was rewarded by a magical light and atmosphere.

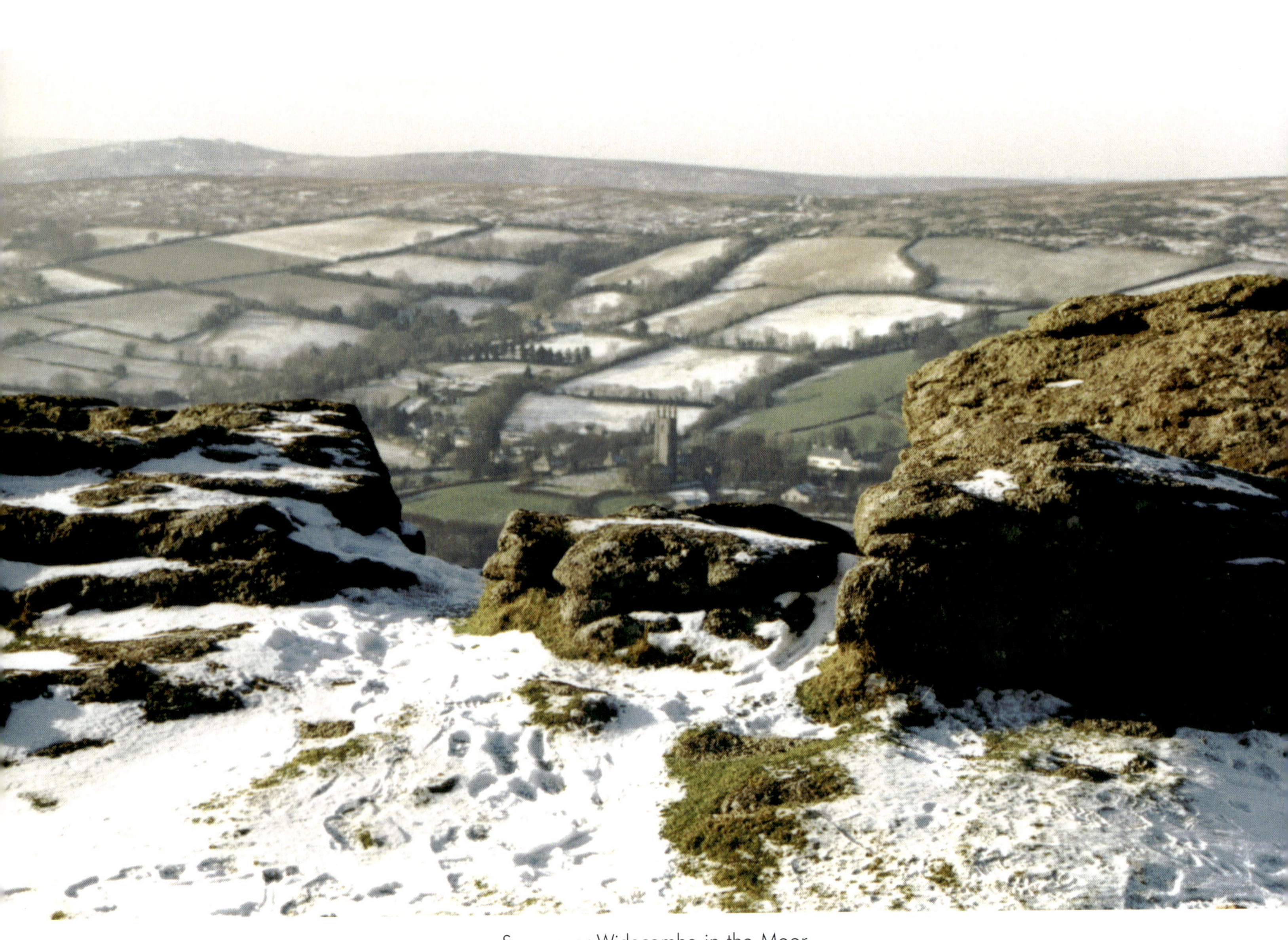

Snow over Widecombe-in-the-Moor.

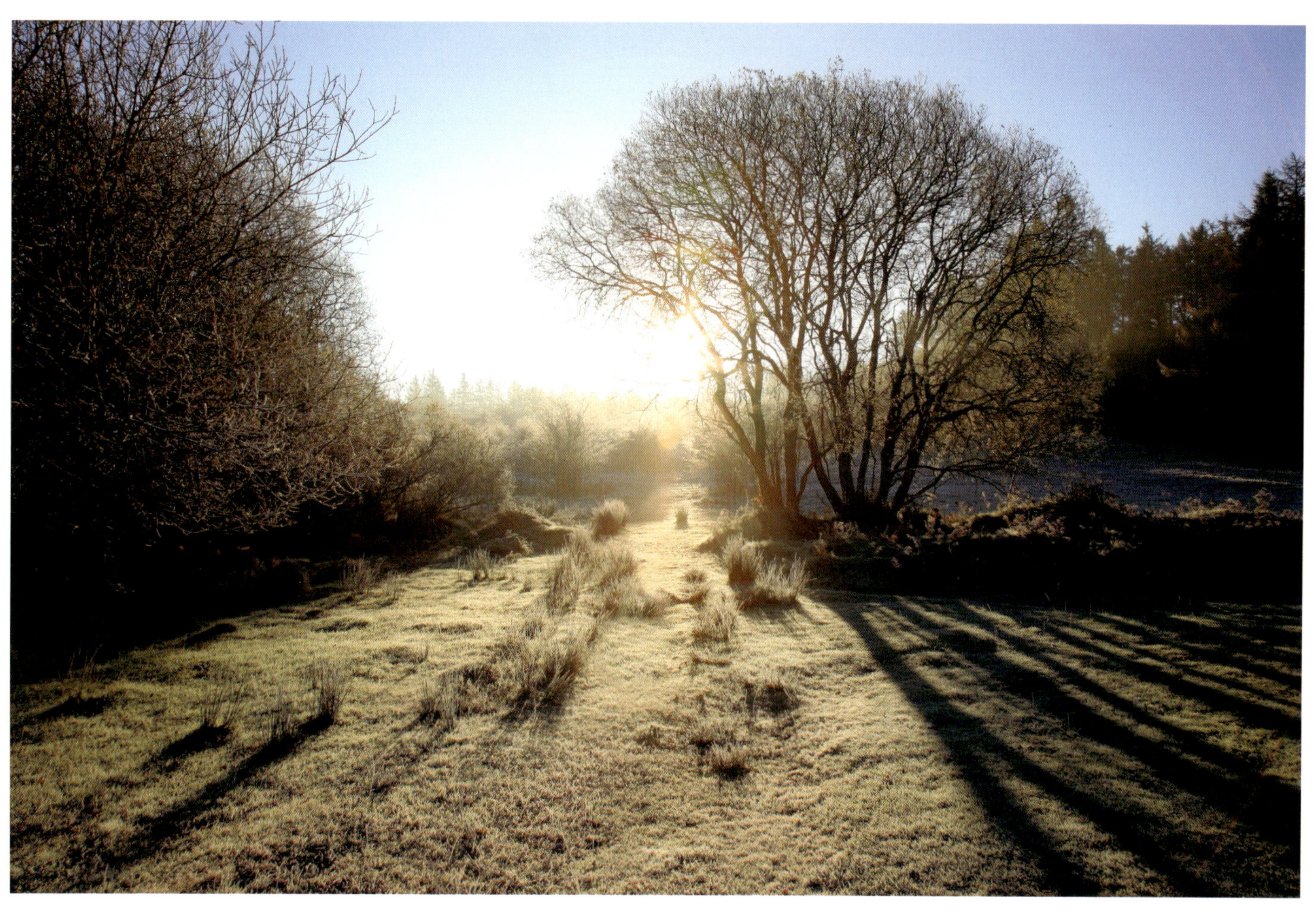

The sun breaks through on a frosty morning.

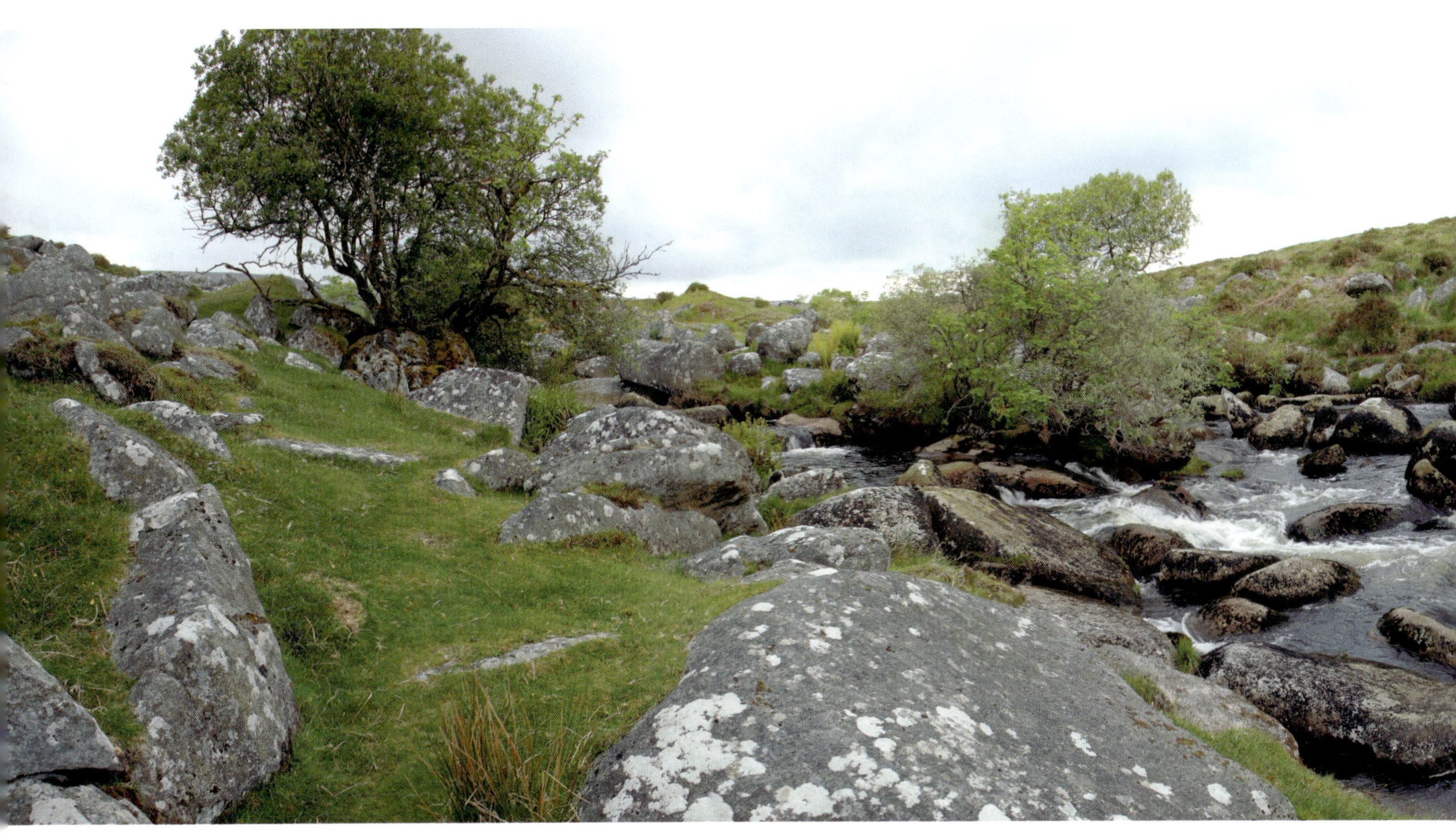

Panorama of the North Teign River and falls.

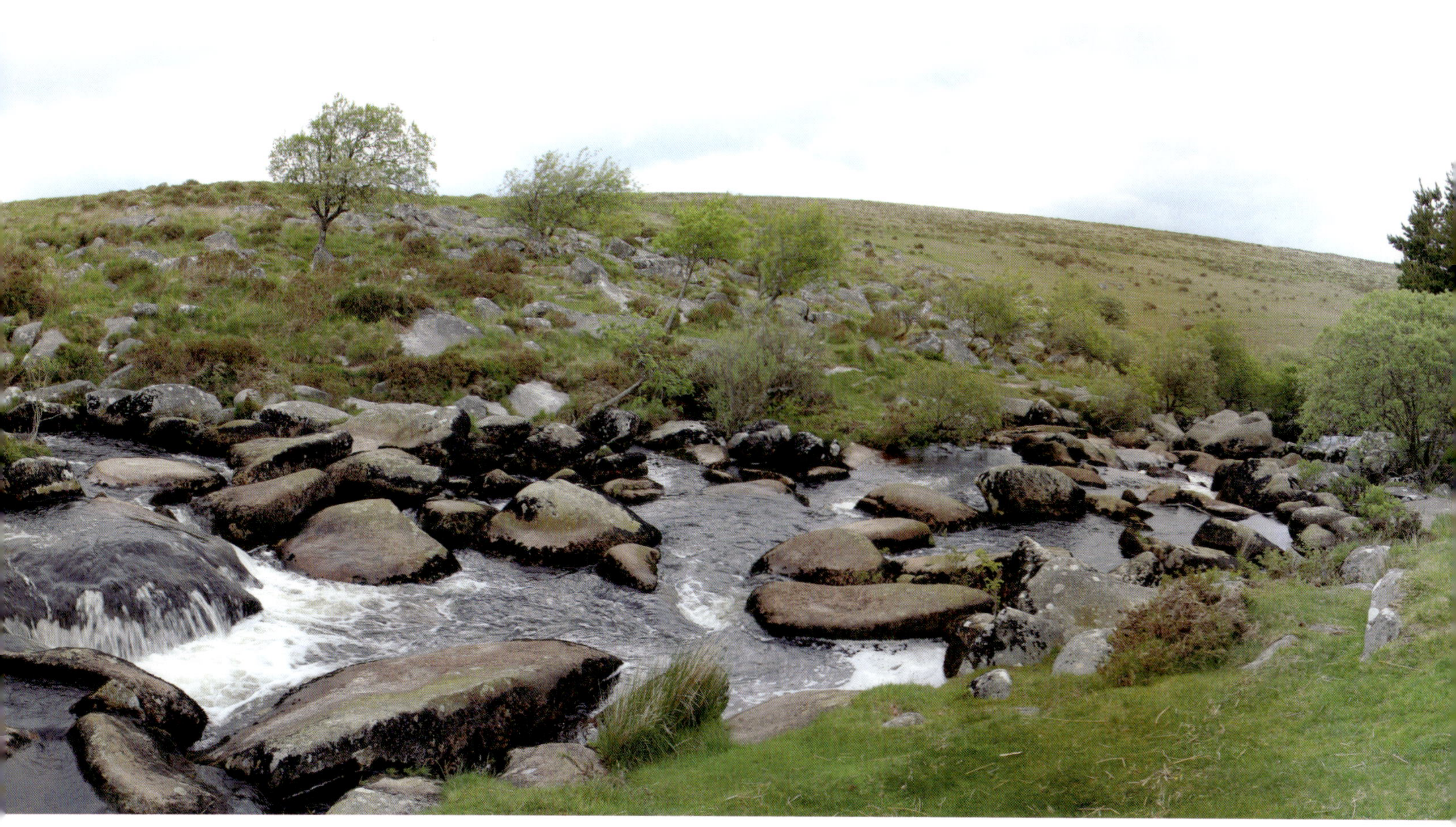

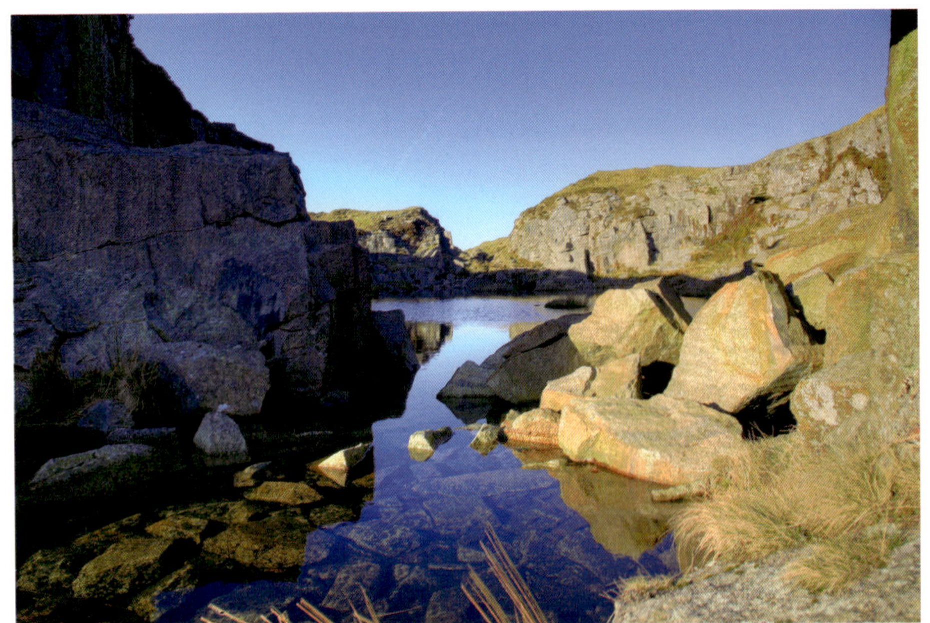

Late afternoon light at Foggintor quarry. The quarry once supplied granite for many London buildings most notably for Nelson's Column and Princetown prison. The sheer faces give an idea of the volume of granite that was removed.

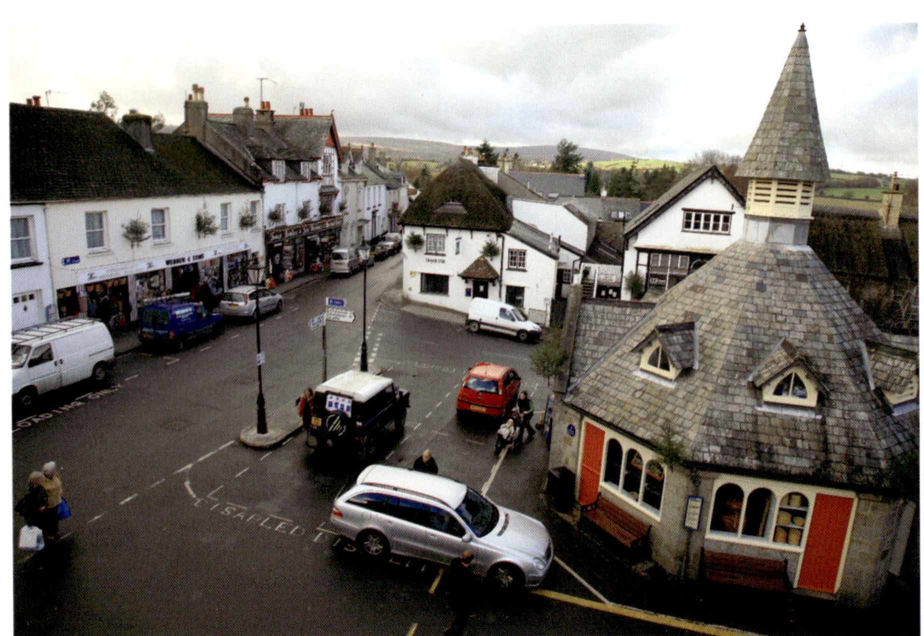

Chagford Square at Christmas.

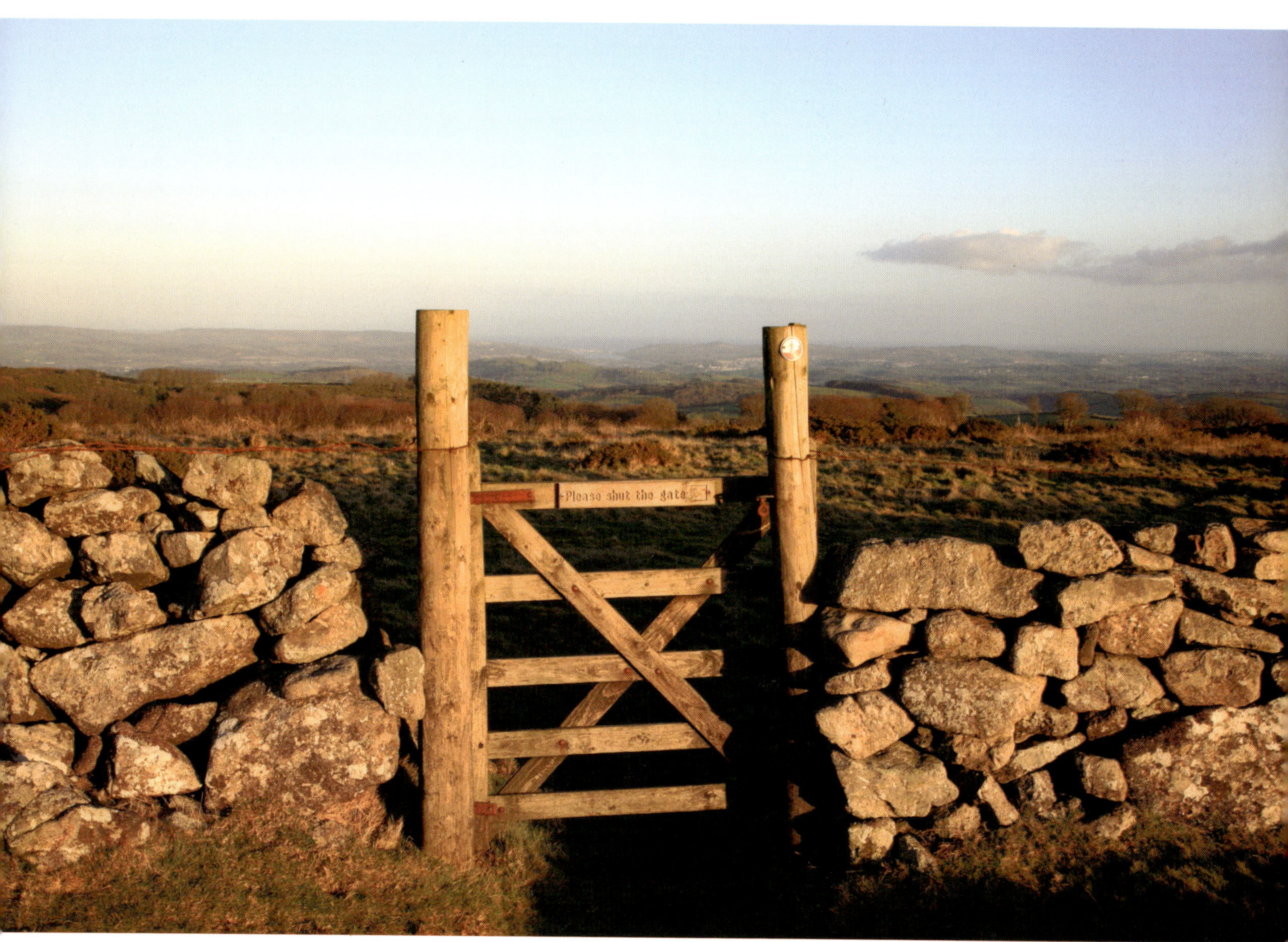

This gateway offers a view to the sea between the uprights.

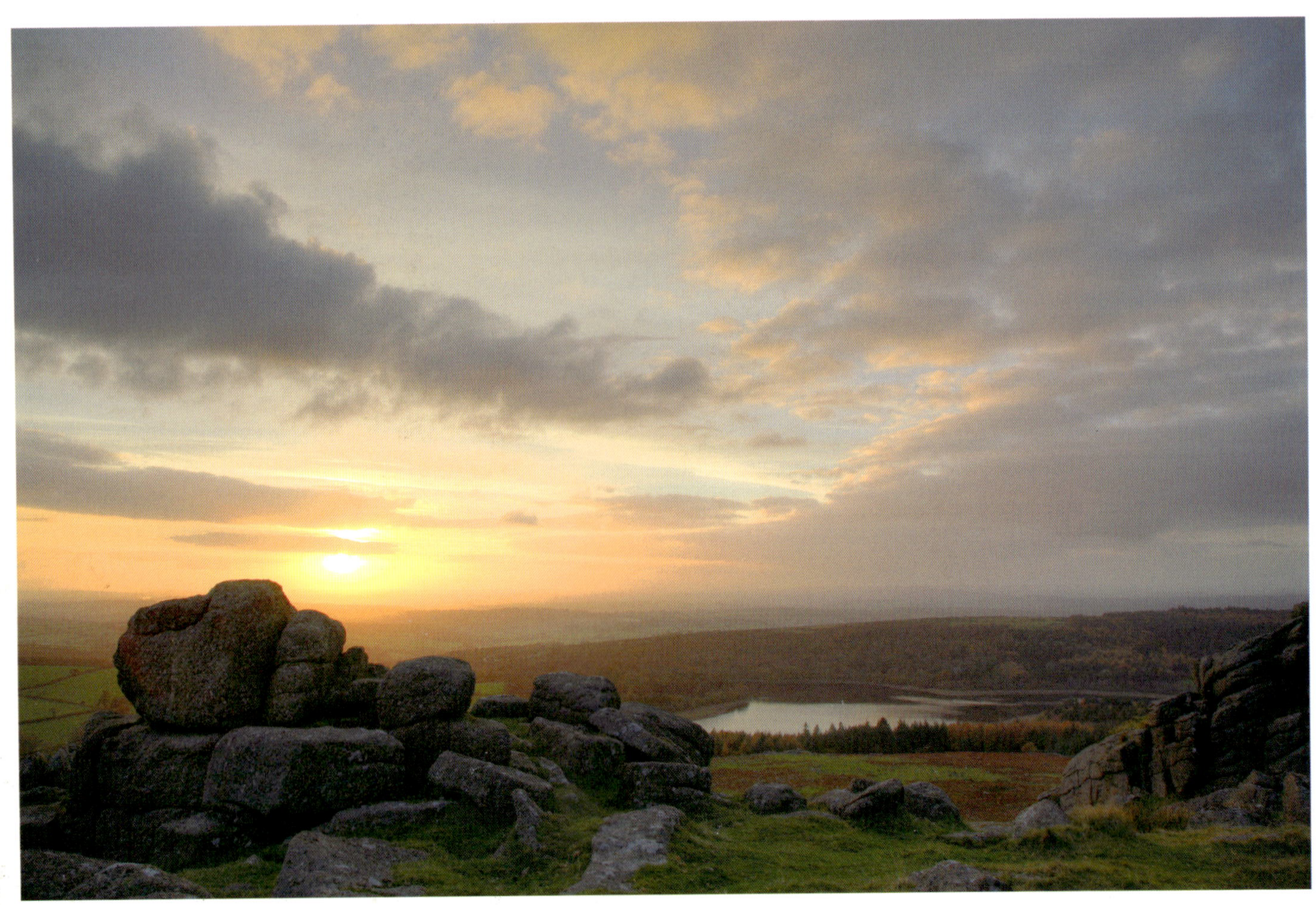

Sunset over Burrator reservior.

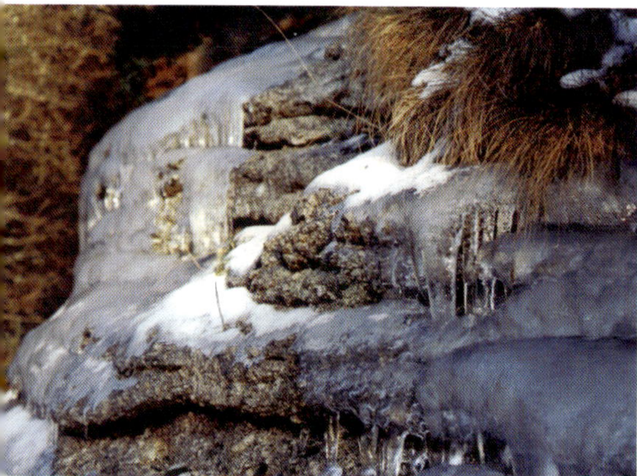

Thick ice hangs from
a giant granite boulder.

The end of another enjoyable and tiring day was rewarded with this beautiful scene as the sun set behind one of Dartmoor's characteristic weathered trees.

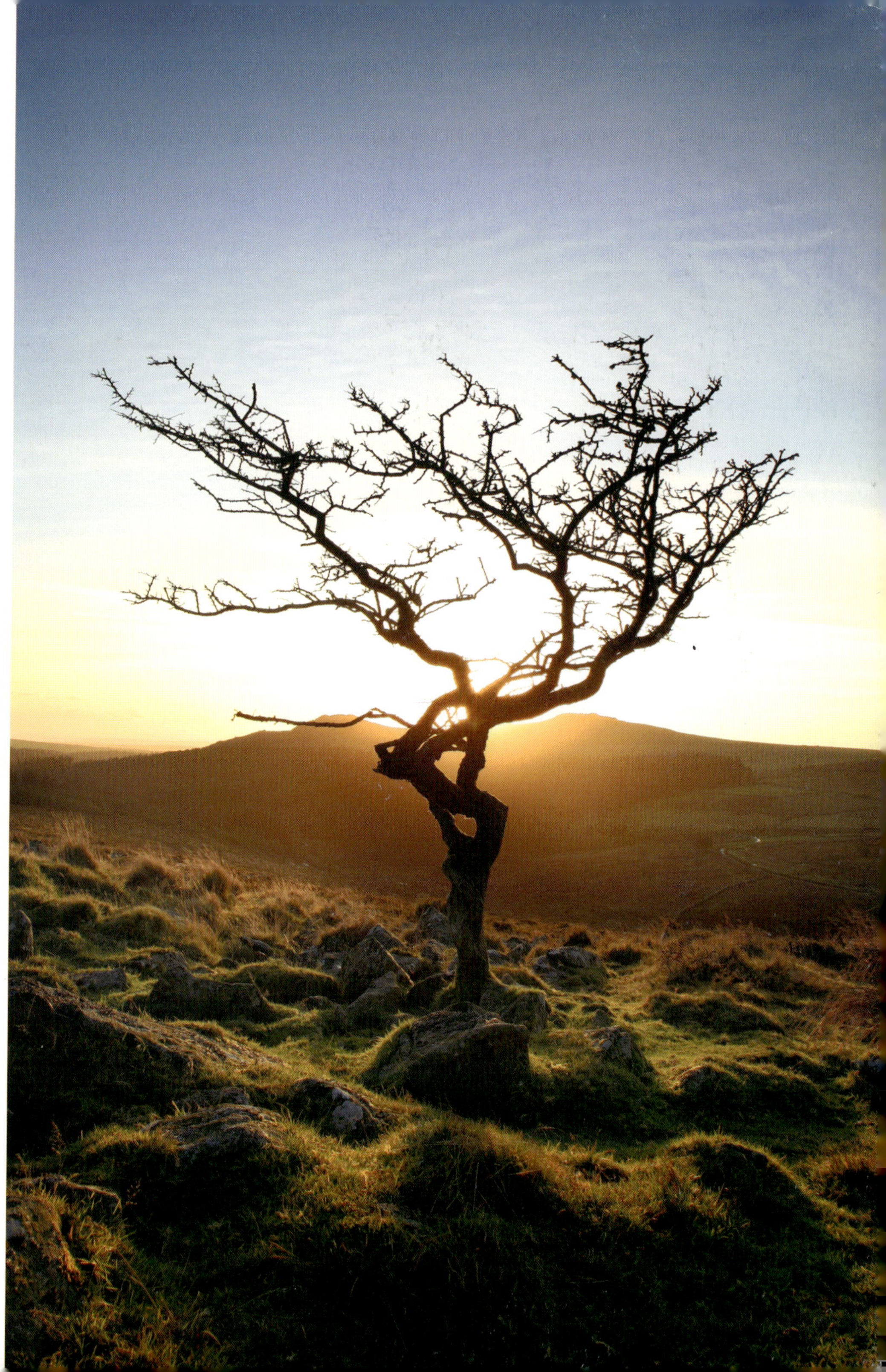

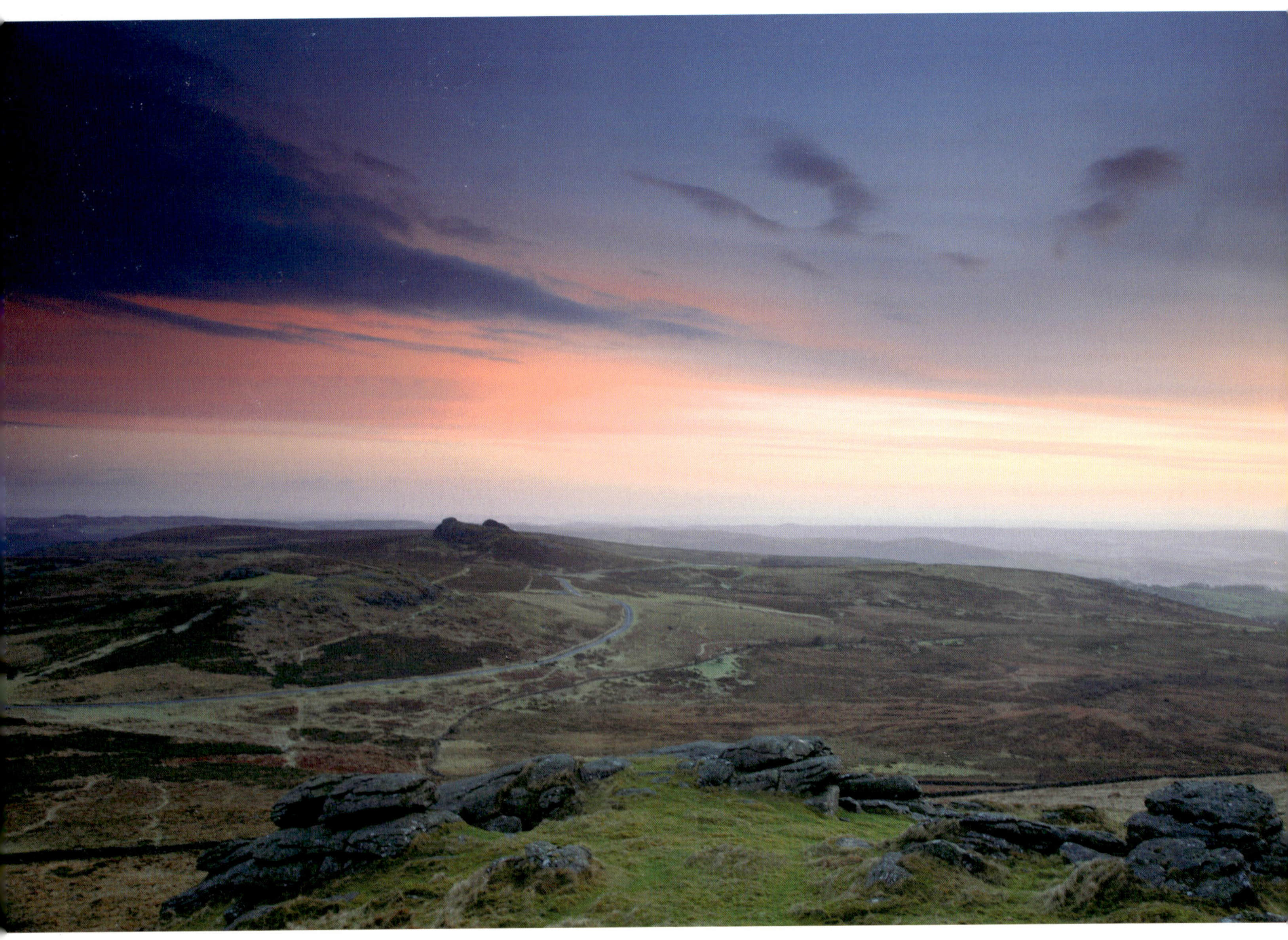

Looking over Haytor from the top of Rippon Tor just before sunset in winter.